ELEMENTS OF S ⎯⎯ LAW

ELEMENTS OF SCOTS LAW

by

David J. Field

*Solicitor for Prosecutions, Queensland, Australia.
Formerly Head of the Department of Law,
Napier Polytechnic of Edinburgh
and
Stipendiary Magistrate for the City of Glasgow*

W. GREEN / Sweet & Maxwell
EDINBURGH
1994

First published 1994

© 1994
W. GREEN & SON LTD.

ISBN 0 414 01049 3

A catalogue record for this book is
available from the British Library

Printed in Great Britain by
Hartnolls Ltd., Bodmin

PREFACE

When I began teaching Scots Law, some 16 years ago, the subject itself was more straightforward, and those responsible for examining the subject had an obliging habit of adhering to a standard syllabus. Changes in educational philosophy have created a situation in which each academic institution sets its own syllabus, and this has much to recommend it. Student and lecturer alike can concentrate on those topics most applicable to the course in question, and the only nostalgia for the old system comes from those who have the temerity to attempt textbooks on the subject.

No-one was more surprised than myself to be contacted by my former publishers, from another hemisphere, with a request to consider a new textbook on Scots law which would incorporate the essential elements of most college undergraduate study programmes. The challenge, however, proved irresistible. I have probably spent more on postage than I will ever receive in royalties, but I am delighted to be re-associated with Scots law after a gap of almost five years.

A swift perusal of the contents page will reveal nothing revolutionary. I have chosen to concentrate on those topics which students cannot avoid being called upon to study, and I have endeavoured to cover as many of those topics as possible. By this means, I have hopefully produced an introductory text which will be of use to most students on most courses.

I make no claim to academic niceties, but have endeavoured to convey the basic principles of the subject in the clearest manner available to me, with appropriate illustrations from case law. Every lecturer, and every author, has his strong and weaker subjects, and no doubt the more discerning reader will be able to identify mine. However, it is my hope that the material within these covers will be sufficiently detailed to be of use to both student and lecturer alike, without deterring the most casual of readers.

It is traditional in a preface for the author to thank the editorial staff of his publishers. On this occasion, these thanks have been amply justified by the effort involved in dispatching volumes of law reports, proofs, etc. to the other side of the world, and by allowing me to overshoot at least three editorial deadlines. My grateful thanks are also due to my executive secretary, Mrs Virginia McCaw, for taking over and reorganising the typing of the manuscript, in which I had proved myself particularly inept.

The law is intended to be as it was on January 1, 1994. If it is not, then I alone bear the blame.

June 1, 1994

DAVID J. FIELD,
Brisbane.

CONTENTS

TABLE OF CASES

TABLE OF STATUTES

TABLE OF REGULATIONS

1. THE SCOTTISH LEGAL SYSTEM

1.1 Before anyone may embark upon a study of even the most basic principles of Scots law which are contained in the chapters which follow, it is both important and advantageous to be aware of the legal system within which these principles operate. In particular, it is essential that the student of law be at least conversant with the sources of that law, the courts within which it is administered and those whose profession it is to apply the law. These essential elements are further explored in this introductory chapter.

SOURCES OF LAW

1.2 The modern law of Scotland emanates from a variety of sources, some of them more historical than of modern importance, others very modern and pragmatic. The main sources of law may in fact be itemised as follows:

1. Legislation.
2. Judicial precedent.
3. Authoritative writings.
4. Custom.
5. Equity.

Legislation

1.3 Legislation may be defined in general terms as the laying down of rules of law by a body or person authorised to do so. That authority comes constitutionally, of course, and the best example of a legislative body is the United Kingdom Parliament, although it is by no means the only one. The following main sources of legislation are in fact the three of greatest practical importance.

1. Acts of Parliament.
2. Delegated legislation.
3. Legislation of the EC (now European Union).

Acts of Parliament (Statutes)

Statutes Applicable to Scotland

1.4 Not every statute passed by the United Kingdom Parliament applies to Scotland, since Scotland retains its own distinct legal system despite the Act of Union of Parliaments in 1707. Acts passed prior to 1707 in Scotland ("Scots Acts") may still apply, but are likely to be held to have fallen into "desuetude" (disuse) by being overtaken by a contradictory statute since 1707, or by simply falling out of use or becoming totally inappropriate for modern life. Even a court decision to the contrary may be sufficient to in effect abolish a Scots Act.

1.5 Acts since 1707 passed in Westminster apply to Scotland unless there is a clause in a specific Act stating that it does not. Some acts apply *only* to Scotland, and have the word "Scotland" in brackets as part of their title.[1] Sometimes Parliament resorts to the crude expedient of extending what is primarily an English Act to Scotland by simply substituting for a certain English concept (*e.g.* "tort") a Scottish concept which is almost, but sometimes not quite, equivalent (*e.g.* "delict").[2]

Classification of Statutes

1.6 Statutes may be classified in one or more of several ways. They may, for example, be general (*i.e.* applicable to the whole community), local (applicable only in respect of a particular locality) or personal (for the benefit of an individual or a small group). A general Act begins life as a public bill before the whole Parliament,[3] promoted either by the Government or by a private member, whereas a local or personal Act begins as a private bill competing hopefully for increasingly limited parliamentary time.

---

[1] *e.g.* the Age of Legal Capacity (Scotland) Act referred to in 2.93 below.
[2] A process known cynically in Parliamentary drafting circles as "putting a kilt on it."
[3] See 1.7 below.

Parliamentary Procedure for Public Bills[4]

1.7 This consists of the following 5-stage process:

1. *First reading.* A formal "reading" and an order that the Bill be printed ready for the

2. *Second reading.* A more detailed discussion of the main points of the Bill. A purely Scottish Bill will be considered by the Scottish Grand Committee, which consists of all of the Scottish MPs plus additional members to maintain the political balance of Parliament as a whole.

3. *Committee stage.* A detailed examination of every word of the Bill by a committee to which it is referred for that purpose at the second reading. Scottish Bills are considered once again by a special committee, the Scottish Standing Committee.

4. *Report stage.* The committee reports back to the full House, and amendments may be made to the original Bill.

5. *Third reading.* A formal proposal that the Bill be read a third time, which in practice is a motion that it be passed.

1.8 If a Bill originates in the House of Commons, it is sent, once passed, to the House of Lords, where a similar process is followed. Sometimes a Bill will be introduced into the Lords first,[5] and then passed to the Commons. After being passed by both Houses, it goes to the Queen for the Royal Assent.

---

[4] Which are on the whole the only ones of importance for the purpose of this book.
[5] N.B. that financial legislation must originate in the Commons.

Purpose of Statute

1.9   While all statutes are in a sense designed to enact new law, in practice some of them have a technical legal purpose. They may, for example, be codifying Acts,[6] designed to bring together all the law on a particular subject, or they may be consolidating Acts,[7] which collect in one single statute the provisions of several previous statutes on the same subject, sometimes codifying the law at the same time. A declaratory Act is designed to restate the law after an unpopular court decision,[8] while a statute law revision Act is designed quietly to repeal statutes which are obsolete anyway. In the reverse direction, a Law Reform (Miscellaneous Provisions) Act is one designed to instigate minor reforms in various unrelated areas of law.[9]

Commencement, Amendment and Repeal of Statutes

1.10   Unless indicated to the contrary, an Act comes into force on the date of the Royal Assent. Alternatively, a commencement date may be nominated in the Act itself, or it may be left to come into force in stages fixed by delegated legislation.[10]

1.11   A statute may later be amended by another statute,[11] and a later statute may totally repeal an earlier one, usually by restating the law on the subject.

Delegated Legislation

General Nature of Delegated Legislation

1.12   Parliament does not possess sufficient time to devote to every single new law, regulation, etc. which may require to be passed in

---

[6] Such as the Partnership Act of 1890—see 8.1 below.
[7] Such as the Sale of Goods Act of 1979—see 5.1 below.
[8] *e.g.* the War Damage Act 1965, designed to neutralise the effect of the House of Lords decision in *Burmah Oil Company Limited* v. *Lord Advocate*, 1964 S.C.(H.L.) 177, requiring the Government to pay compensation for the deliberate arson of British owned oil terminals in the path of the invading Japanese.
[9] See, for example, the Law Reform (Miscellaneous Provisions) (Scotland) Act 1985 considered in 14.32 below.
[10] For which see 1.12 below.
[11] *e.g.* Married Womens Policies of Assurance (Scotland) (Amendment) Act 1980, considered in 14.38 below.

the course of a single year on matters as diverse as the correct loading strain for a jib crane or the state of the effluent on an Ayrshire beach. For that reason, it is obliged to delegate some of its law-making powers to other persons or bodies, who are usually more qualified to legislate on the subject anyway. Such legislation, assuming that the correct procedures are followed, has the same force as an Act of Parliament, but is also controlled by Parliament and the courts.

1.13 Parliament controls this delegated legislation by ensuring that it is authorised and enacted within the correct procedural framework, while the courts control it by interpreting it, and ensuring that it is *intra vires* (*i.e.* within the limits of the delegated authority).

Types of Delegated Legislation

1.14 The following forms of delegated legislation may be regularly observed in action:

1.15 *1. Statutory Instruments.* These take the form of regulations, orders, etc. enacted by someone such as a government minister who has authority to do so for his own area of responsibility under powers granted to him in an enabling Act.[12] In practice there are two broad categories of statutory instrument, namely the Ministerial Regulations referred to above, and Orders in Council, which are orders made by the Queen in Privy Council, and which are part of the last remaining royal prerogative to the Queen under the modern parliamentary system. Even that is controlled politically in the sense that Orders in Council are a device by means of which a government can bypass the parliamentary procedure in time of national emergency (*e.g.* the sudden outbreak of war).

1.16 *2. Bye-laws.* These are regulations passed by some public body (and principally by local authorities) in connection with the management of matters within their responsibility (highways, schools, etc.). They normally derive this authority from an enabling Act,[13] and any local special Act which may have been passed for the purpose (*e.g.* to control a local harbour).

---

[12] *e.g.* Health and Safety at Work etc. Act 1974, referred to in 12.92 below.
[13] *e.g.* the Local Government (Scotland) Act 1973.

1.17 Such legislation normally requires to be confirmed by a government minister before it becomes effective, and is once again challengeable both procedurally and in the courts.

1.18 3. *Acts of Sederunt and Acts of Adjournal.* An Act of Sederunt is a rule made by the Court of Session to regulate the procedure in any civil court,[14] while an Act of Adjournal is the equivalent process observed by the High Court of Justiciary in respect of criminal procedure. They are normally now found in the form of statutory instruments.

1.19 4. *Sub-delegated legislation.* Normally, the person or body to whom the power to enact delegated legislation is given may not delegate it further. However, on rare occasions there may be such a sub-delegation, as in the case of Orders in Council, in which the Queen's powers may on occasions be exercised by ministers.

The Need for Delegated Legislation

1.20 The most obvious argument in favour of delegated legislation is the sheer impossibility of Parliament dealing with every tiny rule and regulation for the governing of the entire country, some of them of limited or specialist application. Another argument is the relative speed of delegated legislation as opposed to the somewhat cumbersome Bill process referred to in 1.7 above. Equally important is the flexibility of delegated legislation, and the ease with which it may be amended swiftly to cope with changes in requirements or unseen emergencies. It also allows for new control systems to be tried out and to be replaced speedily if unsuccessful.

Criticisms of Delegated Legislation

1.21 The main criticisms against delegated legislation centre around the lack of effective control over what is being enacted. These controls have been briefly referred to in 1.13 above, but many regard them as illusory because of the need for Parliament to attend to more important issues, and the fact that the courts are

---

[14] Including the Sheriff Court, see 1.43 below.

powerless to act against abuse of authority unless a suitable case
is referred to them.

1.22 Other criticisms surround the lack of publicity given to delegated legislation before it is passed, the lack of general consultation which the Bill procedure theoretically provides, and the wide
discretionary powers sometimes given to ministers under enabling
statutes to enact delegated legislation whenever they see fit.

Legislation of the EC (now European Union)

1.23 The EEC began with the Treaty of Rome in 1957, and treat-
ies are still the primary legislation under which the considerably
enlarged European Economic Community[15] (now European Union)
operates. However, of far greater interest to lawyers are the various
forms of secondary EC legislation, consisting of regulations, directives and decisions.

1.24 Regulations are directly applicable to every nation within
the EC, and have the effect of law without passing through any of
the parliaments of the individual member states. They also allow
United Kingdom citizens (and all other EC citizens) direct access
to the courts of the United Kingdom[16] and all other state courts if
the laws thus enacted are not observed, and they over-ride any
United Kingdom law inconsistent with them.

1.25 Directives are not directly applicable, but they oblige each
member state to bring its laws within line on a particular topic. As
will be seen in Chapter 12, the United Kingdom has received several
salvos in this regard with respect to its attitude on sexual equality
in employment.

1.26 Decisions of the European Court of Justice, as well as being
binding upon the litigants themselves, may be adopted by the EC
Commission or the Council of Ministers and directed to a particular nation, or to certain corporations and individuals, upon whom
they then also become binding.

---

[15] Which the U.K. effectively joined on January 1, 1973.
[16] And from there to the European Court of Justice.

Judicial Precedent

1.27 The second most important source of law after legislation is what is referred to as judicial precedent or case law. The principle underlying it is that a court of law, when faced with a decision which has previously been made by another court of higher status, is bound by it, assuming that certain other conditions, considered below, are satisfied. In more formal Latin, the principle is known as *stare decisis*, or "standing by decisions." A previous decision which must be followed by the present court is said to be "binding," whereas one which it is free to follow or not is merely "persuasive."

1.28 In order to be binding, as indicated above, the decision must come from a senior court of higher status in the hierarchy of courts.[17] At the top of the hierarchy comes the European Court of Justice, whose decisions bind all the courts of the United Kingdom, although it reserves the right to depart from its own decisions. The highest court in the United Kingdom, the House of Lords, will only hand down binding precedents for Scotland insofar as they relate to interpretation of United Kingdom-wide statutes, or cases which come on appeal from the highest *civil*[18] court in Scotland, the Court of Session. This court in turn is divided into the more senior Inner House, and its decisions bind both itself[19] and the Outer House, as well as the lower sheriff courts. Outer House and sheriff court decisions are never binding precedents, but may well be persuasive, in the sense that they command respect and consideration.

1.29 Judicial precedent does not apply so strictly in criminal cases, and not even the High Court of Justiciary regards itself as bound by its own decisions, and High Court judges and sheriffs sitting in trials, while they will regard High Court of Justiciary decisions as highly persuasive, and will normally follow them, are not formally bound by them.

---

[17] Considered more fully in 1.43 and 1.63 below.
[18] *N.B.* the House of Lords has no status in Scottish *criminal cases*. *N.B.* also that since 1966, the House of Lords does not regard itself as bound by its own decisions.
[19] Where it has sat in division; a bench of seven Inner House judges may, however, sit in order to over-rule a divisional decision.

1.30 The other important factor to be satisfied before a previous decision will be binding is that such previous decision must have dealt, as its main point, with precisely the principle of law with which the present court is faced. All judgments are divided into two sections, namely the *ratio decidendi* (or more commonly simply the *ratio*), which is the point of law which the previous court was obliged to decide in order to deal with the case, and the *obiter dicta*, which is everything else which the court may have decided to given an opinion on at the time. Only the *ratio* can become a later precedent of the binding variety, although the *obiter dicta* of a senior court will normally be treated as at least persuasive.

1.31 A system of case law clearly relies on a network of accurate and reliable law reports from which lawyers can research precedents for cases in which they may be involved. The most important modern case reports are the Session Cases, devoted to Court of Session cases and Scottish cases of the House of Lords, and the Scots Law Times which reports major cases in all Scottish courts including the Court of Session.

1.32 The main advantages with a system of judicial precedent are that by referring to court decisions, lawyers and their clients can build up a picture of the law on a particular topic, there is consistency between cases, and the law may develop in a swift but orderly fashion in order to meet new situations, without the need for parliamentary intervention.[20] Against this is some times argued the contrary, namely that precedent can be too rigid, that some distinctions can be artificial and impracticable, and that searching for the right precedent can often be something of a lottery, depending primarily on the case having been reported in the first place, which is by no means guaranteed.

Authoritative Writings

1.33 In the days before modern communication technology, and indeed before any regularised system of law reporting, certain famous and influential lawyers of their day took the trouble to

---

[20] A classic example being the decision in *Donoghue v. Stevenson*, considered in 10.31 below.

record the law as they understood it and saw it developing in the early courts. These works are still referred to today, partly as a source of "grass roots" feeling for the precise principles upon which modern law is based, and partly to fill a gap in judicial precedent, an increasingly unlikely event.

1.34 Such is their status in the history of Scots Law that they have become literal "institutions," in that they are referred to as the "Institutional Writers." Chief among them are Viscount Stair (*Institutions of the Law of Scotland*, 1681), Professor John Erskine (*An Institute of the Law of Scotland*, 1773), Baron David Hume (*Crimes*, 1797), Professor George Bell (*Commentaries*, 1810), and Sir Archibald Alison (*Criminal Law*, 1832).[21]

Custom

1.35 "Custom" is a word used in many different contexts in Scots Law, for example to describe a former trade practice which has now become statutory[22] or absorbed into case law,[23] or to show how the parties, in agreeing the terms of a contract, chose to incorporate a well-recognised and understood principle of their trade.

1.36 But in a special sense, "custom" can be a source of law, in that a court will be bound by the terms and conditions of a particular practice when it has been around for so long that everyone believed that it was the law anyway, it is definitive and certain, and it is fair and reasonable. It must not be inconsistent with the major sources of law, namely legislation and judicial precedent, but it may operate as an exception to them.

Equity

1.37 "Equity" in the sense of a source of law refers to "fairness," and it is not so much a source of law in itself as the process by

---

[21] The others are Sir Thomas Craig, Sir George McKenzie and Lord Bankton.

[22] *e.g.* a large proportion of what is now the Sale of Goods Act 1979; see 5.1 below.

[23] The origins, for example, of a widow's right to succeed to her deceased husband's estate.

which the harsher aspects of the operation of ordinary law are mitigated or softened in appropriate cases in order to ensure that justice is done. It is seen in our courts almost daily, when decrees of specific implement[24] and interdicts[25] are granted, since they are both discretionary remedies which the court will only grant if satisfied that the pursuer is deserving of such a remedy.

1.38 There is also a more specific source of law referred to as "equity," and this is the power known as the *nobile officium*[26] of the Court of Session and the High Court of Justiciary to grant a remedy in a situation in which the strict law does not provide one.

COURTS OF LAW

Introduction

1.39 The Scottish courts of law are organised into two hierarchies (although some courts such as the sheriff court exist in both) which reflect the division between civil and criminal law. Civil law is the law which governs disputes between private individuals or entities such as companies and local authorities, while criminal law is the law which governs the behaviour and conduct of the individual in terms of the "criminal law" of Scotland at any given time, being behaviour deemed by society to be sufficiently injurious to its wellbeing to require sanctions (*e.g.* fines and/or imprisonment) to discourage it.

1.40 A party bringing a civil action is referred to as a pursuer, and the person against whom it is brought as the defender. The civil process is known as litigation, and the pursuer will normally be seeking damages and/or some court order such as specific implement or interdict.

1.41 The person against whom criminal actions are raised is the accused or the defendant.[27] The person instituting the procedure

[24] See *e.g.* 4.96 below.
[25] See *e.g.* 10.53 below.
[26] "Equitable Power".
[27] *N.B.* that in indictable cases he is sometimes still referred to by the old name of the "panel'.

will be the procurator fiscal,[28] although in indictable cases he will do so in the name of the Lord Advocate.

1.42 In addition to the civil and criminal courts, there are a handful of specialised courts which exist to hear technical matters of limited application. Finally, as an alternative to the traditional courts, there are tribunals, while the parties may in some cases choose to refer their differences to arbitration.

Civil Courts

1.43 The following are the courts within the civil hierarchy referred to above:

1. Sheriff Courts.
2. Court of Session (Outer and Inner Houses).
3. House of Lords.

Sheriff Courts

1.44 The sheriff court, although strictly speaking the lowest court in the civil court structure, is strategically the most important, since it provides ready access to civil justice at a local level, and deals with by far the highest volume of cases.

Organisation of Sheriff Courts

1.45 Scotland is divided into six sheriffdoms[29] each presided over by a sheriff principal. Each of the sheriffdoms is then further subdivided into sheriff court districts,[30] thus ensuring that every centre of population of any size has access to a local sheriff court, presided over by one or more sheriffs who may exercise jurisdiction anywhere within the sheriffdom. Temporary sheriffs may be appointed to assist with heavy workloads, and "floating" sheriffs may, for similar reasons, move from sheriffdom to sheriffdom.

---

[28] See 1.100 below.
[29] Grampian Highland and Islands, Tayside Central and Fife, Lothian and Borders, Glasgow and Strathkelvin, North Strathclyde and South Strathclyde, Dumfries and Galloway.
[30] Which is currently 49 in total.

Jurisdiction of Sheriff Courts

1.46 Although the jurisdiction of the sheriff court is very wide, a case cannot be brought within any particular court unless the *defender* is subject to its jurisdiction, and the *subject matter* is one which it is competent for the sheriff court to try.

1.47 So far as concerns jurisdiction over the *defender*, the Civil Jurisdiction Judgments Act of 1982 makes the defender subject to the jurisdiction of a particular sheriff court if he is personally cited in it,[31] the case concerns a contract which was performable within the sheriffdom, the case concerns a delict[32] committed within the sheriffdom or the case is a "consumer contract" case in which the pursuer/consumer is domiciled within the sheriffdom. Additionally, in terms of the Sheriff Court (Scotland) Act 1907 the defender will be subject to the jurisdiction if he resides there, or having resided there for 40 days, he has ceased to reside there for less than 40 days and has no known residence in Scotland. He will also be subject to the jurisdiction if he has a place of business within the sheriffdom and is cited either personally or at his place of business. The same will apply if the action is concerned with heritable property[33] within the sheriffdom of which the defender is the owner or tenant, or with a contract performed within the sheriffdom, and the defender is personally cited there.

1.48 In relation to jurisdiction over the *subject matter*, the rule is that any action may be brought within the sheriff court other than ones within the privative[34] jurisdiction of the Court of Session, which will include cases involving a person's status (*e.g.* marriage), actions for reduction[35] and actions for proving the tenor of a lost document such as a will.[36] Similarly, other specialist courts[37] will have their own privative jurisdictions.

---

[31] But only in cases in which he has no fixed residence.
[32] For which see Chapter 10.
[33] For which see 13.5 below.
[34] *i.e.* exclusive. N.B. that since 1983, divorce cases may be heard in the Sheriff Court as well as the Court of Session.
[35] Setting something aside such as a contract.
[36] See 15.37 below.
[37] See generally the section on "specialised courts" below.

1.49 At the same time, sheriff courts have a privative jurisdiction, which means that certain types of case *must* be brought within them. Most notable among these are actions for £1500 or less, and actions for eviction from heritable property.

Procedure in the Sheriff Courts

1.50 Sheriff court civil actions may be one of three types, small claims causes, summary causes and ordinary causes. Small claims procedure is for cases under £750 in value, in which the parties may appear for themselves,[38] legal expenses against the unsuccessful party are limited to £75[39] and the rules of evidence are to a certain extent relaxed. The only right of appeal is to the sheriff principal on a point of law.

1.51 The next stage up is the summary cause, for actions of between £750 and £1500 in money, and eviction orders. The action originates on a special pre-printed form which only requires the filling in of blanks, and decree (*i.e.* judgment) is automatic if the defender does not "enter an appearance" (by returning his portion of the form by the stated "return day"). An appeal from a summary cause finding may be to the sheriff principal on a point of law, and from him to the Inner House of the Court of Session if the sheriff principal certifies that the point is suitable for such an appeal.

1.52 All sheriff court actions which do not fall within the small claims or summary cause categories are referred to as ordinary causes.[40] They proceed by means of an initial writ drafted by the pursuer's solicitor, which will normally be met by written defences from the other side. After various adjustments to the pleadings by both parties, the remaining ground between them becomes the subject of a hearing. Further detail on sheriff court procedure is outwith the scope of this book. Appeal against ordinary cause finding is either as for a summary cause or directly into the Inner House of the Court of Session.

---

[38] N.B. they may retain solicitors, but Legal Aid is not available.
[39] *Nil* if the action is for less than £200.
[40] And will include *e.g.* claims for more than £1500, divorce actions, and "succession" cases, for which see Chapter 15.

Court of Session

1.53 The most senior civil court exclusively within Scotland is the Court of Session in Edinburgh, which is divided into an Outer House (primarily hearing new cases) and an Inner House (primarily hearing appeals).

Outer House

1.54 The Outer House of the Court of Session consists of several separate courts, each of them presided over by a junior "Lord of Session" known as a Lord Ordinary. Very rarely[41] there will be a jury of twelve, but normally the hearing is before the Lord Ordinary alone.

1.55 The Outer House is primarily a court of first instance, which means that it hears a case for the first time. Jurisdiction extends over anyone domiciled[42] in Scotland, where such a person is the intended defender, while in various matrimonial proceedings, only one of the parties need be so domiciled when the action is raised; alternatively it is sufficient if either of the parties was "habitually resident" in Scotland for one year immediately prior to the raising of the action. A final possibility giving jurisdiction against the defender is that he is resident in Scotland or is the owner or tenant of heritable property in Scotland.[43]

1.56 As explained in 1.48 above, the Court of Session may hear any action which is not privative to the sheriff court, and in some cases exercises privative jurisdiction itself. It may also exercise the *nobile officium* referred to in 1.38 above. This means that in many cases not within the privative jurisdiction of either court, the pursuer has a choice of courts between the sheriff court and the Court of Session. However, the expense of a Court of Session action tends in practice to reserve only the most important[44] cases for the Outer House.

---

[41] And normally only in certain personal injury claims.
[42] *i.e.* usually or habitually.
[43] *N.B.* the action need not relate to that heritage.
[44] In the legal and/or financial sense.

1.57 Procedure in the Outer House is normally by written sum-mons[45] to which are sent defences in response unless the action is to be undefended. Written pleadings are then adjusted on the "open record," until the pleadings are closed and the matter set down for hearing, whether by "proof" on the facts or by the arguing of "pleas in law."

1.58 Appeals from Outer House findings lie to the Inner House by way of what is known as a reclaiming motion, and it will norm-ally be restricted to a question of law, the facts being as recorded in the shorthand writer's transcript.

Inner House

1.59 The Inner House of the Court of Session is in effect solely an appeal court,[46] sitting in two divisions of three Lords of Session, or senior Court of Session judges. A majority decision will normally suffice, and the divisions may be combined for the hearing of important cases, and may even be extended to bring in Outer House judges so as to produce a full court of fifteen.

1.60 The principal work of the Inner House consists of hearing appeals from the decisions of sheriffs, sheriffs principal and the Outer House, as indicated above. The procedure for such appeals normally consists of taking the evidence "as read" from the trial transcript, and dealing with legal argument from counsel before producing an opinion.

1.61 Appeals may be brought from the rulings of the Inner House by means of a petition to the House of Lords, which may be on a mixed question of fact and law,[47] but will normally be restricted to cases involving the most important and wide-ranging principles of law.[48]

---

[45] The alternative form of procedure being by "petition" in matters such as the winding up of a company.
[46] *N.B.* it has limited "first instance" jurisdiction in special cases such as "stated cases" on issues of taxation law.
[47] Law only when the matter originated in the sheriff court.
[48] One case which went all the way to the House of Lords was *Donoghue* v. *Stevenson* considered in 10.31 below.

House of Lords

1.62 In terms of its role in the hierarchy of Scots courts, the House of Lords[49] operates solely as a final court of appeal on points of civil law of considerable public importance referred to it by the Inner House of the Court of Session. It does so by means of petition to the Lords of Appeal in Ordinary, as the House of Lords judges are known. Their judgment is not a decree in itself, but only has legal effect when applied by the Inner House. By convention, two of the "Law Lords" are Scottish in origin and judicial experience, but there is no binding rule that a Scottish Law Lord must sit on a Scottish case. Although the official quorum is three, there are normally five Lords sitting on every appeal.

Criminal Courts

1.63 The criminal courts of Scotland consist of the following, in ascending order of seniority:

1. District courts.
2. Sheriff courts.
3. High Court of Justiciary.

As indicated in 1.41, all crimes in Scotland are prosecuted by the local procurators-fiscal, on authority from the Lord Advocate acting through the Crown Office in Edinburgh.

1.64 The least serious crimes proceed by way of "complaint," and are dealt with "summarily," *i.e.* without a jury, in either the District Court or the Sheriff Court. More serious crimes proceed "on indictment" in the Sheriff Court or the High Court before a jury of fifteen.

1.65 Whereas at the highest end of the scale, some cases (*e.g.* murder and rape) can only proceed on indictment before the High Court, at the lowest end of the scale only summary procedure can be adopted for certain cases (*e.g.* under various statutes dealing with matters such as being drunk and incapable). For the vast majority of cases in between, it is a matter for the procurator

---

[49] Which exercises a much wider jurisdiction in England.

fiscal's discretion which court a matter is raised in, since he is "the master of the instance." Against this background, the individual courts may be examined more fully.

District Courts

1.66 Except in Glasgow,[50] the district courts consist of local courts (one for each local authority district, as the name suggests) staffed by lay magistrates sitting with legally qualified "assessors," whose function it is to deal with the most lowly crime of all (*e.g.* drunkenness, shoplifting and breach of the peace) committed within the district. The maximum penalty is 60 days imprisonment or a fine of £1000 from a lay magistrate, and £2000 and three months' imprisonment[51] from a stipendiary magistrate who is legally qualified, and who sits without an assessor. A district court presided over by a stipendiary magistrate may also, of course, deal with more serious offences (*e.g.* robbery and drunken driving), up to the limits of the jurisdiction of a sheriff sitting summarily.

Sheriff courts

1.67 As indicated above, the sheriff court, as it does in civil matters, occupies a pivotal role in the criminal court hierarchy, since in addition to dealing with the more serious summary cases, it deals with all but the most serious indictable offences as well, the sheriff in such cases sitting with a jury. As with the district court, there is a jurisdictional limit in the sense that the crime in question must have been committed within the sheriffdom. In summary cases, the sheriff's sentencing power is limited to £2000 and three months' imprisonment, while in indictable (sometimes referred to as "solemn") cases there is a limitless fine and a three year imprisonment. A sheriff may, however, remit suitable cases for sentence to the High Court, if he feels that his sentencing powers are inadequate.

---

[50] Where Stipendiary Magistrates have been appointed with jurisdiction equivalent to that of a sheriff sitting summarily; see 1.68 below.
[51] Six months in the case of a second or subsequent offence of dishonesty or violence.

High Court of Justiciary

1.68 The High Court of Justiciary, headed by the Lord Justice-General[52] and staffed by the Court of Session judges who in the exercise of criminal jurisdiction are known as Lords Commissioners of Justiciary, deals with certain privative criminal cases[53] at first instance (*i.e.* as a court of trial with a jury) while acting as a court of appeal from the district and sheriff court criminal jurisdictions.

1.69 In its first instance jurisdiction, and unlike the Court of Session which remains fixed in Edinburgh, the High Court of Justiciary goes on circuit to various cities in Scotland as the need demands. There is no limit on the sentencing power of a High Court judge, who sits with a jury of fifteen.

1.70 Appeal cases to the High Court of Justiciary are divided into appeals from summary findings (the justiciary roll) and solemn findings (the criminal appeal roll).

1.71 On the justiciary roll, the accused may appeal on both sentence and findings of fact, while the procurator fiscal may appeal against sentence and against a point of law which led to an acquittal. The appellant may bring additional evidence, but normally the appeal proceeds on a stated case (*i.e.* facts found as proved) from the trial judge. A retrial may be ordered, the appeal may be upheld or dismissed, and a higher sentence may be imposed if the appeal was against sentence. Irregularities in procedure are appealed against by way of bill of suspension (by the accused) or bill of advocation (by the prosecutor).

1.72 In criminal appeal roll cases, only the accused may appeal, against conviction and/or sentence,[54] and new evidence may be led. A new trial may be ordered, and the sentence may be increased in

---

[52] Who in his Court of Session civil capacity is known as the Lord President of the Court of Session.

[53] *i.e.* treason, murder, incest and rape, known as the "Crown pleas," in which the High Court has exclusive first instance jurisdiction.

[54] But not when the sentence is fixed by law, as in the case of life imprisonment for murder.

sentence appeal cases. The Secretary of State may refer a case to the High Court of Justiciary whether an appeal has been lodged or not, and the *nobile officium*[55] may be appealed to in suitable cases. The Lord Advocate may also refer a point of law to the High Court of Justiciary following an acquittal, although it will not affect the acquittal, since there is no right of appeal against a jury verdict, only the legal summary by the judge, or the evidence allowed in, which led to it.

Specialised Courts

1.73   In addition to the regular courts of law, in their criminal and civil hierarchies, there exist within the Scottish legal system certain courts which exercise limited and specialist functions in certain areas delegated to them, normally by statute. The following are among the more important.

Court of the Lord Lyon

1.74   This court specialises in matters relating to heraldry, and the right to bear arms and use heraldic devices or clan badges. It is presided over by the Lord Lyon King of Arms and has the power to fine and imprison offenders, and seize unauthorised goods. Right of appeal lies to the Inner House of the Court of Session, and from thence to the House of Lords.

Scottish Land Court

1.75   This court deals with issues of agricultural landholding, notably crofting, and one of its members[56] must speak Gaelic. Appeal is by way of stated case to the Inner House to the Court of Session.

Lands Valuation Appeal Court

1.76   This deals with appeals against rating decisions over land which have already been heard by local valuation appeal committees and the Lands Tribunal for Scotland. It is normally staffed by

---

[55] For which see 1.38 above.
[56] Only the chairman requires to be legally qualified.

one Court of Session judge,[57] and the appeal is by way of a stated case. There is no further right of appeal.

Restrictive Practices Court

1.77 This is not exclusively a Scottish court at all, but a United Kingdom court established under various statutes to deal with issues relating to unfair trade practices, monopoly agreements and unhealthy price maintenance agreements. In Scotland, it is chaired by a Court of Session judge sitting with lay members (normally two). Appeals on point of law lie to the Court of Session.

Children's Hearings

1.78 The Social Work (Scotland) Act of 1968 set up children's hearings to deal with persons under 16 who appear to be "in need of compulsory measures of care."[58] Each local authority area has a children's panel consisting of lay members, to whom a matter is referred by the local "reporter," a specialist officer of the relevant local authority.

1.79 If the child admits the facts upon which the referral is based, the panel disposes of the case; if not, the matter is referred to the sheriff to make findings of fact. If the sheriff upholds the allegations by the reporter, the matter is referred to the panel. A right of appeal against the decision of the panel lies to the sheriff, while a right of appeal in cases of alleged procedural irregularity, or on a point of law, lies to the Court of Session.

1.80 A child who commits a serious offence may by-pass the children's panel system and be charged in the normal way in the sheriff court or High Court.

Courts Martial

1.81 Once again, these are not exclusively Scottish courts, but simply courts established within the armed forces network to deal

---

[57] Three on an appeal from the Lands Tribunal.
[58] Normally, but not necessarily, evidenced by the child's criminal behaviour.

with offences against the military code. A Courts Martial Appeal Court, if established for a case in Scotland, will consist of three (or five) Lords Commissioners of Justiciary. A further appeal in cases involving only points of law of general public importance will lie to the House of Lords.

Administrative Tribunals

1.82 Administrative tribunals began life historically as an informal, inexpensive means by which the individual could challenge the actions of officialdom in matters which affected him personally, such as taxation, social security payments, etc. Once the popularity and success of such alternatives to the traditional courts became obvious, they came to be used in a whole host of contexts, perhaps the best known of which today are the industrial tribunals established to hear employee grievances against unfair dismissal, sex discrimination etc., and which are considered more fully in context in Chapter 12.

1.83 The composition of such tribunals varies markedly according to the context in which each was established, and in terms of the statute which established it. On the whole, however, they will normally be found to consist of a legally qualified (often full time) chairman assisted by lay members drawn from a panel established for the purpose and intended to reflect the interests of those affected by the tribunal's decision. The industrial tribunals, for example, draw their two lay members per tribunal from two panels, reflecting employee and employer interests generally.

1.84 Judicial control over tribunals is maintained by rights of appeal built into the tribunal system by the legislation setting up each new tribunal, and this right of appeal will normally be to a traditional court such as the Court of Session. Political control in a general sense is exercised by the Council on Tribunals (with a Scottish Committee for Scottish Tribunals) which reports in Scotland, to the Lord Advocate.

1.85 It is the hallmark of tribunals, generally, that they are quicker, cheaper, less formal and more experienced in the particular matters in hand than the traditional courts, which could not in any case cope with the massive case load now handled by tribunals, whose decisions are normally as binding upon the parties as any courts.

Arbitration

1.86 Another alternative to referring a dispute to a traditional court of law is for the parties to refer the matter to arbitration, a process whereby their differences will be considered and ruled upon by an independent third party (the arbiter), or sometimes more than one (with an "oversman" to make the final decision should an even number of arbiters fail to agree).

1.87 The decision to arbitrate may even be taken before any dispute arises, by means, for example, of an "arbitration clause" in a contract. Alternatively, the decision to go to arbitration may be made post-dispute, which requires the parties to prepare a "reference" or "submission" to arbitration, which is in effect a report to the arbiter on the issue(s) which he has to decide. Some statutes[59] provide for arbitration rather than litigation, and a court may refer a matter to an arbiter at the request of the parties (known as a judicial reference to arbitration), in which case the arbiter's findings will normally be incorporated into any eventual decree.

1.88 The advantages of arbitration are obviously speed, simplicity, relative cheapness, privacy and technical expertise. The parties may also agree on a greater degree of informality in the proceedings as compared to what would prevail in a court of law.

1.89 Although the parties may in theory choose any arbiter(s) they wish, in practice the person(s) chosen will normally have expertise in the subject matter of the submission, and may even be a named office-bearer (*e.g.* President of the Royal Incorporation of Architects for Scotland) or a person selected from a standing panel of arbiters maintained by a professional body. Above all, he must be independent, and any personal interest he may have in the out-

---

[59] For example the Agricultural Holdings (Scotland) Act 1949 for matters relating to agricultural tenancies.

come of the matter, however remote,[60] will disqualify him unless the parties, in full knowledge of his interest, have waived it.

1.90 In general, once the parties have agreed to submit to arbitration, they cannot later seek to avoid the consequences of the finding by seeking to re-open the issue in the courts. The successful party may, however, seek a decree conform to the finding from the court, so as to enforce it against the unsuccessful party as if it had been a court ruling.

1.91 The court may also set aside or reduce an arbiter's decision on one or more of the grounds that it is tainted by corruption, bribery or falsehood, that the arbiter had an undisclosed interest in the outcome, that the arbiter has gone beyond the terms of reference set by the parties, that he has failed to fully deal with all the issues raised with him, or that there has been a breach of natural justice.[61]

THE PERSONNEL OF THE SCOTTISH LEGAL SYSTEM

1.92 The main personnel in the Scottish Legal System are the legal practitioners (solicitors and advocates), the judges and the Law Officers of the Crown.

Solicitors

1.93 Solicitors may accurately be described as the general practitioners of the Scottish Legal System, dispensing legal advice on a wide range of topics to clients in every city and town in the country. Most firms invite the public simply to walk in, and there is no need for a prior reference from any other professional. As well as giving legal advice, solicitors will normally draft documents such as wills and contracts, and will appear on behalf of clients in all but the highest courts in the country.[62] In addition to private practice, soli-

---

[60] *e.g.* shares in the company which is one of the parties, as in *Sellar* v. *Highland Ry.*, 1919 S.C.(H.L.)19.
[61] *e.g.* the parties were not given equal rights of audience.
[62] *N.B.* that the provisions of the Law Reform (Miscellaneous Provisions) (Scotland) Act 1990 allow suitably authorised solicitors the right to appear even in those courts (*e.g.* the Court of Session and the High Court) which were previously the exclusive preserve of advocates.

citors may also be found in the public sector, working in local government, banking, insurance, the procurator fiscal service and so on. Many of them are now sheriffs. Entry to the profession is normally via a university law degree, a post graduate Diploma in Legal Practice and a two-year period of traineeship in a solicitor's office. Thereafter a practising certificate is issued by the Law Society of Scotland, the profession's governing body.

Advocates

1.94 Advocates[63] offer a more specialist service, either in the higher courts pleading a case on behalf of a client, or in chambers giving expert opinions. In all cases, they act only when a case is referred to them by a solicitor, who instructs the advocate on behalf of the client.

1.95 The professional body to which advocates belong is known as the Faculty of Advocates, and its leader is the Dean of the Faculty. Professional qualification is by a similar route to that of solicitor training. A year's traineeship in a solicitor's office is required and nine months as the "pupil" or "devil" of an established and practising advocate. In practice, many advocates are qualified, and often experienced, solicitors prior to admission to the Faculty.

1.96 Senior advocates may at a suitable time apply to "take silk,"[64] and become a Queen's Counsel (Q.C.).

Judiciary

1.97 The identities of the various members of the Scottish judiciary have been noted in passing when dealing with the courts of law in which they sit. Appointment to the Court of Session and the High Court of Justiciary has hitherto been exclusively granted to senior Q.C.s, but the Law Reform (Miscellaneous Provisions) (Scotland) Act of 1990 allows the appointment to this rank of sheriffs of not less than five years standing, and many such qualified sheriffs are solicitors. Those solicitors made eligible for a right of

---

[63] In England known as barristers.
[64] A term derived from the fact that a Q.C.'s gown is made of silk.

audience in the Court of Session and High Court of Justiciary under the 1990 Act will also become eligible for appointment to the benches of those courts after five years minimum experience in this new role.

1.98   Sheriffs, as indicated above, may be advocates or solicitors of 10 years standing, while for stipendiary magistrates the equivalent period is five years. Lay magistrates are of course not qualified legally.

Law Officers of the Crown

1.99   The main crown law officers in Scotland are the Lord Advocate and the Solicitor General for Scotland. Their appointments are political, and they are normally MPs whose office is likely to change with a change in government. They are both normally former senior advocates, and may on occasions appear in court for the crown on important or sensitive matters, as well as heading the departments which advise the crown (through the Secretary of State for Scotland) on legal issues affecting Scotland.

1.100   The Lord Advocate also presides over the Crown Office, which is the public prosecution network for Scotland. The Lord Advocate himself has under him a team of full time senior advocates known as the advocates-depute, who normally appear for the crown in High Court of Justiciary matters, both first instance and appellate. Within the Crown Office is another second in command to the Lord Advocate, the Crown Agent, who supervises the procurator fiscal system of local prosecution referred to in 1.63 above. Procurators fiscal in turn are normally solicitors by profession, but can also be advocates, since appointment is open to both professions.

2. THE NATURE AND FORMATION OF CONTRACT

THE NATURE OF CONTRACT

Intention to Create Legal Relations

2.1 A contract may be defined as: "An agreement which creates, or is intended to create, a legal obligation between the parties to it."[1]

2.2 The essential distinction between a legally binding contract and all other forms of agreement is the intention of the parties that their negotiated terms shall be enforceable in law. A contract may therefore be distinguished from a mere social agreement. If, for example, a man agrees to play for his football team on Saturday, and opts to go fishing instead, his club would not normally be able to sue him. It would be a different story, however, if he were a professional player under contract to the club.[2]

2.3 The "intention to create legal relations" which the parties to an agreement must display before that agreement becomes a contract is something about which one cannot generalise. Not every domestic agreement will be downgraded to non-contractual status if the context in which it was made was a commercial one; thus, in *Merritt* v. *Merritt*[3] it was held that an agreement between a husband and wife which affected the wife's financial claim on a deserting husband was a contract because the parties clearly intended thereby to affect their legal relations, while in *Simkins* v. *Pays*[4] the court awarded to a lodger the one-third share he was claiming in the proceeds of a newspaper competition entered into weekly by

---

[1] Jenks, *Digest of English Civil Law*, 2.1.

[2] In *Skerret* v. *Oliver* (1896) 23 R. 468, a similar distinction was made between the expulsion of an ordinary congregation member from a church (non-contractual) and the expulsion of the minister (contractual if the minister derives income from his position).

[3] [1970] 2 All E.R. 760.

[4] [1955] 3 All E.R. 10.

a syndicate which comprised the plaintiff, his landlady and her grand-daughter.

2.4   Similarly, even those agreements which by every other yard-stick would be regarded as commercial will be refused contractual status when the parties manifest their unwillingness to create a legal relationship. The clearest example of such an agreement is one which is stated by the parties to be "binding in honour only;" in *Jones* v. *Vernon's Pools*,[5] such a clause was upheld so as to prevent the winner of a football pool from claiming a first dividend.

2.5   Occasionally the position is regulated by statute, one of the clearest examples being section 18 of the Trade Union and Labour Relations Act 1974, which expressly provides that "collective agreements" in writing between trade unions and employer organ-isations will be presumed *not* to be legally binding unless the agree-ment itself states to the contrary.

2.6   Unlike the position under English law, there is no need for both parties to provide "consideration"[6] before an agreement will be legally enforceable. Thus, in *Morton's Trs.* v. *Aged Christian Friend Society of Scotland*[7] it was held that the Society could legally enforce a written promise by the late M. to pay annual instalments to the Society even though he received nothing (except presumably satisfaction) in return.

Agreement

2.7   As is implicit in the definition of contract given above, there can be no legally binding contract unless and until the parties have at least reached agreement on the basic terms which will sub-sequently bind them. This agreement is still dignified by the Latin phrase *consensus in idem*,[8] and in the vast majority of cases pro-vides no problems, in that the parties have clearly expresseed

---

[5] [1938] 2 All E.R. 626.
[6] *i.e.* something of value. But *N.B.* the special rule requiring proof of such contracts by writ or oath, considered in 2.72 below.
[7] (1899) 2 F. 82; 7 S.L.T. 220. *N.B.* that the undertaking by M. was in his own handwriting.
[8] A "meeting of minds."

(orally or in writing) what they wish to agree, or this wish can be clearly inferred from their actions.[9]

2.8 Inevitably, when later being called upon to construe the parties' intentions,[10] the courts are obliged to apply some objectivity in hindsight, and it frequently comes down to what a "reasonable man" would have concluded were the parties' intentions, having regard to their words and actions at that time.

2.9 One of the clearest examples of this process arose in *Muirhead and Turnbull v. Dickson*,[11] one of the first cases on hire-purchase contracts, in which D. agreed to buy a piano for £26, payable in monthly instalments. There was no written agreement, but the piano was delivered and after five months D. stopped payment. The deceptively simple question for the court was whether or not the firm of M. and T. could recover the piano, and in concluding that it could not, but could recover the unpaid instalments, the court pointed out that the onus was on M. and T. to record in the agreement its continuing right to recover the piano if that was what had been intended, since "Commercial agreements are arranged according to what people say."[12]

2.10 As will be seen later[13] a genuine failure on the part of the parties to reach any form of agreement which the courts can construe may lead to the so-called contract being "void" for "mutual error." A later section[14] also illustrates how the parties' intentions may be construed entirely from the circumstances in which they placed themselves.

2.11 In the vast majority of cases, however, the agreement between the parties is both reached and recorded by means of

[9] As, for example, when a customer takes a morning newspaper from the shop counter and silently hands the exact money to the assistant. Not a word has been spoken, but the parties are *ad idem* and a contract has been made.
[10] By which stage it can be guaranteed that the parties themselves offer conflicting interpretations.
[11] (1905) 7 F. 686; 13 S.L.T. 151.
[12] *Ibid.*, a powerful reason for "reading the small print."
[13] In 3.15—3.20 below.
[14] 2.44.

a process known as "offer and acceptance," which may now be examined.

OFFER

The Nature of an Offer

2.12   An offer may be described as a statement by a person seeking to enter into a contract (the "offeror") which contains all the essential terms upon which he wishes to do business with the person to whom it is made (the "offeree") which, if it is met with a simple "yes," will result in the making of a binding contract. It may be made orally, in writing, or by means of silent action (*e.g.* taking an item from a shop display counter and handing it to the assistant with the required money). It may be by an agreed symbolic action, as in the case of a hand bid in an auction, or it may be by implication, as in *Chapelton* v. *Barry U.D.C.*[15] in which it was held that the silent display of deckchairs on a beach was an implied offer to holidaymakers to take one at the advertised hire price.

2.13   Before any statement or action may be said to have the quality of an offer, however, it must be definite and unequivocal in its terms, and the offeror must clearly intend to be bound by its terms. For this reason, it is sometimes necessary to distinguish between true offers and other statements which can, superficially, look like offers, but which cannot simply be accepted so as to lead to a binding contract. Chief among these are 1. invitations to treat, 2. quotations of price and 3. expressions of intention.

1. *Invitation to Treat*

2.14   An invitation to treat is nothing more than a request for offers, and as such is something which occurs *before* an offer is made, the important distinction being that whereas an offer can be accepted in order to form a binding contract, an invitation to treat cannot, since the response which it generates, however enthusiastic,

---

[15] [1940] 1 K.B. 532, considered more fully in 2.49 below.

can only itself be an offer, which the original "inviter" may accept or reject.

2.15 There are some clear and obvious examples of invitations to treat, such as the request for the submission of tenders for a project, or an advertisement in a newspaper that goods are for sale.[16] There have, however, been some problem cases in the past which have required judicial intervention.

2.16 For example, it is now authoritatively settled that in an auction situation, it is the bidder who makes the offer, which may or may not be accepted by the auctioneer, as agent for the seller, which acceptance is signified by the fall of the hammer. This is so even though the auction is stated to be "without reserve."[17] In *Thornton* v. *Shoe Lane Parking*[18] it was held that a silent ticket machine (in this case at the entrance to a multi-storey car park) was *not* an invitation to treat but a firm offer accepted by the motorist taking a ticket, while in *Gibson* v. *Manchester City Council*[19] it was held that a letter from the Council to a tenant in which it indicated that it might be prepared to sell the house to him for a given purchase price was only an invitation to treat.

2.17 But, without doubt, the most controversial of the situations in which the courts have had to distinguish between offers and invitations to treat has been the display of goods in a shop, and the matter was settled authoritatively in *Pharmaceutical Society of Great Britain* v. *Boots Cash Chemists (Southern) Ltd.*[20] in which, in order to avoid conviction on a criminal charge of selling drugs in a supermarket without the presence of a qualified pharmacist, Boots were required to convince the court (which they did) that the sale took place at the cash desk, when an offer to purchase was

---

[16] N.B. however that some newspaper advertisements may be classed as offers—see the *Carbolic Smoke Ball* case in 2.24 below.

[17] *i.e.* without a minimum price below which the auctioneer is instructed not to go; see *Fenwick* v. *Macdonald, Fraser & Co.* (1904) 6 F. 850.

[18] [1971] 2 Q.B. 163, considered again in 2.47 below. Other silent machines which are generally regarded as being standing offers are food vending machines and petrol pumps.

[19] [1979] 1 All E.R. 972.

[20] [1952] 2 Q.B. 795.

made by the customer and accepted (or not) by the cashier, who was attended by a pharmacist. The mere display of the goods on the shelves was therefore only an invitation to treat.

2. *Quotation of Price*

2.18   When a person wishing to do business with another, or with people generally, announces the price or prices of his product, his announcement will normally be taken to be something short of an offer. However, such a statement can, in context, be taken as being a firm offer, and should therefore be made cautiously. It is all a question of interpretation in the circumstances, as may be illustrated by contrasting the two leading cases.

2.19   In *Philp* v. *Knoblauch*[21] K.'s letter to P., which included the phrase, "I am offering today plate linseed for January/February shipment to Leith, and have pleasure in quoting you 100 tons at 41/3 such plate terms. I shall be glad to hear if you are buyers" was held to be a firm offer because it was "an absolutely definite offer of a specific quantity at a specific price." In *Harvey* v. *Facey*,[22] on the other hand, H. sent a telegram to F. asking whether he would consider selling the "Bumper Hall Pen" in Jamaica, and asked him to telegraph his lowest cash price. F.'s reply of "lowest cash price for Bumper Hall Pen £900" was held not to be an offer, which H. claimed to have accepted by return telegram, but simply a price quotation, which might or might not lead to an offer, but was not itself an offer.

3. *Expression of Intention*

2.20   A simple announcement by someone that he has something for which offers may be made, or will make something available for sale, is not normally a binding offer to sell. For example, an announcement that an item will be exposed for auction on a given day does not oblige the seller to put it up that day, nor does the person inviting the submission of tenders thereby incur an obligation to accept any of them, not even the best.

---

[21]   1907 S.C. 994.
[22]   [1893] A.C. 552.

2.21 In *Paterson* v. *Highland Ry.*[23] it was held that an announcement by a railway company that a reduced rate would apply for a certain period did not preclude the company from withdrawing the concession before the expiry of that period.

Who May Accept an Offer

2.22 An offer may be made to a given individual (*e.g.* the seller of a car), or to a defined group of people (*e.g.* the members of a particular profession), or to anyone legally capable of accepting (as in the case of the holidaymakers selecting deckchairs in the *Chapelton* case referred to above).

2.23 In extreme cases, an offer may be made to the whole world, in the sense that an offeror exposes himself to acceptance by anyone and everyone who feels moved to accept. Such a policy is doubly dangerous when all that is required by way of acceptance is some action on the part of the offeree which need not be signalled in advance to the offeror.

2.24 This lesson was learned—the hard way—by the manufacturers of a proprietary medicine known as the Carbolic Smoke Ball. So confident were they of its efficacy as a preventative against influenza that they offered, in a newspaper advertisement, to pay £100 to anyone who purchased the item, used it as directed, and caught flu. Mrs. Carlill did all of these things, and in her subsequent test case[24] was awarded the £100. It was held that the newspaper advertisement constituted an offer to the whole world, which anyone might accept by simply doing what was requested, without formally notifying the company that they were about to put their product to the test.

2.25 In the normal course of business, however, an offer will be made to a particular person or business entity, who alone is capable in law of accepting.

---

[23] 1927 S.C.(H.L.) 32.
[24] *Carlill* v. *Carbolic Smoke Ball Ltd.* [1893] 1 Q.B. 256.

Communication of Offer

2.26 With the exception of those contracts which may only be formed or proved by a particular method (normally writing), an offer may be made in any form which is capable of adequately communicating to the offeree what is being offered. But before it will be valid, an offer must be so communicated.

2.27 This is perhaps a somewhat obvious proposition which is unlikely to cause many difficulties in practice, but among the problems which are occasionally encountered are offers made without authority (normally held to be invalid) and offers which take a long time to reach their intended destination. The general rule is that an offer received after the expiry of either a period specified by the offeror or a "reasonable" time in the circumstances will simply lapse, and be incapable of acceptance. The implications of this become more obvious below.

Revocation of Offer

2.28 As a general rule, an offer may be revoked by the offeror at any time before it is accepted by the offeree; during this period the offeror is said to have *locus poenitentiae* (which roughly translated means time for second thoughts or "room for repentance"). Assuming that he does so clearly before there has been an unqualified acceptance by the offeree, there will normally be no difficulty, but questions of law can arise when it is alleged that the offeror undertook to keep his offer open for a certain period of time, and therefore cannot lawfully revoke within that period.

2.29 The general rule is illustrated by the leading case of *Littlejohn* v. *Hadwen*,[25] in which, at the foot of a letter describing an estate of land which was for sale, the seller's solicitors indicated that the potential purchaser had an option to purchase which would remain open for 10 days. It was held that the offeror was legally bound to keep the offer open for that period. However, in the more recent case of *Effold Properties* v. *Sprot*[26] it was held that

---

[25] (1882) 20 S.L.R. 5.
[26] 1979 S.L.T. (Notes) 84.

there was a world of difference between that situation and one in which the offeror states that his offer must be accepted within a certain time. In this latter situation, the offeror is still free to withdraw his offer within the specified time.

2.30 An offer is also normally revoked automatically upon the expiry of a period specified by the offeror as being that during which it must be accepted. In the absence of any such fixed period, the court will also deem an offer to have been revoked after the expiry of a period which is "reasonable" in the circumstances. This is obviously a question of fact,[27] and in some cases the relevant period may be a very short one, particularly if it involves a commodity which fluctuates in price over a short period. Thus, in *Wylie and Lochhead* v. *McElroy and Sons*,[28] it was held to be unreasonable for contractors to wait five weeks before purporting to accept an offer to carry out ironworks for a new stable block.

2.31 An offer is also impliedly revoked by the death of either party, by the offeror's bankruptcy or insanity and by outright rejection by the offeree. The same effect is produced by a "counter-offer" from the offeree, which is best considered separately.

Counter-Offer

2.32 Since the parties must clearly be *ad idem* before a valid contract is formed, it follows that an offer by A which is answered by B in the form of proposed new terms cannot be regarded in law as having given rise to a contract. A's original offer has been impliedly revoked and replaced by a new offer from B which A can either accept or reject.

2.33 The effect of such a process is clearly illustrated by the facts of *Wolf and Wolf* v. *Forfar Potato Co.*,[29] in which F. telexed an offer to sell potatoes to W., which was open for acceptance by 5

---

[27] In which assistance may be obtained from a variety of sources, such as trade custom.

[28] (1873) 1 R. 41. It was held that in such cases, acceptance by return of post was more appropriate.

[29] 1984 S.L.T. 100. For another example of this process, see *Rutterford* v. *Allied Breweries*, 1990 S.L.T. 249.

p.m. the following day. A purported acceptance was telexed by W. the following day, but it set out proposed new terms. Having learned by telephone that these new terms were unacceptable, W. then sent an unconditional acceptance of the original offer, again by telex, before the deadline. It was held that, having killed the original offer by their counter-offer, and no similar offer having been reissued by F., W. had nothing to accept in their second telex, and there was therefore no contract.

2.34   However, the general rule does allow for some fine points of distinction. It is not, apparently, a counter-offer if the acceptance contains some meaningless additional terms which may safely be ignored, allowing the contract to proceed on the original conditions.[30] Similarly, it will not create a counter-offer if the offeree includes in his acceptance proposals as to how the contract may be executed.

ACCEPTANCE

Forms of Acceptance

2.35   Provided that an acceptance may be said to be an unqualified assent to the terms of an offer, it does not matter, as a general rule, whether it is express or implied. If the offeror specifies a particular method of acceptance (*e.g.* by letter), then this method must be used if acceptance is to be validly made. Thus, a stipulation that acceptance be "by notice in writing to the intending vendor" of a house is not validly met by a telephone call.[31]

2.36   In all other cases, acceptance may be by any normally accepted means, although the safest policy is probably to accept by the same medium as that by which the offer was made (*i.e.* a letter for a letter, telex for telex, etc.). Acceptance may even be

---

[30] *Nicolene Ltd.* v. *Simmonds* [1953] 1 Q.B. 543, the term in question being to the effect that "the usual conditions of acceptance apply," when no such conditions existed.
[31] *Holwell Securities* v. *Hughes* [1974] 1 W.L.R. 155.

validly effected by a silent action,[32] particularly if it is preceded by a silent offer.

2.37 But an offeror may not impose contractual obligations on an unwilling offeree by stipulating that continued silence on his part will be construed as acceptance. A popular commercial trick in the 1960s was for traders to send unsolicited goods to unwilling purchasers, along with a letter to the effect that they would be taken to have purchased them if they did not return them within a specified period. The Unsolicited Goods and Services Act of 1971 made this officially unlawful and awarded the goods in question to the recipient if the sender did not collect them within a certain period.

Time of Acceptance

2.38 In order to be validly made, an acceptance must be communicated to the offeror, in just the same way that an offer is only valid when communicated to the offeree. However, the moment of "deemed" communication will vary according to the medium chosen. Clearly, a verbal acceptance will normally be instantly communicated to the offeror,[33] but dangers may arise if a method of communication normally regarded as equivalent to the spoken word is chosen.

2.39 For example, in *Brinkibon Ltd.* v. *Stahag Stahl*[34] it was held that a telex acceptance is only valid when printed out at the offeror's end, and the same rule would no doubt apply to a fax, although at least in such cases the sender normally has a mechanical confirmation that the transmission has been received.

2.40 In cases in which acceptance is sent by post, however, there is a special rule to the effect that acceptance is valid as soon as the

---

[32] *e.g.* a shop assistant handing over the item requested, or a purchaser performing an act in respect of goods delivered to him which is inconsistent with the continuing rights of the seller; see Sale of Goods Act 1979, s. 35, considered in 5.101 below. See also the *Carbolic Smoke Ball* case in 2.24 above.

[33] Leaving aside those highly unlikely scenarios beloved of examiners in which the noise of an aircraft or a passing truck drowns out the words.

[34] [1983] 2 A.C. 34; [1982] 1 All E.R. 293.

letter is lawfully placed within the control of the postal authorities
(*e.g.* by putting it into a pillar box). The importance of this rule is
that any communication by the offeror purporting to revoke his
offer which arrives after such a letter of acceptance has been posted
(even if it arrives before the letter of acceptance is received by the
offeror) is invalid. It is simply too late.

2.41   Two classic examples of this rule in action were *Jacobsen*
v. *Underwood*,[35] in which the offeror's condition that the offeree
reply by a certain date was held to have been satisfied when a letter
of acceptance was posted on that date, even though it did not arrive
until the following day, and *Thomson* v. *James*[36] in which T. posted
an acceptance on the same day that J. posted a revocation of his
offer. The two letters crossed in the post and reached their respective destinations on the following day. It was held that since the
acceptance (valid when posted) had occurred before the revocation
(valid when received), there was a contract.

Revocation of Acceptance

2.42   A tantalising question is whether or not an acceptance, once
validly communicated, can be revoked before it is received by the
offeree. In practical commonsense terms this can only happen in
cases in which communication of acceptance is separated in time
from its receipt by the offeror (*e.g.* in postal cases), and in the only
apparent recorded case on the subject, *Countess of Dunmore* v.
Alexander,[37] it was held that an acceptance may be revoked by a
communication which arrives before, or at the same time as, that
acceptance.

2.43   However, later cases[38] have cast doubt on the extreme
application of such a rule, and it is probably safer to conclude that
it only applies when the revocation arrives *before* the acceptance.

---

[35] (1894) 21 R. 654.
[36] (1855) 18 D.1.
[37] (1830) 9 S. 190, involving an acceptance of a servant's offer to commence work
which arrived in the same post as a letter cancelling the acceptance.
[38] *e.g. Holwell Securities*, considered in 2.35 above.

IMPLIED CONTRACTS

The Construction of an Implied Contract

2.44 As will be noted in later sections of this book, there are many situations in which the courts are prepared to imply specific terms into an existing contract,[39] but very rarely will the courts imply the very existence of an entire contract without some overt sign by the parties that they intend to enter into one.

2.45 However, on occasions it is both possible and sensible to infer that when two parties took certain actions, it must have been obvious to them that they were thereby bringing a contractual relationship into being. One (admittedly rare) example was the case of *Clarke* v. *Dunraven*,[40] in which it was held that competitors in an amateur yacht club race had, by virtue of entering into the race in terms of the club rules, contracted to pay full compensation to any other competitor whose vessel they damaged. Although there was no obvious formal offer and acceptance procedure between each of the members and the others, the court was prepared to construct one in order to give effect to what it clearly believed to be a contract.

INCORPORATION OF CONTRACTUAL TERMS

The General Rule

2.46 In the ideal situation, the parties to a contract will set out at length, in advance, all the terms and conditions of the proposed contract, hopefully in a document which leaves nothing to chance. On occasions, however, they are not so obliging, and the courts are required to rule upon the question of whether or not a particular term or condition (written or oral) has validly become part of the contract. The specific implications of this process, so far as

---

[39] *e.g.* the implied terms in a sale of goods contract (for which see 5.61–5.88 below), and equality clauses in contracts of employment (for which see 11.28 below).
[40] [1895] P. 248; [1897] A.C. 59.

concerns purported "exemption clauses," will be considered in
4.2—4.15 below.

2.47 The first general rule is that no additional terms may be
incorporated into the contract after it has been formed (*i.e.* after the
offer has been accepted). Thus, in *Olley* v. *Marlborough Court*[41] it
was held that a notice displayed in a hotel room which contained
an exemption clause was not part of the contract because the guest
to whose attention it was directed had already entered into the
contract of booking at the reception desk, and it was by then too
late to include additional terms and conditions. In a more modern
context, the English Court of Appeal, in *Thornton* v. *Shoe Lane
Parking*,[42] said the same of a purported exemption clause contained
(a) in the ticket paid for by a motorist when he entered a multi-
storey car park, and (b) in a notice on the wall of the car park.
Both attempts at incorporating a term into the contract occurred
after the making of the contract.

2.48 Tickets have provided special difficulties for the courts, and
a series of "ticket cases" raised the question of whether or not,
when receiving a ticket, the customer in each case was merely
obtaining a receipt or in fact receiving an important contractual
document which contained terms by which he was bound.

2.49 As has already been seen, it was held in *Chapelton* v. *Barry
UDC*[43] that a customer taking a deckchair from a pile on a beach
was accepting the silent offer which the pile itself constituted, and
that therefore the subsequent issue of a ticket was merely the handing over of a receipt, and could not validly be used to incorporate
an exemption clause. The same decision was given closer to home
in *Taylor* v. *Glasgow Corporation*,[44] in the context of a ticket
issued to bathers paying for entrance to a public baths. The principle would seem to be that tickets of this type can only become
contractual documents when they are clearly identified as such in
advance of the contract being entered into.

[41] [1949] 1 K.B. 532.
[42] [1971] 2 Q.B. 163.
[43] [1940] 1 K.B. 532, considered in 2.12 above.
[44] 1952 S.C. 440.

2.50 Thus, in *Hood* v. *Anchor Line*,[45] it was held that the operators of a shipping line had successfully incorporated an exemption
clause into a contract when it was handed to the passenger in an
envelope which read, "Please read contents of enclosed contract."
The same effect can sometimes be achieved when the party seeking
to assert that the clause has been validly incorporated into the
contract can show that the other party was aware of its existence
by virtue of previous dealings between the parties.[46]

2.51 Finally, it should be emphasised that any party unwise
enough to sign a contract which contains conditions which he later
wishes to challenge will have considerable difficulty in persuading
the court that the clause in question was not brought to his attention before the contract was entered into. Hence the wisdom of
"reading the small print."

The Battle of Forms

2.52 A recent phenomenon in the law relating to the incorporation of terms into a contract has involved the practice of larger
commercial organisations seeking to do business only on their own
standard terms and conditions, incorporated into a form which is
simply handed to the other party for his signature. The implications
of this practice when the terms and conditions are unfair to the
recipient party, who is an ordinary domestic consumer, are considered in 4.9 below, but the other problem which has beset the courts
is that which arises when two contracting organisations seek to do
the same thing at the same time, so that their contractual negotiations turn into what has become known as "a battle of forms."

2.53 One of the earliest examples of this process was *Butler
Machine Tool Co.* v. *Ex-Cell-O Corpn.*,[47] in which an offer from
B. contained a standard clause allowing a possible subsequent price
increase pre-delivery. The standard-form acceptance sent by E. con-

---

[45] 1918 S.C.(H.L.) 143.
[46] Although ironically such an attempt failed in the leading case of *McCutcheon* v.
McBrayne, 1964 S.C.(H.L.) 28, in which the possibility of such a constructive notice
was confirmed.
[47] [1979] 1 All E.R. 965.

tained a different condition, and incorporated a tear-off portion which B. signed and returned to E., as requested, signifying that E.'s standard terms were acceptable. However, B. enclosed with it a letter which sought to reinstate the terms of B.'s original offer. It was held that a contract had been formed on E.'s standard terms (*i.e.* not allowing for a price rise) because B. had, by returning the tear-off slip, accepted the counter-offer by E.[48]

2.54   Another device is for the original offer to contain what is called an "overriding clause," which states that the terms of the offer will prevail unless and until the offeror himself confirms a variation in writing; the validity of such a device was confirmed in *Roofcare Ltd.* v. *Gillies*.[49]

FORMALITIES

The General Rule

2.55   The general rule under Scots law is that no formalities are required in order to make a valid contract, and that a contract will therefore be enforceable whether made orally, in writing, or by implication arising from the parties' actions.

2.56   To this general rule there are two important categories of exception, namely:

1. *Obligationes literis.* These are contracts which must be constituted by formal writing in order to be valid.

2. *Contracts requiring proof by writ or oath.* This group of contracts cannot be enforced unless and until their existence is proved by either a written acknowledgment by the person alleged to be

---

[48] For a similar case in which an original offeror was taken to have accepted a counter-offer (constituted by the offeror's standard form contract) by virtue of having taken delivery of the goods, see *Uniroyal Ltd.* v. *Miller and Co. Ltd.*, 1985 S.L.T. 101. But see also *Continental Tyre and Rubber Co.* v. *Trunk Trailer Co.*, 1987 S.L.T. 58.

[49] 1984 S.L.T. (Sh.Ct.) 8.

bound by the contract, or his testimony on oath in court that the contract exists.

2.57 Each of these exceptional categories may now be examined more fully.

Obligationes Literis

Applicable Categories of Contract

2.58 The following are the remaining categories of contract which under Scots law require to be constituted by means of formal writing:

2.59 1. *Contracts concerning heritable property.*[50] This category includes not only offers and acceptances ("missives") for the sale of houses and other buildings, but also leases for property which are to operate for more than one year. A classic example of this requirement in practice was the leading case of *Goldston* v. *Young*,[51] referred to in 2.82 below.

2.60 2. *Contracts of employment for one year and all contracts of apprenticeship.* In reality, the old common law rule has tended to take second place to the more modern requirements of the Employment Protection (Consolidation) Act of 1978, considered in Chapter 9.

2.61 3. *Formal submissions to arbitration and decrees-arbitral which discharge such submissions.*

2.62 4. *Contracts which the parties agree should be constituted by formal writing.*

2.63 5. *Contracts which, by operation of statute, require to be constituted in writing.* Examples of such contracts which are found elsewhere in this book are the memoranda and articles of a regis-

---

[50] *i.e.* property such as land and buildings.
[51] (1868) 7 M. 188.

tered company, and "regulated agreements" under the Consumer Credit Act of 1974.

Forms of Writing Required

2.64   When a particular statute specifies a form of writing which must be adhered to,[52] then the contract in question will be validly constituted if this form is followed. In all other instances of *obligationes literis*, the writing in question must either be "probative" (*i.e.* attested) or "privileged" (*i.e.* holograph or *in re mercatoria*). These confusing and forbidding expressions may be simply defined:

2.65   1. *Attested writings.* An "attested writing" is simply one which is signed by the maker in the presence of two witnesses[53] each of whom also signs as a witness to the maker's signature. An "attestation clause"[54] is then completed in a space left above the signatures, which records the date and place of signing, and the names and addresses of the witnesses. A special form of "notarial execution" allows blind or illiterate persons to attest to a deed by the hand of a notary public, solicitor, J.P. or church minister (for wills only) in the presence of two witnesses. Attested writings are normal for the transfer of heritable property by title deed, and are preferable for the making of wills.

2.66   Attested documents are the only ones which are fully "probative" (*i.e.* self-proving) without further procedure.

2.67   2. *Holograph writings.* A holograph writing is one which is entirely, or in all essential parts, written by hand by the maker, who then signs it. A holograph writing is for most purposes as formal as an attested one, unless it is challenged, in which case the person seeking to rely on it must produce other evidence proving

---

[52] *e.g.* the documentation which must be issued to a "consumer" under the Consumer Credit Act, for which see 6.28—6.29 below.

[53] *N.B.* that as an alternative, the maker, having already signed, may acknowledge his signature to the witnesses.

[54] Normally commencing with the words "IN WITNESS WHEREOF." *N.B.* that this clause is not strictly necessary, provided that the witnesses specify their addresses and occupations after their signatures.

that the handwriting is genuinely that of the alleged subscriber, and the date upon which it was signed.

2.68 A further refinement of the process has led to the regular practice whereby a document is typed or printed, and then signed by the party, who writes the words "adopted as holograph" immediately before his signature. This has the accepted practical effect of making the whole document holograph in form, and is a common means of binding communication between solicitors (*e.g.* exchanging "missives" for property sales). This device also allows two parties to adopt the same document as incorporating the terms of their contract.

2.69 3. *Documents in re mercatoria.* Over the years, commercial expediency has resulted in certain forms of business documents being granted validity if they are simply signed. Examples encountered in this book are contracts of agency and orders for goods, but their alleged privileged status is something of a myth, since, if their validity is challenged, full proof is required from those seeking to rely on them.

Contracts Requiring Proof by Writ or Oath

2.70 Some contracts, while not requiring to be constituted by formal writing, can be enforced only if the enforcing party (A) can *either* show that the other party (B) has acknowledged the existence of the contract in writing, *or* force B to admit to its existence on oath in evidence. For all practical purposes, only the former method has the remotest chance of success.

2.71 The following are the remaining categories of contract which fall into this group:

2.72 1. *Gratuitous obligations.* These are agreements in which one party gives "something for nothing," in the sense that he agrees to part with something of material value without any material return. Such a one-sided arrangement can only be enforced if the court is satisfied that the granter has acknowledged it on oath or in writing. Thus, in *Smith* v. *Oliver*,[55] an oral promise by a lady to leave a sum of money in her will for church repairs was held to be unenforceable after her death, when her will proved silent on the subject.

2.73 2. *Loans of money in excess of £8.33.* This is the modern equivalent of £100 Scots, the sum around which the original rule was developed.

2.74 3. *Trusts.* A trust exists when a person who appears to be the absolute owner of property in reality holds it "on trust for" (*i.e.* for the benefit of) some other person (the "beneficiary").

2.75 4. *Obligations of relief.* These are situations in which A expressly agrees with B that he will relieve C of some duty (which may be the future payment of money) to be performed by C towards B. In *Devlin* v. *McKelvie*,[56] for example, it was held to cover a situation in which one director was alleged to have undertaken to relieve his co-directors of the liability to repay a bank overdraft.

2.76 5. *Innominate or unusual contracts.* These are contracts which either do not fall within any of the usual categories of contract, or else are so unusual in their terms that the court will not enforce them without evidence proving their existence in the form of writ or oath. An early leading case was *Garden* v. *Earl of Aberdeen*,[57] in which it was held necessary to prove, by writ or oath, an alleged agreement whereby if a tenant would honour his remaining year of a 19-year lease, the landlord undertook to reimburse him all his losses for the entire 19 years.

2.77 The same rule was applied more recently in *McCourt* v. *McCourt*,[58] in which the court held as both innominate and unusual an alleged gratuitous promise by an estranged wife to hand

---

[55] 1911 S.C. 103; 1910 S.L.T. 304. But see *Morton's* case in 2.6 above, in which a similar sort of undertaking was enforceable because it was made in writing.
[56] 1915 S.C. 180.
[57] (1893) 20 R. 896.
[58] 1985 S.L.T. 335. *N.B.* here, the dual reason for requiring proof by writ or oath.

over to her husband on demand a taxi operator's licence held in her name from Glasgow District Council. In the absence of writ or oath, the husband failed.

2.78 In all cases requiring proof by writ or oath, the "writing" need not itself be probative; thus, in *Paterson* v. *Paterson*,[59] it was held that a loan of £450 made by a man to his mother could be proved by a simple written acknowledgment from her made at the time.

Proposals for Reform

2.79 After much valid criticism of the haphazard and illogical state of the law on the subject of contractual formalities, the Scottish Law Commission, in 1988, recommended that those categories of contract currently requiring proof by writ or oath be abolished,[60] and that the only contracts which should continue to require writing should be those relating to heritage, gratuitous obligations, cautionary obligations,[61] those required to be in writing by statute, and those which the parties themselves have stipulated should be in writing.

2.80 A further proposal is that only one witness should be required in order to make a document probative, and that only a signature should be required for all non-probative writings.[62]

Consequences of Defects in Form

2.81 When, under the current law, a contract falls into the category of *obligationes literis*,[63] then a failure to observe the formalities renders the contract "defective in form," and either party may "resile" (*i.e.* withdraw). During the period in which the defect

---

[59] (1897) 25 R. 144.
[60] So that proof *prout de jure* (*i.e.* by any admissible means) would thereafter be sufficient.
[61] *i.e.* guarantees.
[62] Thus abolishing the need for holograph writings.
[63] *N.B.* not simply one which requires proof by writ or oath.

continues, the parties are said to possess *locus poenitentiae*,[64] and the contract is not binding.

2.82 The classic example of this rule in operation is still *Goldston v. Young*,[65] in which a shop owner, Y., wrote out an offer by G. to purchase his shop, and got G. to sign it. Y. then wrote out and signed an acceptance. The problem was, of course, that G.'s offer was neither holograph nor attested, and since the contract involved the sale of heritable property, Y. was able to resile without penalty when he later changed his mind about selling.

2.83 To prevent this sort of situation arising to the disadvantage of one of the parties after some performance has followed in the belief that a contract exists, the law has developed the "doctrine of personal bar," which may conveniently be considered as a separate topic.

THE DOCTRINE OF PERSONAL BAR

The Operation of the Doctrine

2.84 As indicated above, the law has recognised that in many circumstances it would be inequitable to allow a party to a contract to lead the other party, by his actions, into believing that the contract is to proceed, only to stand on his legal "rights" later on, pointing to the fact that the contract is formally invalid.

2.85 The rule therefore is that if A has either performed some act consistent with the validity of the contract ("homologation"), or allowed B to take such action (*rei interventus*), then A is barred from resiling from the contract, and *locus poenitentiae* has been overridden by personal bar.

2.86 Each of these concepts requires a section to itself, even though homologation and *rei interventus* operate to the same effect.

---

[64] Translated loosely as "room for repentance" or time for second thoughts.
[65] (1868) 7 M. 188.

Rei Interventus

2.87 *Rei interventus* consists of actions on the part of the party seeking to enforce the contract (B) which were either performed with the knowledge of (and lack of challenge by) A, or were such that they were a foreseeable and natural consequence of the informal[66] agreement between the parties. In order for the doctrine to operate, B's actions must be more than trivial, and they must clearly be in furtherance of his belief that a contract exists between himself and A. B must also be able to show that he has thereby altered his circumstances, and would suffer loss and inconvenience if A were allowed to resile.

2.88 Operations of the rule included *Grieve* v. *Barr*,[67] in which, on the basis of an improbative lease, and with the landlord's knowledge, the tenant moved on to a farm and planted seeds, and *Walker* v. *Flint*,[68] in which in similar circumstances the tenant erected expensive buildings. In each case, the tenant succeeded in upholding the lease. It is also generally believed that the actions of Mitchell in the *Stornoway Trustees* case below amounted to *rei interventus* on his part.

Homologation

2.89 Homologation consists of some unequivocal action on the part of the person (A) who later attempts to resile from the contract, by means of which he signifies his intention to proceed with the contract, *after* he becomes aware of his right to resile.

2.90 The leading case is *Mitchell* v. *Stornoway Trs.*,[69] in which a dispute arose as to whether or not a piece of land had been validly

---

[66] N.B. that in the absence of at least an informal agreement containing all the essential terms, the doctrine of personal bar cannot operate at all; see *Morrison-Low* v. *Paterson*, 1985 S.L.T. 255. See also note 68.

[67] 1954 S.C. 414. The landlord was held to be barred by *rei interventus* on the part of the tenant.

[68] (1863) 1 M. 417. N.B. however that in this case the lease was restricted to one year, and not the three alleged by the tenant, because the court held that the basic agreement had to be proved by writ or oath. Fortunately the landlord was prepared to admit a one-year lease.

[69] 1936 S.C.(H.L.) 56. This case also illustrates that homologation and *rei interventus* can arise from the same action or set of facts.

feued to M. After proving the informal agreement, M. was also able to point to the fact that the Trustees, in full knowledge of the fact that no formal agreement had been concluded, had nevertheless given their signed approval for an application to be made for building permission for a garage to be erected on the land by M. They compounded this action by giving evidence on M.'s behalf during the oral application. It was held by the House of Lords that the Trustees had by their actions homologated the informal agreement.

CAPACITY TO CONTRACT

General Rule

2.91 Before a valid contract may be made, each of the parties to it must have the legal "capacity" to make such a contract, *i.e.* each party must be one whom the law recognises as having no restriction or impediment which would prevent them from contracting.

2.92 The general rule is that all natural and artificial (*e.g.* registered companies) persons have full contractual capacity. To this rule there exist certain exceptions, considered in the sections below, in respect of the following:

1. Persons under 16.
2. Persons aged 16 to 18.
3. Insane persons.
4. Intoxicated persons.
5. Enemy aliens.
6. Corporate bodies.

Persons Under 16

2.93 As the result of the reforms introduced under the Age of Legal Capacity (Scotland) Act 1991, children under the age of 16 have virtually no contractual capacity, with the result that any contract made by or with such a person will be null and void.

2.94 To this rule there are certain important exceptions. In particular, section 2(1) of the Act allows a person under 16 to enter into a transaction "(a) of a kind commonly entered into by persons of his age and circumstances, and (b) on terms which are not unreasonable." This very flexible test is clearly designed to allow a young person to acquire increasing contractual capacity as he or she grows older, as social circumstances change, and in accordance with the level of independence which the parents or guardians choose to allow such a person to enjoy.

2.95 The great disadvantage of this new rule is, of course, its uncertainty. Thus, while it is clearly "common" for young people aged 12 to buy sweets, soft drinks and magazines, is it yet the norm for them to acquire personal computers? In such doubtful cases, it may well be safer to contract with the parents, at least until a body of case law is established.

2.96 In recognition of this fact, section 5 of the Act continues the old common law rule whereby a young person with no legal capacity of his or her own may contract via his or her "tutor."[70]

Persons Aged 16 to 18

2.97 Under the new legislation, a person reaches full contractual capacity at 16. This does not mean that he or she wakes up on the morning of their sixteenth birthday with the wisdom of Solomon, and accordingly section 3 of the Act allows a person aged 16 or 17 to apply to the court to have a particular transaction set aside.

2.98 This may be done at any time up until the person in question attains 21, and in order to succeed, the applicant must show that the transaction in question was one which "(a) an adult, exercising reasonable prudence, would not have entered into in the circumstances of the applicant at the time of entering into the transaction, and (b) has caused or is likely to cause substantial prejudice to the applicant." If the application is successful, the effect will be to

---

[70] Who by virtue of the provisions of the Law Reform (Parent and Child) (Scotland) Act 1986 will be the child's mother, or its father if married to the mother at the time of conception or later. Each parent may act as tutor without reference to the other, and provisions exist for the appointment of a tutor by the court or after the death of the surviving parent.

make the transaction void,[71] with all the implications which this has for innocent third parties.

2.99 However, a new concept was introduced under section 4 of the Act, whereby any party dealing with a person aged 16 or 17 who is uncertain about whether or not the transaction will later be challenged may apply to the sheriff court to have that transaction "judicially ratified." The two main practical drawbacks to this system are 1. that the application has to be joint (*i.e.* by the young person as well), and 2. that only intended transactions may be so ratified. Once the transaction is entered into and potentially binding, it is ineligible for judicial ratification.

2.100 The effect of judicial ratification is that thereafter the transaction is unchallengeable on the grounds of lack of contractual capacity by the young person. The test to be used by the court in deciding whether or not to ratify is the same as that used by the court when a transaction is challenged under section 3 (see 2.97–2.98 above).

2.101 The other remaining possibility is that a person, when he or she attains the age of 18, himself or herself ratifies the transaction. Having taken this step when no longer under any lingering limited contractual capacity, it is believed that the young person could then no longer challenge the transaction.

Insane Persons

2.102 Since a genuinely insane person is incapable of giving the free consent upon which the law of contract is based, there is a general rule that a contract entered into by an insane person is void, and a person thus incapacitated may only contract via a *curator bonis* (someone appointed by the court to manage such a person's affairs). There is a statutory exception in the case of "necessaries."[72]

2.103 Where, however, a person only becomes insane *after* a contract has been made, it is possible that the law will allow the

---

[71] For which see 3.36 below.
[72] For which see 5.21 below.

contract to continue, either because the personal involvement of the party concerned is not essential,[73] or because of the operation of statute. Thus, under section 35 of the Partnership Act 1890, even though a partner has become insane, it requires application to the court formally to terminate the partnership.

Intoxicated Persons

2.104 Intoxication on the part of one of the parties only renders a contract voidable when it reaches the stage that he no longer knows what he is doing, in the true sense of that term. Mere impaired judgment will not suffice, as is illustrated by the facts in *Taylor* v. *Provan*,[74] in which, in the evening, after a good few drinks, P. accepted a price for cattle from T. which he had rejected when sober that morning. The court refused to set aside the contract; had he not even been aware that he was buying cattle, it might have been a different matter.

2.105 Even if he satisfies that stringent test, the intoxicated person must still take immediate steps to repudiate the contract once he sobers up and realises what he has done. Otherwise it will remain valid, and all such cases are therefore best regarded as voidable only.

Enemy Aliens

2.106 An "enemy alien" is a person who, at time of war between Britain and nation X voluntarily resides or carries on business in that country. It does not matter what nationality that person is, and he or she may even be British. By the same token, a person of nationality X will not be an enemy alien if he or she resides in Britain, even while it is at war with his country of origin.

2.107 The rule is that at time of war with nation X, any contract made with an enemy alien of that country will be not only null and void but also the subject of criminal charges. Contracts already

---

[73] *i.e. delectus personae* is not involved; see 4.30—4.31 below.
[74] (1864) 2 M. 1226.

in existence at the outbreak of war become void for the period of the war, but revive following the restoration of peace.

Corporate Bodies

2.108   A "corporate body" is an organisation which has a legal life or personality independent of the individuals who control its actions. Although not human, corporate bodies possess contractual capacity. However, that contractual capacity is restricted by the terms and conditions upon which the corporate body was established and, by virtue of what is referred to as the *ultra vires*[75] rule, a body corporate may not contract beyond the powers given to it. If it does so, such contracts are void, and not even the unanimous approval of the individuals controlling that body can validate the situation.

2.109   It is therefore a question of examining the contractual capacity of each corporate body, as evidenced by its founding constitution, as amended, *before* entering into a contract with it. There are three broad types of corporate body:

2.110   1. *Corporate bodies established by Royal Charter.* Such a body may enter into any contract not expressly forbidden by its charter.

2.111   2. *Corporate bodies established under Act of Parliament.*[76] Such bodies will have their contractual capacity defined in the clauses of the statute, and any purported contract outside that definition will be *ultra vires*.

2.112   3. *Registered companies.* The registered company is the most familiar corporate body of all, the commercial trading company, and the contractual capacity of such a body is set out in the "objects" clause of the Memorandum of Association of that company, which formerly limited its contractual capacity to the objects for which the company was formed. However, by virtue of

---

[75] Literally "beyond the powers."
[76] Which term includes most Scottish local authorities, under the Local Government (Scotland) Act 1973.

the Companies Act 1989, and in order to protect innocent persons dealing with companies, the *ultra vires* rule has been all but abolished for registered companies by a new provision that no contract entered into by a company may be challenged on the grounds that it exceeds the objects clause of the Memorandum. Nor will anyone contracting with the company be prejudiced by any lack of authority on the part of a director with whom they dealt.

3. VITIATING FACTORS

3.1 A "vitiating factor" is one which affects the validity of a contract even though it is formally valid, in the sense that there has been offer and acceptance, the contract is in the correct form, and both parties to it possess the contractual capacity to make it. It normally arises from the circumstances in which the contract was made, or from its purpose.

3.2 The following vitiating factors may be considered separately, before the chapter concludes with an examination of the possible consequences for a contract of the presence of a vitiating factor[1]:

1. Error.
2. Misrepresentation.
3. Illegality.
4. *Sponsiones ludicrae.*
5. Force and fear.
6. Facility and circumvention.
7. Undue influence.

ERROR

Nature of Error in Law

3.3 An "error" in law arises when one or both of the parties to the contract have entered into it as the result of a mistaken belief on their part. Where that error has been induced by the words or actions of the other party, it is more correct to describe the vitiating factor involved as a misrepresentation, dealt with in a separate section of its own below. Only self-induced mistakes are here considered under the heading of "error."

3.4 Even then, it is by no means every error which will vitiate a contract. No mistake of law, for example, can ever constitute the

---

[1] N.B. contracts affected by a vitiating factor are not always automatic nullities.

sort of error which will invalidate a contract,[2] although it can sometimes be difficult to distinguish between a mistake of law and a mistake of fact. Only the latter may qualify as an "error" which may vitiate a contract, but the mere fact that one of the parties has made a bad bargain will not entitle him to avoid the consequences.

3.5 Over the years, the categories of error which the courts have been prepared to recognise as vitiating a contract have been reduced to three:

1. Error in transmission.
2. Error of expression.
3. Error of intention.

Error in Transmission

3.6 It is probably inaccurate to describe as an "error" in the legal sense those mistakes which come within the category of "error in transmission," since their effect is to prevent a contract arising in the first place, due to lack of *consensus ad idem*.[3]

3.7 An error in transmission occurs when an offer which A intended to make to B is incorrectly transmitted to B, and is "accepted" by him. Since there is no true *consensus*, the courts will not enforce the contract, and a clear example of this was *Verdin v. Robertson*,[4] in which R. sent a telegram to V. placing an order for salt, but a misreading of his instructions by a telegraph operator resulted in delivery being made to another firm entirely. The court refused to make R. pay for the salt delivered by V.

Error of Expression

3.8 In this group of situations, the parties have reached consensus orally, and having decided to reduce their agreement into written form, succeed in incorrectly expressing their true agreement. In this

---

[2] By virtue of the maxim "ignorance of the law is no excuse."

[3] *i.e.* it is more accurate to say that no contract comes into existence at all than to say that it is vitiated by an error in transmission.

[4] (1871) 10 M.35.

situation, the courts will "rectify" the agreement[5] so as to restore the parties' original intentions.

3.9 The classic example of this sort of error was the case of *Krupp* v. *John Menzies Ltd.*,[6] in which the parties agreed that K. would be employed by M. as an hotel manageress with a wage determined as one-twentieth of the net annual profit. The clerk given the task of drawing up the contract was supplied, as a style, with the previous manager's contract (which had been for one-tenth of the profit), and was instructed simply to "halve it." He mistakenly took one half of one-tenth to be one-fifth, and the court refused to allow K. one-fifth, since it was not what the parties had agreed.[7]

Error of Intention

3.10 An error which is identified as being one of "intention" is a more fundamental one than the two previously considered, in that one, or possibly both, of the parties is mistaken as to the nature of the contract being entered into. However, the mere fact that one party is in error as to what he is contracting for[8] will not of itself affect the contract if the court is able to conclude that the purpose of the contract was clear, when viewed objectively, and the mistaken party simply deluded himself.[9]

3.11 The only true errors of intention are therefore those in which the parties are *both* in error, or have so confused the situation, and are at such cross-purposes, that the court cannot in all equity hold that a consensual contract has been formed between them. These are described traditionally[10] as "bilateral errors," and may be sub-categorised into:

---

[5] By a streamlined process now available in either the Court of Session or the sheriff court under s. 8 of the Law Reform (Miscellaneous Provisions) (Scotland) Act 1985. For a recent unsuccessful attempt to invoke s. 8, see *Shaw* v. *William Grant (Minerals)*, 1988 S.C.L.R. 416.

[6] 1907 S.C. 903.

[7] N.B. that the court may examine any relevant evidence in order to establish the true agreement.

[8] A "unilateral error."

[9] A possible exception being "gratuitous obligations," considered in 2.72 above.

[10] If inaccurately.

1. Common errors.
2. Mutual errors.

Common Errors

3.12   These arise when both parties have made the *same* mistake, and even in this apparently straightforward situation the court will only invalidate the contract when it can be shown that the fact concerning which the common error arose is one which is "material" to the contract.

3.13   A good example of such a material factor is that supplied under section 6 of the Sale of Goods Act 1979, which states that when a contract exists for the sale of "specific" goods,[11] and the goods have, without the knowledge of the seller, perished at the time when the contract is made, then the contract is void. The common error which the parties are making in such a case is in respect of the very existence of the goods themselves.

3.14   This process will not, however, be available to rid the parties of the consequences of a common error of judgment, as opposed to one of fact. Thus, in *Dawson* v. *Muir*,[12] the courts refused to reduce a contract for the sale of certain vats sunk in the ground simply because neither party was aware that they contained white lead, which made them more valuable, and in *Leaf* v. *International Galleries*[13] the same principle was applied to the sale of a painting incorrectly believed by both parties to be a Constable. In each case the parties were *ad idem* as to what was being sold, and the quality or value of that thing was not regarded as material to the contract.

Mutual Errors

3.15   A mutual error arises when the parties have been at cross-purposes, *and* the court is unable, objectively, to conclude that one party's understanding of the agreement must be taken to be the correct one. Even in such cases, the courts display their natural

---

[11] For which see 5.46 below.
[12] (1851) 13 D.843.
[13] [1950] 2 K.B. 86.

reluctance to set aside contracts by distinguishing between an error *in substantialibus*,[14] which will be allowed, and an error *concomitans*,[15] which will not be allowed to invalidate the contract.

3.16 A good example of a non-effective error *concomitans* occurred in *Cloup v. Alexander*,[16] in which a group of entertainers booked an Edinburgh theatre for their performances. It transpired that their performances were illegal in that particular theatre, but the court held that they must still pay the hiring fee because the fact concerning which the error arose was merely collateral to the contract of hire, which was the main contract.

3.17 When the mutual error is one *in substantialibus*, and the courts cannot choose objectively between the conflicting interpretations of the two parties, they have no choice but to declare the contract void for lack of *consensus*. It is possible to identify four major examples of this process, but it is also probably incorrect to regard the list as fixed, and unwise to regard the categories as rigid.

3.18 1. *Error as to identity.* If A believes himself to be contracting with B, but is in fact contracting with C, then if the identity of the other party to the contract is material to it so far as A is concerned, the contract is void. If B's identity is not material to the contract, then of course it continues, and it is for A to prove the materiality. The rule is best illustrated by contrasting two cases.

3.19 In *Morrisson v. Robertson*,[17] M. contracted to sell cattle to T. in the belief that he was the son of W., with whom he had done business in the past. He therefore gave the cattle to T. on credit, and saw neither the money nor the cattle again. T. sold the cattle to R., from whom M. successfully recovered them, on the ground that since the identity of T. had been material to M.'s decision to

---

[14] Literally translated as "an error in the substantials," but more fluently regarded as an error in respect of some material fact.
[15] *i.e.* an error in respect of some fact which is "collateral to" (*i.e.* not material to) the contract.
[16] (1831) 9 S. 448. It is arguable, in any case, that the "error" was either unilateral, or one of law only.
[17] 1908 S.C. 332.

part with the cattle, the contract was void, and not even an innocent third party like R. could acquire a valid title to the cattle.[18]

3.20 In *McLeod* v. *Kerr*,[19] on the other hand, M. was happy to
sell his car to the person who offered to buy it, and the question
of his identity only became relevant when it came to his request to
pay by cheque. M. believed the purchaser to be the person named
on the chequebook, and parted with the car, which was promptly
resold to K. before the cheque was not honoured. It was held that
the contract was valid because the identity of the purchaser was
not material. His creditworthiness might well have been, but that
was not sufficient to invalidate the contract.

3.21 2. *Error as to subject-matter.* In this group of cases, the
parties are at odds as to what precisely is the item which is the
subject of the contract, and the courts cannot reasonably choose
one or the other as the one which the parties must have had in
mind.

3.22 The classic illustration of this process is *Raffles* v. *Wichel-
haus*,[20] in which the parties contracted for the sale of a consignment
of cotton sailing "ex Peerless from Bombay." Unfortunately, two
vessels of the same name were due to load cotton from Bombay,
one in October and the other in December. It was impossible on
any objective analysis of the parties' dealings with each other to
choose one vessel or the other, and the court therefore ruled that
no contract had been made because the parties had not been *ad
idem*.

3.23 The same rule can also apply when the parties are at cross-
purposes concerning the quality, quantity or extent of the subject-
matter, but only when this is material to the contract, and of course
when the parties are not making the *same* mistake.[21] In *Patterson*

---

[18] On which point, see 3.73 below.
[19] 1965 S.L.T. 358.
[20] (1864) 2 H. and C. 906.
[21] As in *Leaf* v. *International Galleries*, note 13 above.

v. *Landsberg and Son*,[22] for example, P. was able to set aside a
contract for the purchase of several items of jewellery which she
believed to be genuine antiques but which the London suppliers
had all along intended to be mere reproductions.

3.24   3. *Error as to the nature of the contract.* The contract may
be avoided when one of the parties can show that he was mistaken
as to the very nature of the contract which he was entering into,
or indeed did not believe himself to be entering into a contract at
all.[23] In such a case, he may be able to avoid the contract by means
of the plea of *non est factum* ("it is not my deed"). English cases
suggest that this plea is only available when the mistaken party
acted without negligence, and most of the cases involving *non est
factum* arise from fraud which, when it is committed by the other
party, is best dealt with as misrepresentation.

3.25   4. *Error as to price.* In a case in which the parties believe
the price to have been fixed, but have different prices in mind, then
if the price has not been fixed, and the contract has not yet been
carried out, the contract may be void for error. If the contract has
already been carried out, then the courts will normally fix the price
quantum meruit[24] or under the "reasonable price" provisions of
the Sale of Goods Act 1979, section 8.[25] In a case in which no
actions have yet occurred, it is perhaps best to regard the contract
as not yet having left the ground, since there is no *consensus* on a
vital factor.

---

[22] (1905) 7 F.675. In *Matthew Middleton* v. *Newton Display Group Ltd.*, 1990
G.W.D. 40–2305, the court set aside a contract for the painting of display panels
at the Garden Festival in Glasgow when it was proved that the contractors believed
the surfaces to be flat, whereas the organisers thought that they knew that they
were three-dimensional, and therefore more costly to paint.
[23] As for example when he believes that he is simply witnessing a signature. However, the courts remain very reluctant to upset clear written undertakings; see *The
Royal Bank of Scotland* v. *Purvis*, 1990 S.L.T. 262.
[24] "As much as has been earned."
[25] Thus, in *Wilson* v. *Marquis of Breadalbane* (1859) 21 D.957, in which cattle
changed hands in confusion over the price, the court applied the market price of
£15 per head.

MISREPRESENTATION

Nature of Misrepresentation

3.26 A "misrepresentaion" is a false statement of fact, or mis-leading conduct, by A which induces[26] B to enter into a contract with him. This misrepresentation may be made innocently, fraudulently or negligently, but its effect on the contract itself is the same regardless of A's intentions. When the misrepresentation induces B into an error in the substantials of the contract,[27] then the contract will be void; if the error is only *concomitans*,[28] then the contract is only voidable. The distinction between "void" and "voidable" is considered in 3.73 below.

3.27 Even then, it is only possible for the contract to be set aside when *restitutio in integrum* may occur, *i.e.* when the parties may be restored to their original positions. If this is not possible, then the law of contract has exhausted its remedies for the injured party, and the contract must therefore stand. Only if the misrepresentation was made fraudulently or negligently will the victim receive damages, and then only under the law of delict, and not contract.

3.28 In order to be a misrepresentation, a mis-statement must be one of fact, and not, for example, one of law. Nor may it be a statement of future intention,[29] or of opinion. Thus, in *Hamilton v. Duke of Montrose*,[30] the court refused to set aside a contract based on a landowner's own assessment of the stock capacity of his land.

3.29 Special problems arise, however, in connection with non-disclosure of material facts.

---

[26] N.B. it need not be the only inducement, but it must be a material factor in B's decision.
[27] For which see note 14 above.
[28] For which see note 15 above.
[29] Except in the unlikely event that it is possible to prove that such intention was not genuinely held.
[30] (1906) 8 F.1026.

Non-Disclosure of Material Facts

The General Rule

3.30 The general rule is that mere silence can never constitute misrepresentation, since there is no general obligation placed upon a party to a contract to disclose all the facts known to him. The parties are said to be at "arm's length," and the courts leave it to them to assess the value of what they are contracting for.

3.31 Thus, in *Gillespie* v. *Russell*,[31] the court refused to set aside a mineral lease simply because the tenant was aware, when the bargain was struck, of the existence in the ground of a seam of coal which made the lease more valuable, while in *Royal Bank of Scotland* v. *Greenshields*,[32] the court took the same view of an agreement in which G. agreed to guarantee H.'s overdraft at the bank, unaware of an additional debt which H. owed the bank. It was held that the bank was under no obligation to reveal to G. the existence of the additional debt.

Exceptions

3.32 To this general rule there are, however, four exceptions.

3.33 1. *Contracts uberrimae fidei.* These are contracts in which one of the parties is under a legal duty to disclose all the material facts known to him. The best example is a contract of insurance, and woe betide any applicant for life insurance who omits to mention on his application form a pre-existing heart condition. Other examples of such contracts are guarantees of employee honesty and contracts of partnership.

3.34 2. *Fiduciary relationships.* Into this category of contracts come those in which one of the parties is in a position of authority or trust *vis-à-vis* the other, and the clearest examples of fiduciary relationships are those between parent and child, principal and

---

[31] (1856) 18 D.677.
[32] 1914 S.C. 259.

agent and trustee and beneficiary. Contracts made between such persons may also be challengeable on the ground of undue influence (for which see below), but in the context of misrepresentation the rule is that the dominant party must reveal all material facts to the other party prior to the contract being entered into.

3.35 3. *Half-truths.* It is one thing to remain totally silent on a matter and let the other party form his own opinion. It is another matter altogether to tell half the story and thus induce the other party into a false belief. For example, the intending purchaser of a second-hand car would be most heartened to read that "this vehicle has been thoroughly examined prior to sale;" he would be less than impressed to learn that this examination revealed 27 defects, none of which had been remedied. For this reason, half-truths are regarded as misrepresentations.

3.36 Into this category come also statements which were true when they were made, but are rendered inaccurate by changing circumstances prior to the finalisation of the contract. In such cases, the party making the original statement must correct it, or the contract may be tainted by misrepresentation. This principle is well illustrated by the case of *Shankland v. Robinson,*[33] in which the seller of a machine stated, correctly at the time, that it was not to be requisitioned by the Government. It was held that the seller should have notified the purchaser when it appeared that the Government's attitude had changed.

3.37 4. *Fraudulent concealment.* When one of the parties acts fraudulently in positively concealing facts from the other party, then the courts will regard this concealment as a fraudulent misrepresentation. The process is most easily seen in the case of physical concealment, as in *Gibson v. NCR,*[34] in which the defendants, having contracted to supply G. with a new cash register, supplied him with an old one, reconditioned so as to look new. G. was awarded damages for fraud.

---

[33] 1920 S.C.(H.L.) 103.
[34] 1925 S.C. 500.

Fraudulent Misrepresentation

3.38 A fraudulent misrepresentation is one which is made "(1) knowingly, or (2) without belief in its truth, or (3) recklessly, careless whether it be true or false."[35]

3.39 In the case from which this leading definition is taken, the directors of a company issued a prospectus inviting the public to take shares in the company, stating that the company had authority to operate steam trams. They honestly believed that they had, but were refused the all-important consent of the Board of Trade for this new venture. P. sued the directors for fraudulent misrepresentation, but it was held that because of the honest belief, however mistaken or negligent, they could not be taken to have acted fraudulently.[36]

3.40 Once honest belief is proved, fraud is disproved, however ill-advised the statement may have been. This principle is also well illustrated by the facts in *Boyd and Forrest* v. *Glasgow and South Western Ry. Co.*,[37] in which B. contracted to carry out the construction of a railway cutting on the basis of a soil survey report supplied to them by the railway. The notes made by the rock-borers, which revealed the presence of a large quantity of rock, were altered by the railway's own engineer so as to reduce the quantity of rock disclosed, before B. received the report. The engineer was, however, able to persuade the court that he honestly believed the original notes to be wrong, and the court therefore refused to categorise his action as a fraudulent misrepresentation.

3.41 In addition to being entitled to resile from the contract in suitable cases, the victim of a fraudulent misrepresentation may also seek damages for the "delict"[38] of fraud. This right is independent of the reduction of the contract, so that, for example, in *Smith* v. *Sim*,[39] the purchaser of a public house whose turnover

---

[35] Lord Herschell in *Derry* v. *Peek* (1889) 14 App. Cases 337 at p. 374.
[36] The law now gives a statutory right to damages for inaccurate prospectuses, but this case still provides the best definition of fraudulent misrepresentation.
[37] 1912 S.C.(H.L.) 93.
[38] *i.e.* actionable civil wrong.
[39] 1954 S.C. 357.

had been fraudulently doubled in figures supplied by the seller was able to keep the public house while receiving almost a complete year's turnover in damages.

Innocent Misrepresentation

3.42 An innocent misrepresentation is one which is not only made with an honest belief in its truth, but has not even been made negligently. As indicated above, no damages are awardable, and the only remedy available to the victim is to have the contract set aside if *restitutio in integrum* is possible. If it is not, then he has no remedy at all, not even in delict.

3.43 This point is forcefully illustrated by the *Boyd and Forrest* case considered in the previous section. Since the alterations made by the engineer were held to be non-fraudulent, and since the law of negligence had not at that time developed to the point at which it offered any remedy to B. in damages,[40] B.'s only possible remedy was recission of the contract. However, by the time that the action reached the courts, large quantities of earth and rock had been removed from the cutting, and the court ruled that the parties could not realistically be returned to their pre-contract positions. B. therefore not only had no remedy, but were obliged to proceed with a contract in which they were doomed to lose money through no fault of their own.

Negligent Misrepresentation

3.44 The law on negligent misrepresentation is essentially the same as that for innocent misrepresentation, with the important addition that the law of delict allows the victim to sue for damages, as an alternative, or in addition, to the right to resile from the contract in suitable cases.

3.45 In order to receive damages, however, the victim must be able to show that he was owed a "duty of care" by the other party. It is by no means the case that every party to a contract owes a duty of care to the other, but it is difficult to see, for example, how

---

[40] N.B. that it almost certainly would now.

the railway company in the *Boyd* case could avoid liability for the negligent actions of their engineer were a similar case to arise again.

3.46 In special cases, even though the contract between A and B would remain intact, it may be possible for A to sue a third party, C, for negligence on his part which led to A entering into a contract with B, under the principle established in *Hedley Byrne and Co. v. Heller and Partners*[41] which is considered more fully in 10.36 below.

ILLEGALITY

General Rule

3.47 The general rule is that illegal agreements (*pacta illicita*), since they are prohibited by law, are void, and of no legal effect, and not even innocent third parties[42] can obtain a valid title to property under them.

3.48 This state of affairs is described in two Latin phrases, *ex turpi causa non oritur acta* ("out of an immoral situation no action may arise"), and *in turpi causa melior est conditio posidentis* ("in an immoral situation the position of the possessor is the better one"), which make it clear that no one may normally expect any assistance from the courts if they enter into an illegal agreement. Thus, in *Barr v. Crawford*,[43] the court refused to allow the wife of a publican to recover £8,000 paid in bribes to two men in connection with a Licensing Board renewal application by her husband.

3.49 However, even this normally strict rule can be waived in the interests of justice, as when the parties are not equally at fault (*in pari delicto*), or it is possible to sever an illegal section of a contract from the rest of it, so as to enforce the unobjectionable portion. An example of the latter process may be seen in 3.68 below, while an example of the former was the case of *Cuthbertson v. Lowes*,[44]

---

[41] [1964] A.C. 465. See also *Bank of Scotland v. 3i plc*, 1992 G.W.D. 6–321.
[42] *e.g.* the purchaser of a stolen car.
[43] 1983 S.L.T. 481.
[44] (1870) 8 M. 1073.

in which the parties had agreed on the price of a consignment of potatoes using the old Scots measure rather than the imperial measure required by statute. The potatoes had been delivered, and the purchaser simply refused to pay for them, hiding behind the illegality, but in the exercise of its equitable jurisdiction the court ordered him to pay the value of the potatoes at the market price.

3.50 An agreement may be rendered illegal in one (or both) of two ways, namely under statute or by the operation of the common law.

Illegality under Statute

3.51 A contract may be rendered unlawful by statute in one of two ways, either by an outright statutory declaration that a particular agreement is outlawed, or by the imposition of a penalty in respect of a particular agreement. A clear example of the former process was the Weights and Measures provision which prohibited the use of Scots measures in *Cuthbertson* v. *Lowes* above, and other examples encountered elsewhere in this book are the banning of certain types of exemption clause under the Unfair Contract Terms Act 1977, and the prohibition of various forms of sexual and racial discrimination under the Sex Discrimination Act of 1975 and the Race Relations Act of 1976 respectively.

3.52 So far as concerns the second category, the fact that a penalty has been prescribed against a particular type of agreement will normally raise a presumption that such an agreement is regarded as illegal, unless it can be shown that the primary purpose of the provision is to raise revenue (for example the requirement that certain deeds be stamped—they may be unenforceable until they are, but they are not necessarily illegal).

3.53 A statute may, alternatively, simply make a particular type of agreement unenforceable; a good example of this process is the Trade Union and Labour Relations Act of 1974, which provides that "collective agreements" between employers and unions are not legally enforceable unless they contain a written provision to that effect.

Illegality under Common Law

3.54 The following are the main types of agreement rendered void at common law on the basis that they are unlawful.

1. *Contracts for Criminal, Fraudulent or Immoral Purposes*

3.55 Obviously, the courts will not enforce agreements which involve the commission of crime,[45] or the perpetration of a fraud. They are equally sensitive when it comes to apparently condoning sexual immorality, as in *Pearce* v. *Brooks*,[46] in which a court refused to enforce the hire fee for a carriage engaged by a prostitute who, with the knowledge of the hirer, employed it to hawk her charms around the streets of London.

2. *Contracts Contrary to Public Policy*

3.56 Into this category come many types of agreement which are unacceptable to the Government of the day, including agreements which conflict with international or economic policy, agreements which interfere with the freedom of the courts, or agreements which restrict the free exercise of discretion by a public office-holder.

3.57 But by far the most important group of agreements to be found under this heading are those which restrict individual liberty, particularly in matters of trade, and the rest of this section is devoted to this important group.

Contracts in Restraint of Trade

3.58 This type of contract (known also as a "restrictive covenant") is rejected as being contrary to public policy because it is restrictive of free market forces, and therefore, so the theory goes, contrary to the economic well-being of the nation. Agreements in

---

[45] See, *e.g. Barr* v. *Crawford*, above. This also puts paid to the fictional concept of a "contract" being put out on someone's life.
[46] (1886) L.R. 1 Ex.213.

restraint of trade are normally encountered in one of four groups, namely:

3.59 1. *Contracts between employer and employee.* In this type of agreement, the employee, normally as a term of his contract of employment, volunteers to restrict his behaviour in some way if and when he moves on.

3.60 2. *Contracts between the seller and purchaser of a business.* As part of the sale contract, the seller gives an undertaking not to carry out certain specified activities for an agreed period of time.

3.61 3. *Joint agreements among manufacturers and traders.* This type of agreement normally has as its primary objective the exploitation of some monopolistic power, for example to fix prices or limit production capacity. The normal weapon used by governments to combat this type of agreement is statutory (*e.g.* the regulation of "resale price maintenance" under the Resale Prices Act of 1964, and the requirement for the prior registration of restrictive trade agreements under the Restrictive Trade Practices Act of 1956).

3.62 4. *Solus agreements.* Under this type of agreement, a businessman (*e.g.* a publican or the owner of a petrol filling station) agrees, usually in return for some financial incentive, to restrict his source of supply, usually to that of the other party. This explains why, for example, most filling stations supply only one brand of petrol.

3.63 The general rule in all these cases is that such agreements will only be valid if the restraint in question can be shown to be "fair and reasonable," not only so far as the parties themselves are concerned, but also in the general public interest. While each case will primarily be decided on its own individual facts, there is some guidance to be derived by contrasting different judgments in broadly similar cases.

3.64 Thus, in *Nordenfelt* v. *Maxim Nordenfelt Guns and Ammunition Co. Ltd.*,[47] it was held to be reasonable for the seller of an

---

[47] [1894] A.C. 535.

arms business to agree with the purchaser not to engage in the sale of cannon anywhere in the world for the following 25 years, because of the nature of the business, whose customers were limited to national governments.

3.65 On the other hand, in *Dumbarton Steamboat Co. Ltd.* v. *MacFarlane*,[48] it was held to be unreasonably wide for the seller of a river carriage business in the lower Clyde to be required to refrain from similar business activity anywhere in the United Kingdom for the next 10 years. The interesting point in this case was that the purchasers were seeking only to interdict the sellers from working the Glasgow to Dumbarton route, but because of the way in which the clause had been drafted it was impossible to restrict it except by in effect rewriting it, which the court refused to do. The objectionable portion of the contract was, in other words, not "severable" from the unobjectionable.

3.66 The most common context in which modern restraint clauses are found is that of employer/employee contracts. In *Stewart* v. *Stewart*,[49] for example, it was held reasonable for an employee of a photographer (who was also his brother) to bind himself not to commence a rival business within 20 miles of Elgin, for an unspecified period, but in *Mason* v. *Provident Clothing and Supply Co. Ltd.*,[49a] it was held to be unreasonable for a travelling salesman with a clothing firm with branches throughout the United Kingdom to be required to refrain from such work for a three-year period within 25 miles of London.

3.67 However, employers may only enforce restraint clauses against former employees when they do so in protection of legitimate interests such as trade contacts, secret formulae and so on, and not simply to prevent the employee leaving for fear of being out of work. This is why, in *Rentokil Ltd.* v. *Kramer*,[50] the former employers were able to interdict K. against canvassing former cli-

---

[48] (1899) 1 F.993.
[49] (1899) 1 F.1158.
[49a] [1913] A.C. 724. See also *Dallas McMillan and Sinclair* v. *Simpson*, 1989 S.L.T. 454, where the court refused to interdict an outgoing partner of a firm of Glasgow solicitors from practising within 20 miles of Glasgow.
[50] 1986 S.L.T. 114.

ents of his with Rentokil for a two-year period after leaving them, while in *Bluebell Apparel Ltd.* v. *Dickinson,*[51] a former management trainee with Wrangler jeans was successfully interdicted from working at all for Levi Strauss, under a clause in his contract which prohibited him from performing any services for a trade rival within two years of leaving Wrangler.

3.68 Reference was made, in the context of the *Dumbarton* case above, to the possibility of an enforceable section of a restraint clause being successfully severed from an unenforceable one. This can happen with all types of restraint clause, as in *Mulvein* v. *Murray,*[52] in which the court was able to sever an enforceable restraint against canvassing former customers in the boot trade from an unenforceable restraint against travelling in any of the areas previously covered by the former salesman. Equally, in *Esso Petroleum Co. Ltd.* v. *Harpers Garages (Stourport) Ltd.,*[53] the court was able to refuse to enforce a 21-year solus agreement in respect of one filling station while enforcing a four-and-a-half-year one between the same parties but in respect of a different filling station.

SPONSIONES LUDICRAE

3.69 Somewhat akin to illegal contracts are agreements condemned as *sponsiones ludicrae* ("sportive promises"),[54] which the courts refuse to enforce because they are not worthy of the court's time. They are largely controlled by statute anyway, while at common law bets and wagers will not normally be enforceable. However, since such agreements are not downright illegal, matters incidental to them[55] will still be enforceable.

---

[51] 1980 S.L.T. 157.
[52] 1908 S.C. 528.
[53] [1968] A.C. 269.
[54] *e.g* the Gaming Act 1968, which will allow certain gaming contracts to be enforced if the strict regulations established by the Act are followed, and the Lotteries and Amusements Act of 1976, which makes lotteries unlawful unless conducted in conformity with the Act.
[55] *e.g.* the recovery of betting agents' fees. But not, apparently, the cashing in of gaming chips; see *County Properties and Development* v. *Harper,* 1989 S.C.L.R. (Sh.Ct.) 597.

FORCE AND FEAR

3.70 So-called consent obtained by threats of, or actual, physical violence, is, in the eyes of the law, no consent at all, and any contract obtained by these means will be void. The rule extends to threats to close relatives, and even to threats by a person who is not a party to the contract. The principle may even extend to threatened loss of employment, but not to legitimate actions which a party may lawfully take in respect of the subject-matter of the contract.[56]

FACILITY AND CIRCUMVENTION

3.71 "Facility" refers to a frailty or weakness of mind which falls short of insanity, but makes a person vulnerable to fraud, while "circumvention" is misleading behaviour which falls short of fraud. The combination of the two is sufficient to render any contract thus obtained voidable at the option of the victim. In view of the special tests which have to be satisfied, it is hardly surprising that there are few decided cases, but a rare example was *MacGilvray* v. *Gilmartin*,[57] in which the court set aside a conveyance to a daughter made by a mother during a depression brought on by the death of her husband. Presumably only the relationship of the parties (*i.e.* the victim being the mother) prevented the matter being considered under the heading of undue influence.

UNDUE INFLUENCE

3.72 When the relationship between the parties is such as to place one of them in a dominant position over the other, then the contract will be voidable at the instance of the weaker party. Relationships which are recognised as falling within this category are those of parent and child, clergyman and parishioner, doctor and patient and solicitor and client. The giving of independent advice prior to the making of the contract may well satisfy the court that the dominant party has not abused his or her position, but the courts

---

[56] *e.g.* the threat of bankruptcy proceedings which results in the granting of a security for an existing debt.
[57] 1986 S.L.T. 89.

will always be suspicious of situations such as that in *Gray v. Binny*,[58] in which a mother and a solicitor (who was also the mother's creditor) persuaded a son to transfer his estate to her. The conveyance was reduced by the court on the ground of undue influence.

THE EFFECT OF VITIATING FACTORS

The Distinction between Void and Voidable Contracts

3.73   As indicated at the start of this chapter, the effect of a vitiating factor will vary from factor to factor. In some cases, the contract is rendered "void," *i.e.* of no legal effect and totally unenforceable by anyone. Even innocent third parties acquiring an interest in the subject matter[59] are left with no remedy. In others, the contract is merely "voidable," in that the innocent party may, if he so chooses, take steps to have it "reduced" by the court, and possibly also claim damages.

3.74   However, in the latter case, the right to reduction may be lost if certain supervening events have occurred, and these events may be summarised as follows.

1. *Restitutio in Integrum Impossible*

3.75   As has already been noted, the court will not reduce a contract if it is impossible to restore the parties to the position they occupied prior to the contract; the case of *Boyd and Forrest* considered above (at 3.40) is a good example of this process in action.

3.76   However, if the item in question has merely diminished in value,[60] the court will not refuse to reduce the contract provided that the item in itself may be handed back.

2. *Innocent Third Parties have Acquired Rights*

3.77   Whereas in the case of a void contract the court will take no account of the rights of innocent third parties, in the case of

---

[58]   (1879) 7 R.332.
[59]   *e.g.* the purchaser of a stolen car, who will be required to hand it back.
[60]   *e.g.* the car has completed more mileage, or the shares have fallen in value.

voidable contracts they will, in that once an innocent third party acquires a right in the subject-matter of the contract which depends upon the validity of the suspect contract,[61] then the court will not upset that contract.

3.78 However, the third party must always act innocently, in good faith and without knowledge of the circumstances which are later founded upon in an attempt to avoid the contract. Also, the innocent third party will acquire no better title than the party from whom he acquired it, under the principle of *assignatus utitur jure auctoris*, which is considered more fully in 4.33—4.34 below.

3. Personal Bar has Intervened

3.79 If, between the circumstances of the making of the contract and the date upon which the injured party seeks to have it reduced, the same party has "homologated" it,[62] or if he "unduly" delays bringing the action (which will obviously be a question of fact in each case), then the court has the power to refuse to reduce the contract on the ground that the pursuer is "personally barred" from such a remedy.

Summary of Vitiating Effects

3.80 It is convenient to conclude this chapter with an outline summary of the effect on the contract of each of the vitiating factors which have been considered.

Error

3.81 (a) in transmission—no contract;
          (b) of expression—rectification;
          (c) of intention:
                (i)   unilateral—contract valid;
                (ii) common—contract void, but only if *in substantialibus*;

---

[61] As when B buys goods from A, and resells them to C. The court will not reduce the contract between A and B, because this would rob C of his title to the goods.
[62] For which see 2.89 above.

(iii) mutual—contract valid if *concomitans* but void if *in substantialibus.*

Misrepresentation

3.82 (a) fraudulent and negligent—contract voidable if *concomitans* and void if *in substantialibus.* Damages in either case, but in delict, not contract;

(b) innocent—as above, but no damages.

Illegality

3.83 Void.

Sponsiones Ludicrae

3.84 Unenforceable.

Force and Fear

3.85 Void.

Facility and Circumvention and Undue Influence

3.86 Voidable.

4. EXCLUSION, ASSIGNATION AND EXTINCTION OF CONTRACTUAL LIABILITY

4.1 In this final chapter on the law of contract, it is proposed to examine the rules which govern the extent to which contractual liability may be excluded under the contract itself, the means by which contractual rights and duties can pass to persons other than the original parties to the contract, and the ways in which contractual liability may be extinguished, with legal remedies where appropriate.

EXCLUSION CLAUSES

4.2 Sometimes referred to as an "exemption clause," the intention behind the incorporation of an exclusion clause into a contract is to divest one of the parties of legal liability should something go wrong with that contract, or should he not perform to the other party's satisfaction. As an alternative to making the exclusion clause an integral part of the contract, the party seeking to rely on it may simply refer the other party to another document (*e.g.* a set of "conditions," which is available on application), which is to be deemed as incorporated into the contract.

4.3 Traditionally, the courts have been reluctant to enforce such clauses, and have developed barriers to their validity which the party seeking to rely on the clause must surmount in order to succeed. In recent years, the common law has been assisted in this task by the intervention of statute, and each of these hurdles may now be considered in turn.

Incorporation into the Contract

4.4 Like any other clause in a contract, an exclusion clause must be validly incorporated into it before the courts will enforce it, and the courts are particularly vigilant to ensure that this has occurred in the case of a clause under which one of the parties seeks to avoid liability for breach of contract. The rules relating to incorporation of clauses into a contract were considered in 2.46 above.

The Contra Proferentum Rule

4.5 Under this rule of interpretation, any ambiguous or unclear condition which appears in a contract is interpreted *contra proferentum*, *i.e.* against the party seeking to rely upon it. The rule is applied particularly vigorously in relation to exclusion clauses.

4.6 For example, in *North of Scotland Hydro-Electric Board* v. *D. and R. Taylor*,[1] a sub-contractor to the Board was required, as a term of his contract with them, to indemnify the Board against "all claims from third parties arising from the operations under the contract." Due to the Board's own negligence, one of T.'s employees was electrocuted, and the question arose as to whether or not the clause covered claims arising from the Board's negligence. Since the clause itself was ambiguous, it was interpreted *contra proferentum*, *i.e.* against the Board, and T. was not required to indemnify it.

4.7 Similarly, in *Life Association of Scotland* v. *Foster*,[2] ambiguity was built into a clause in a life insurance policy in which the proposer agreed that the policy would be void if any of the statements made by her in the proposal form turned out to be untrue. Unknown to her at the time, she was already suffering from the disease which ultimately killed her, but when the company attempted to avoid the policy, it was held, *contra proferentum*, that the clause did not make it clear whether or not it was restricted to illnesses known to the proposer, and that therefore the exclusion clause could not be used to avoid payment under the policy.

Unfair Contract Terms Act 1977

4.8 One of the primary purposes of this Act was to prevent parties in a dominant bargaining position from exploiting that position so as to enforce on the other party an exclusion clause which is

---

[1] 1956 S.C. 1.
[2] (1873) 11 M. 351.

considered to be unfair or contrary to public policy. By virtue of an amendment in 1990,[3] and with effect from April 1, 1991, the Act also applies to "non-contractual notices."[4]

Types of Contract Covered

4.9 The Act applies to a whole range of contracts, including those for employment, the transfer of goods, services of all kinds, and occupation of land. Excluded from the ambit of the Act are contracts of insurance and contracts for the formation of companies and partnerships. Only partially covered are contracts of marine salvage or towage, and for the carriage of goods by sea.

4.10 One potentially serious limitation on the operation of the Act is that it only applies to the attempted exclusion of liability by a "business;" however, this term is interpreted in the Act itself so as to include professions, and the operations of local and central government departments.

Liability for Negligence

4.11 By virtue of section 16 of the Act, strict limitations are placed upon the use, in a business contract, of a clause which seeks to limit or exclude liability for a breach of a duty of care owed by one party to the other, either under the contract (expressly or by implication), or under the common law or the Occupier's Liability Act 1960.[5]

4.12 When the clause in question relates to death or personal injury, it will be void, *i.e.* of no legal effect. In all other cases, it will be unenforceable unless it may be said to have been "fair and reasonable" at the time when it was made.

---

[3] Law Reform (Miscellaneous Provisions) (Scotland) Act 1990, s. 68.

[4] *e.g.* notices in public places seeking to exclude liability for loss or damage to persons using the facilities free of charge. Another important change introduced with effect from April 1, 1991, is that the Act applies to survey reports prepared for building societies and other mortgagees which negligently cause loss to the purchasers.

[5] For which see 10.47—10.49 below. *N.B.* that "strict" liability is not affected.

Consumer and Standard Form Contracts

4.13 A "consumer contract" is one in which one of the parties deals "in the course of a business," and the other does not.[6] The burden of proving that the contract is not a consumer contract lies on the party who is not the consumer. A "standard form" contract,[7] on the other hand, is one in which one of the parties has succeeded in persuading the other to enter into the contract on a standard set of terms and conditions normally employed by him.

4.14 In both cases, the effect of section 17 of the Act is that such contracts may only contain exclusions relating to the liability of the dominant party for breach of contract, for failure to perform at all, or for giving a performance which is substantially less than was reasonably expected, when such exclusions were "fair and reasonable," in the light of the facts as they were at the time of the making of the contract.

Indemnity Clauses in Consumer Contracts

4.15 Under section 18 of the Act, clauses in consumer contracts which seek to impose upon the consumer a contractual duty to indemnify some other person[8] from liability for negligence or breach of contract will also be unenforceable unless they can satisfy the "fair and reasonable" test applied as at the time of the making of the contract.

"Fair and Reasonable" Test

4.16 In applying the "fair and reasonable" test referred to above, the courts may have regard to the relative resources of the two parties, the ability of the party seeking to rely on the exclusion to have covered himself by insurance, any inducement offered to the other party to accept the exclusion clause, the relative bargaining strengths of the parties, the availability of alternative sources of

---

[6] This concept is further considered in 5.71 below, in the context of sale of goods.

[7] In which neither party need be a consumer, and which has already been considered in 4.30 above.

[8] Who need not be the other party.

supply to the consumer at the time, and whether or not goods were made to the special order of the consumer, or the consumer had accepted such exclusions in the past.

✳ **4.17**   The onus of proving that an exclusion is fair and reasonable lies on the party seeking to rely on it. The rules also apply to conditions seeking to limit a party's right to claim.[9]

TITLE TO SUE AND ASSIGNATION OF CONTRACT

4.18   During the life of a contract, and for various reasons, it may be important to ascertain precisely who may sue under the contract, and if the rights and duties thereunder may be assigned to another party.

The Doctrine of *Jus Tertii*

4.19   The phrase *jus tertii* (which ironically translates as "the right of a third party") is used to describe the effect of the general rule that persons who are not parties to a contract cannot sue under it, since this right is normally reserved to the parties themselves. A third party may have an interest in a contract, but that does not mean that he may sue under it as if he were a party.

4.20   This general rule is simply illustrated by the old case of *Finnie* v. *Glasgow and South Western Ry. Co.*,[10] in which a contract had been signed between two railway companies, agreeing the rate for the haulage of coal along a particular stretch of line. When one of the companies increased its charges, one of its customers sought in effect to enforce that agreement, but the court held that the agreement was *jus tertii* so far as that customer was concerned. He had an interest in seeing it enforced, but no legal right to enforce it himself.

4.21   To the general rule there are certain important exceptions.

---

[9]   *e.g.* by requiring all claims to be made within a certain time limit.
[10]   (1857) 3 Macq. 75.

Agency[11]

4.22 If A makes a contract with B while he is acting as agent for C, then his "principal" (C) may sue under the contract.

Death or Bankruptcy

4.23 When a party to a contract dies, the right to sue under the contract passes to his "executor," unless the contract may be said to involve *delectus personae* (which is explored below), in which case the contract dies with him. A similar rule allows the "trustee in bankruptcy"[12] to continue with a contract which had been entered into by the bankrupt, assuming that the trustee elects to do so; once again, the principle of *delectus personae* may prohibit him from doing so.

4.24 The main difference between the two situations is that a trustee who elects not to proceed with a contract may expose the estate to an action for breach of contract, which cannot occur in the case of a contract terminated by death.

Jus Quaesitum Tertio

4.25 This phrase translates as "a right accruing to a third party," and is used to describe those limited situations in which the law allows that third party to enforce the contract in his own right. Before this may happen, the *tertius* (as such a third party is called) must be able to show that the contract itself refers to him either as an individual or as one of a class of people, and that the original parties to the contract intended to benefit him.

4.26 For example, in *Lamont v. Burnett*,[13] B. agreed to buy L.'s hotel for £7,000, and also undertook to pay a further £100 to Mrs. L. for her assistance to him during his visits to inspect the hotel. L. accepted the offer in its entirety, and it was held that Mrs. L.

---

[11] The law of agency is considered more fully in Chapter 7, below.
[12] *i.e.* the person appointed to administer the bankrupt's estate.
[13] (1901) 3 F.797.

could sue him separately for the £100 when he refused to pay it at a later date.

4.27   Similarly, in *Morton's Trs.* v. *Aged Christian Friend Society*,[14] it was held that the Society, which had only been in formation when M. offered to pay annual instalments to it in a contract entered into between him and the steering committee of the Society, could sue under that contract.

Assignation

4.28   When rights and/or duties under a contract are formally assigned to a third party who was not a party to the original contract, he acquires the rights and duties of the assigning party. This may conveniently be considered under a separate section.

Assignation of Contractual Rights and Duties

4.29   In a limited number of cases, an original party to a contract may be replaced by someone else. However, only some contracts are assignable, and even then the effect of the assignation is limited.

Assignability of Contract

4.30   One must distinguish between "executed" contracts (which have been fully completed apart from the payment of money or the handing over of an article) and "executory" contracts, which still require some action or forbearance from action by at least one of the parties. An executed contract is assignable unless there is an express provision to the contrary in the contract itself, whereas an executory contract cannot be assigned if *delectus personae* is involved.

4.31   This phrase (literally translated as "choice of person") indicates that one of the parties has been chosen for his personal skill or reputation,[15] and the general rule is that such contracts cannot be assigned. Frequent examples of contracts rendered non-

---

[14] (1899) 2 F. 82; 7 S.L.T. 220. Considered also in 2.6 and 2.72 above.
[15] Obvious examples being a portrait painter or an opera singer.

assignable by this rule are contracts of an artistic or professional nature, contracts of employment and contracts of partnership.

4.32 It is another question entirely whether or not one of the parties to a contract may delegate his performance of it. This will depend upon the facts of each individual case, but even when it is permitted, the original party will remain liable for any breach of contract by the substitute.

Effect of Assignation

4.33 When contractual rights and obligations are assigned, the person making the transfer is known as the cedent, and the person to whom the transfer is made is known as the assignee. The most important underlying rule in such cases is described in the Latin phrase *assignatus utitur jure auctoris*, which translates loosely into a rule whereby the assignee has no more legal rights than those enjoyed previously by the cedent. In particular, if the cedent's legal position has become prejudiced by some action on his part, then the assignee will be equally prejudiced.

4.34 A good example of this principle in action is provided by the frequent practice of assigning the benefits of a life insurance policy.[16] The perils of relying on assignation in such cases are well highlighted by the facts of *Scottish Widows* v. *Buist*,[17] in which B had the benefits of A's life insurance assigned to him, only to discover that the policy had been invalidated by false statements made by A on the proposal form concerning his state of health.

4.35 One clear exception to the *assignatus* rule applies in the case of "negotiable instruments,"[18] since the "holder in good faith and for value"[19] of such an instrument is not affected by any defect in title to that instrument further up the chain of negotiation. If the cheque is not honoured, he may still seek repayment from the person who negotiated it to him.

---

[16] *e.g.* in an endowment mortgage.
[17] (1876) 3 R. 1078.
[18] *e.g.* bills of exchange.
[19] *e.g.* someone who has a cheque endorsed over to him.

EXTINCTION OF CONTRACTUAL LIABILITY

4.36 There are many ways in which the rights and obligations under a contract may come to an end. One of these is breach of contract by either or both of the parties, which may give the injured party a right to one of the various remedies considered in the next section of this chapter. This section concentrates on the various means by which a contract may be extinguished, including breach, leaving until last those which require fuller explanation.

Performance

4.37 Clearly, if the parties perform their obligations to the letter, the contract will be fulfilled and will thereby expire. If one of the parties fails to perform satisfactorily, and his lack of performance is not so marginal that the court may ignore it,[20] then the injured party may well be entitled to a remedy, but for reasons which emerge later in this chapter, the contract may still not be at an end.

Payment

4.38 When the contractual obligation is to make payment of money, then performance of it will take the form of payment on time. The creditor is entitled to insist on whatever method of payment is stipulated in the contract itself, failing which by "legal tender."[21]

Acceptilation

4.39 When a creditor under a contract simply discharges the debtor of all further obligation, by whatever means, the contract is said to be "discharged by acceptilation." Proof by writ or oath is required[22] when the original contract was in writing.

---

[20] Under the principle *de minimis non curat lex*—the law takes no account of trifles.
[21] Defined under the Coinage Act 1971, but excluding cheques which are returned immediately by the creditor. Payment by cheque is conditional on the cheque being honoured.
[22] For which see 2.70 above.

Confusion

4.40 When the original creditor in a contract becomes the debtor (or vice versa), then the contract is said to be discharged *confusione* (*i.e.* by the combination of the two original parties into one). However, the person occupying both roles must do so in the same capacity (for which see below). Confusion can only occur in the context of obligations for the payment of money.

Novation

4.41 A "novation" is said to occur when contract A between two parties is replaced by contract B between the parties in circumstances which make it clear that the old obligations are being extinguished. An example might be a debtor to a bank entering into a new repayment scheme designed to extinguish his current overdraft.

Delegation

4.42 Delegation is simply a form of novation in which the debtor in the new contract is not the same party as in the original one. The consent of the creditor is obviously required before this may occur, but the modern habit of "restructuring" commercial loans is a good example. It is sometimes difficult to distinguish between delegation and a mere guarantee.

Compensation

4.43 When a creditor in one contract finds himself the debtor to the same party in another, then he may set off ("compensate") one debt with another, so as to extinguish or reduce his indebtedness to the other party. The two debts must be "liquid" (*i.e.* of an ascertained amount) and the parties must act in the same capacities in each of the contracts. For example, the treasurer of the local golf club may not extinguish or reduce his dentist's bill when the dentist is in arrears with his subscription. Compensation is one of those devices used by the major clearing banks to process the countless number of debits and credits which arise between them daily.

Prescription

The Nature of Prescription

4.44   "Prescription" is the term used to describe the process whereby a contractual obligation may simply extinguish itself by the passage of time during which no action is taken in respect of it. The same process in other areas of law may be used to establish legal rights (see, *e.g.* rights of way, considered in Chapter 10), and this operates so as to create a "positive" prescription. The main effect of the process in the law of contract, however, is to extinguish legal rights by means of "negative" prescription.

4.45   The effect of the Prescription and Limitation (Scotland) Act of 1973 was to abolish all that had gone before, and to establish two new, simplified, negative prescriptions, the "long negative prescription" (20 years) and the "short negative prescription" (five years). According to which category a particular obligation falls within, it may be extinguished after five or 20 years, if the remaining essential conditions are satisfied. Some rights are said to be "imprescriptible," and are therefore immune from both periods.

The Short and Long Periods

4.46   The vast majority of all contractual obligations will expire under the "short negative prescription," *i.e.* after five years if the necessary conditions considered below are satisfied. The main exception to this general rule concerns obligations contained within a "probative writing,"[23] and the clearest example of these will be those relating to land (*e.g.* the purchase price of a house).

4.47   However, before either of these categories of obligations will prescribe, the relevant period of time must have passed without any "relevant claim" by the creditor, or any "relevant acknowledgment" by the debtor.

---

[23] For the meaning of which, see 2.66 above.

Relevant Claims and Relevant Acknowledgments

4.48 A "relevant claim," for the purposes of the 1973 Act, is a claim in a court of law, or in an arbitration, or a lodgment of a claim in the debtor's sequestration or liquidation. Also classed as a relevant claim will be the execution of any diligence in pursuit of the debt, or the enforcement of the obligation.

4.49 For a "relevant acknowledgment" to occur, there must be some performance on the part of the debtor which indicates that he regards the obligation as still existing, or an unequivocal admission in writing, by or on behalf of the debtor, to the creditor or his agent.

4.50 If neither of these events occurs within the relevant prescriptive period, then the obligation is extinguished by prescription. However, excluded from the computation of this period is any time during which the making of a claim was delayed due to fraud on the part of the debtor, or an error on the part of the creditor induced by the debtor. Also excluded is any period during which the creditor was under a "legal disability" (*i.e.* was under age or of unsound mind).

4.51 The prescriptive period begins to run from the date when the obligation becomes enforceable.

Imprescriptible Rights and Obligations

4.52 There are some rights and obligations which, for reasons of public policy, are not allowed to prescribe simply by the passage of time without enforcement or acknowledgment. Among the main ones are:

1. "Real" rights of ownership in land.
2. The "real" rights of a lessee under a recorded lease.
3. A right which falls within the category of *res merae facultatis*, *i.e.* exercised as a matter of mere power. The chief examples of these relate to ordinary uses of property, such as the right to feu-duty, or the right to open a door.
4. Rights to recover property outside the normal commercial sphere; these are limited to public property or property belonging to the Crown.

5. The right to recover stolen property.
6. The right to challenge a deed which is invalid on its face, or is forged.

Frustration

Doctrine of Frustration

4.53 In the law of contract, the term "frustration" refers to some supervening illegality or impossibility which creeps into the contract after it has become enforceable. If this occurs before the contract is finalised, then it is void *ab initio* (from the start), but if it occurs later, the legal consequence is that the parties are returned to a position as if the contract had never been concluded, neither party is liable in damages to the other, and any payment made in pursuance of the contract is refundable.

4.54 The concept of illegality was considered in the previous chapter, and contracts which become illegal after they have commenced are just as void as those which were illegal from the start. The same effect is brought about by "supervening impossibility," which must now be examined in more detail.

4.55 Before any supervening event may be said to have the effect of terminating the contract without fault on either side, it must be shown to be one which was outwith the control of both the parties, and was not foreseeable by the parties by any commonsense standard. It will not cover the situation in which one of the parties has simply made an error of judgment and now stands to lose financially on the contract.[24]

4.56 The following are regarded as the most common categories of supervening impossibility.

Rei Interitus

4.57 When specific property which is essential to the contract is accidentally destroyed, then clearly the contract has been "frus-

---

[24] As in *Davis Contractors Ltd.* v. *Fareham U.D.C.* [1956] 2 All E.R.145, in which D. argued, unsuccessfully, that inflation which had escalated building costs was a "frustrating event."

trated." In the case of goods, this is recognised in section 7 of the Sale of Goods Act 1979, which renders void any contract for the sale of specific goods, which perish without the fault of either party before the title to them passes to the buyer.[25]

4.58   A simple example of this principle in action in the case of "heritable" property was *Taylor* v. *Caldwell*,[26] in which a contract for the hire of a music hall was held to be frustrated by the accidental destruction of the property before the date of the hire.

Constructive Total Destruction

4.59   When property, while not totally destroyed, is nevertheless rendered useless for the purpose which the parties had in mind, then this "constructive total destruction" will have the same legal effect as actual total destruction.

4.60   This principle was applied so as to terminate, in *Mackeson* v. *Boyd*,[27] the lease of a furnished mansion which was requisitioned by troops during wartime, and in *Tay Salmon Fisheries Co. Ltd.* v. *Speedie*,[28] the rights to salmon fishing over a stretch of river estuary which came to be used by the RAF for bombing practice.

A Change in the Condition of one of the Parties

4.61   In those contracts which require *delectus personae*,[29] a change in the condition of the performing party (such as his death, bankruptcy, insanity or lingering illness) may constitute a frustrating event, and so terminate the contract. This is recognised in the case of partnership agreements by section 33 of the Partnership Act 1890, which states that in the absence of agreement to the contrary, the bankruptcy of a partner automatically dissolves a partnership.

---

[25] Considered further in 5.47 below.
[26] (1863) 3 B. and S.826.
[27] 1942 S.C. 56.
[28] 1929 S.C. 593.
[29] For which see 4.18 above.

4.62   In *Condor* v. *The Barron Knights,*[30] it was held that an illness which rendered the drummer of an internationally famous pop band fit to perform for only half the band's future engagements had the effect of frustrating the contract he had with the band.

Object of the Contract Defeated

4.63   When the real purpose which underlies a particular contract cannot be fulfilled because of supervening events, then the main contract which was built around it will be frustrated. Thus, in *Jackson* v. *Union Marine Insurance Co. Ltd.*[31] it was held that a contract under which a ship was to sail from Liverpool to Newport, and there load a cargo of iron rails for San Francisco, was frustrated by the ship running aground in Caernarvon Bay, and not being fully repaired until seven months later. The long delay had rendered the original purpose of the contract meaningless.

4.64   It can sometimes be difficult to assess whether or not a particular event is sufficiently material or essential to a contract to render it pointless if the event does not take place. A good illustration of this difficulty arises from the contrast between two cases which occurred in the same year, and were built around the proposed coronation of Edward VII, which was delayed by his illness.

4.65   In *Krell* v. *Henry,*[32] it was held that the hire of a room overlooking the procession route was frustrated by the postponement, since the continued hire of the room on that day would have little purpose, whereas in *Herne Bay Steamboat Co.* v. *Hutton,*[33] it was held that the hire of a vessel to witness the proposed review of the navy by the new king, and to tour the fleet at anchor, could still proceed for its second purpose, and was therefore still valid.

---

[30] [1966] 1 W.L.R. 87. The same was held in *Dunbar* v. *Baillie Bros.* (Contractors) Ltd., 1990 G.W.D. 26–1487, a case in which a man employed as an HGV driver lost his licence on health grounds.
[31] (1874) L.R. 10 C.P. 125.
[32] [1903] 2 K.B. 740.
[33] [1903] 2 K.B. 683.

Breach of Contract

4.66 A breach of contract is simply a failure on the part of one (or both) of the parties to fulfil all contractual obligations. By no means all breaches of contract have the effect of terminating the contract outright, and the only ones which do are those which constitute a "material" breach (which is a question of fact in every case) or those which constitute an "irritancy." Material breaches, and the right of rescission which flow from them, are considered below, and irritancies may conveniently be considered here.

4.67 An irritancy is simply a breach of contract by one party which entitles the other party to regard the contract as being at an end. They may take the form of "legal" irritancies (*i.e.* those imposed by law) of which the only two examples are in respect of non-payment of feu-duty or rent. Both may be "purged" (*i.e.* remedied) at any time before a court declares the contract to be terminated.

4.68 Alternatively, they may be "conventional" irritancies, that is irritancies provided for by agreement between the parties, which cannot normally be purged. However, under the Law Reform (Miscellaneous Provisions) (Scotland) Act 1985, sections 4 to 7, no commercial or industrial landlord may take advantage of a conventional irritancy relating to non-payment of rent without serving a notice on the tenant which gives him a further 14 days to pay after what is in effect a reminder. In the case of any other irritancy in a commercial or industrial lease, a "fair and reasonable" test applies.

4.69 A breach of contract will normally, however, attract a selection of remedies other than the right of recission, and the final section of this chapter examines each of these remedies in turn.

REMEDIES FOR BREACH OF CONTRACT

Introduction

4.70 As a general rule, every breach of contract by one party will at least entitle the other party to damages, even though these may in the circumstances be "nominal" (see below), and probably not worth pursuing. Whether or not the aggrieved party is entitled to other remedies as well will depend upon the nature of the breach.

4.71 However, before A may claim in respect of a breach of contract by B, he must, if challenged, be in a position to show, either that he has himself performed his part of the bargain, or that he is both ready and able to do so, and has not already been in breach of contract himself.

4.72 This "mutuality of obligations" is well illustrated by the fate which befell the pursuers in *Graham* v. *United Turkey Red Co. Ltd.*[34] in which commission agents suing for arrears of commission for a period of three years had their damages restricted to the two-year period before they themselves broke the agreement by selling the products of a rival of the defendants.

4.73 It is always open to the parties themselves to stipulate the remedies available to the injured party in the event of a breach (as in the case of liquidate damages clauses considered below), but otherwise the following are the normally available remedies, depending upon the facts of the case:

1. Damages.
2. Rescission.
3. Specific implement.
4. Defensive measures.

4.74 Each of these may now be considered in turn, before the chapter concludes with a consideration of the problems generated by "anticipatory breach."

Damages

4.75 The object of a court in awarding damages is to compensate the innocent party, and not to penalise the guilty one. Whenever possible, the damages awarded will therefore reflect the true loss suffered by the injured party, even if it consists only of trouble and inconvenience, in which case the damages will be "nominal," and small. In recent years, however, the courts have shown themselves

---

[34] 1922 S.C. 533. See also *Laurie* v. *British Steel Corporation*, 1988 S.L.T. 17.

willing to award realistic sums in respect of the disappointment and frustration generated by a breach.[35]

4.76 When damages are more than nominal, they are described, misleadingly, as "substantial," and this category may itself be further subdivided into "ordinary" and "special."

Ordinary Damages

4.77 These represent compensation to the injured party in respect of those losses which flow naturally from the foreseeable consequences for the victim, according to the facts known by, or reasonably obvious to, the party in breach at the time of the making of the contract. They will be calculated by the court using such guidelines as are available to it (*e.g.* the cost of a replacement, the losses arising from the unavailability of a substitute, etc.), and sometimes following statutory rules.[36]

4.78 In doing so, the court will expect the injured party to have taken such steps as were reasonable at the time to minimise ("mitigate") his loss, and he will not recover any greater sum than would have been payable had he taken such steps. For example, the wrongfully dismissed employee must make reasonable efforts to find another job, and the hotel guest whose room has been double-booked must restrict his alternative accommodation, where possible, to an establishment of similar standard.

4.79 In *Ireland* v. *Merryton Coal Co.*[37] a coal company under contract to deliver 3,000 tons of coal in roughly equal consignments over a four-month period at a fixed price per ton had only delivered about half this quantity by the end of that period. Rather than award damages for the entire shortfall at the market price ruling at the end of that period, the court divided the consignment

---

[35] As in *Jarvis* v. *Swan Tours* [1973] 1 All E.R. 71, in which there was a disastrous failure by a tour company to match the promises of its tour brochure, and *Diesen* v. *Samson*, 1971 S.L.T. (Sh.Ct.) 49, in which a wedding photographer failed to turn up to an occasion upon which invited guests were in national costume.
[36] The provisions of s. 50 of the Sale of Goods Act 1979, considered in 5.105 below.
[37] (1894) 21 R.989.

into nominal 750-ton lots, and calculated the shortfall by the ruling price at the end of each of the four months.

4.80   But there are limits to this duty to mitigate, and the injured party need only take such steps as are "reasonable" in the circumstances. So, in *Gunter* v. *Lauritzen*,[38] the purchaser of a consignment of Danish hay known by the seller to be for resale was held not to have been expected to make good the shortage created by the defendant's complete non-delivery by obtaining alternative supplies from three separate sources around the country.

4.81   The pursuer will also only be able to claim ordinary damages for those losses which flow naturally from the breach of contract by the defender, and if the loss which he is claiming is too "remote" from the breach, then damages will not be awarded in respect of it. The leading case in this area of the law is *Hadley* v. *Baxendale*.[39]

4.82   The owners of a broken flour mill crankshaft (H) handed it to a carrier (B) who undertook to deliver it to the makers for a new one to be patterned from it. He undertook to do so within two days, and failed to do so for a much longer period. All that he knew was that he was carrying a broken millshaft, and the court refused to award damages in respect of the loss of profits which arose from this delay since it was not a naturally foreseeable consequence of his breach, and the carrier had no knowledge of the special circumstances (*i.e.* that the mill would remain idle in his absence).

4.83   In order to claim for this loss, the pursuers would have needed to show that "special" damages were recoverable.

Special Damages

4.84   When it can be shown that the party in breach was, at the time when the contract was negotiated, aware of special circumstances which would make the other party suffer loss over and

[38]   (1894) 1 S.L.T. 435.
[39]   (1854) 9 Ex. 341.

Damages 97

above the ordinary level, in the event of the breach which is later committed, then the injured party may claim for these "special" damages. The knowledge necessary on the part of the party in breach may be actual, or implied from the circumstances, in the sense that he ought reasonably to have known.

4.85 A case which illustrates neatly the essential distinction between ordinary and special damages is *Victoria Laundry (Windsor) Ltd.* v. *Newman Industries Ltd.*,[40] in which the pursuers ordered a boiler from the defenders which arrived 20 weeks late. The pursuers sought to recover loss of business profits not only on their normal business, but also in respect of a particularly lucrative Government contract which they had. The defenders knew the nature of the business carried on by the pursuers, and that the boiler was required as soon as possible, but they had no actual or imputed knowledge of the existence of the Government contract. The pursuers therefore recovered, as normal damages, their regular business profits, but failed in their claim for special losses under the Government contract.

4.86 Each decided case will therefore depend upon its own individual facts. Thus, in *Hobbs* v. *London and South Western Ry. Co.*[41] the court refused to award, as special damages, the loss of the pursuer's wife's services to his business after she caught a cold when they both had to walk from a railway station to which they had been misdelivered. However, in *MacDonald* v. *Highland Ry. Co.*[42] the court awarded special damages in respect of the late delivery of confectionery for the coming-of-age party of Lord MacDonald, when it had been clearly marked "perishable" but had been handled as non-perishable, and had arrived too late for the ceremony and past its best.

Penalties and Liquidate Damages

4.87 It is quite normal, in commercial contracts, for the parties to agree in advance what the "quantum" of damages shall be in

---

[40] [1949] 2 K.B. 528.
[41] (1875) L.R. 10 Q.B. 111.
[42] (1873) 11 M.614.

the event of a breach. Provided that the clause in question appears to be a genuine attempt by the parties to pre-estimate the loss to the injured party (in which case it is referred to in law as a "liquidate damages" clause) then the courts will enforce it, whether the sum provided for is greater or smaller than the actual loss. The parties are therefore bound by that clause.

4.88 Where, on the other hand, the clause appears to be an attempt to terrorise the other party into fulfilling the contract, or penalising him if he does not, then such a "penalty clause" will not be enforceable.

4.89 In attempting to distinguish between the two, the courts have over the years devised the following tests.

1. It makes little difference what name the parties give to such a clause, or how they describe it; the courts will examine its true intention.
2. A single lump sum provision is more likely to be regarded as a penalty than as liquidate damages.
3. The true nature of the clause will be judged in the light of the circumstances of the making of the contract, and not of the breach.

4.90 Among the decided cases which illustrate some of these principles are *Elphinstone* v. *Monklands Iron and Coal Co. Ltd.*[43] in which a provision that lessees of mineral rights should pay £100 per acre for every acre which they failed to landscape at the end of the lease was held to be a liquidate damages clause, even though described by the parties as a penalty, and *Dingwall* v. *Burnett*,[44] in which the court refused to enforce an agreement that the tenant of an hotel pay £50 for the breach of each and every clause in the lease broken by him; the landlord was then in fact free to claim over £300.

4.91 The mere fact that the parties have found it almost impossible to pre-estimate the likely loss will not necessarily prevent their

---

[43] (1886) 13 R.(H.L.) 98.
[44] 1912 S.C. 1097.

agreement constituting one for liquidate damages. In *Clydebank Engineering and Shipbuilding Co. Ltd.* v. *Castaneda*,[45] a contract which contained a "penalty" of £500 per week for every week of delayed delivery of torpedo boats to Spain was held to be a liquidate damages provision, even though it had been impossible to pre-estimate loss with any accuracy, given the Spanish Government's difficulties in Cuba at the time. The parties had made a genuine attempt at a pre-estimate, and that was sufficient.

Rescission

4.92 In addition to any right to claim damages, a party who has suffered a "material" breach of contract by the other party may "rescind" (*i.e.* cancel) the contract. What will be a material breach will obviously vary from case to case, and the parties themselves may, in the contract, designate one or more breaches as having this effect.[46] Alternatively it may be implied from the behaviour of the defaulting party, as when he commits an "anticipatory breach," considered below.

4.93 In the *Graham* case discussed at 4.72 above, for example, the actions of the commission agents in selling rival products was said to be a material breach, and the same was held to be true, in *Blyth* v. *Scottish Liberal Club*,[47] of the refusal of a club manager to carry out certain tasks which he did not believe were part of his contractual duties, but in fact were. In both cases, the employers/principals were held to be entitled to regard the contract as being at an end, with no further obligations due by them.

4.94 In *Wade* v. *Waldon*,[48] on the other hand, the failure of a famous music-hall artist (George Robey) to send publicity material to the management of a theatre at least 14 days before his contrac-

---

[45] (1904) 7 F.(H.L.) 77.
[46] Thus, time may be said to be "of the essence" of the contract (see for example, *Ford Sellar Morris Properties* v. *E.W. Hutchison*, 1990 S.L.T. 500); and insurance contracts contain clauses which give the answers given by proposers on proposal forms a similar significance.
[47] 1983 S.L.T. 260.
[48] 1909 S.C. 571.

tual appearance there was held not to be a material breach by him. It is clearly always a question of fact and circumstance.

4.95 The position may often be covered by a statutory provision which stipulates that a particular breach will be deemed to be material, or will entitle the injured party to rescind.[49]

Specific Implement

4.96 Another remedy available to an aggrieved party is specific implement, which may take the form of a court order, either obliging the defaulter to perform the contract (a decree *ad factum praestandum*) or requiring him to desist from conduct in breach of it (interdict). A common example of the latter arises in the context of restrictive covenants,[50] when courts interdict the offender from taking certain action (*e.g.* working for a rival employer) which would be in breach of such a covenant.

4.97 On the whole the courts will not award specific implement:

1. When the obligation being enforced is the payment of money, since there are other procedures[51] more appropriate to secure this objective.
2. When the contract to be enforced would involve an intimate relationship such as employment.[52]
3. When compliance would be unlawful or impossible.
4. When the court could not enforce the decree, for example because the defender is a foreigner.
5. When there is no *pretium affectionis*, *i.e.* no special reason why the pursuer requires the contract to be performed. Thus, when the subject-matter of the contract is unique (*e.g.* a famous painting), the court may well grant specific imple-

---

[49] As in the case of s. 11 of the Sale of Goods Act 1979, considered below, which entitles a buyer whose seller has not delivered the correct goods to repudiate the contract.

[50] For which see 4.29 above.

[51] Known as "diligence" (*e.g.* arrestment and poinding of goods).

[52] *N.B.* not even an industrial tribunal can enforce a reinstatement order if the employer chooses to pay additional compensation instead.

ment, but it is unlikely to do so in respect of a crate of cabbages.

6. When it would be inequitable to do so.
7. When damages are a perfectly adequate remedy.

Defensive Measures

4.98 In certain cases, the injured party following a breach may be in a position to exact his own method of enforcement by retaining something belonging to the party in breach. This may take the form either of *retention* or *lien*, and both may be exercised whether the breach is a "material" one or not.

Retention

4.99 This right arises in circumstances in which "compensation"[53] could be claimed, where both debts arise under the same contract, or where the *creditor* is bankrupt. In each case, the debtor in the contract (who is the person injured in the breach by the creditor) may simply withhold money which he is due to pay under that contract.

Lien

4.100 This is the very specific right of a person who has performed services in respect of an item of moveable property[54] physically to hold on to that property until his bill is paid. In many cases, this right is enlarged into a right of sale under specific statutory provisions.[55]

Anticipatory Breach

4.101 Occasionally, the defaulting party will announce, well in advance of the date for the performance of the contract, that he has no intention of performing it. The other party then has a choice of regarding the contract as breached materially there and then,

---

[53] *i.e.* the right to discharge one debt against another, considered in 4.29 above.
[54] *e.g.* the car repairer or dry cleaner.
[55] *e.g.* the Innkeepers Act of 1878.

rescinding it and seeking such damages as are assessable at that early stage, or waiting until the date set for completion and resscinding then, claiming appropriate damages. If, in the meantime, the first party changes his mind and performs, the performance will be a valid one, and the right to rescind and claim damages is lost.

4.102   The results, either way, can often be spectacular. In *White and Carter (Councils) Ltd.* v. *McGregor*,[56] for example, a contract to take advertising space on lamp-post rubbish-bins for a three-year period was cancelled by the client on the same day as it had been signed by his manager. Three years later, the contractors were allowed to recoup the full cost of the advertising. Similarly, in *Salaried Staff London Loan Co. Ltd.* v. *Swears and Wells*,[57] the landlords were allowed to claim in respect of the remaining 29 years of a 34-year lease even though the tenants had given notice of their desire to quit after the fifth year.

4.103   A party choosing to "sit it out," however, takes the risk that events may overtake him which entitle the defaulting party to resile from the contract. Thus, in *Avery* v. *Bowden*,[58] the owner of a ship who sat waiting for the expiry of a 45-day period in which the defendant was supposed to be loading it with a cargo (having admitted much earlier that he could not do so), received an unpleasant surprise when the Crimean War broke out within the 45-day period. The cargo port was Odessa, and the entire contract was therefore void for illegality.

---

[56] 1962 S.C.(H.L.) 1.
[57] 1985 S.L.T. 326.
[58] (1885) 5 E. and B. 714.

5. SALE OF GOODS

Introduction

5.1 The modern law on the sale of goods is, for all practical purposes, to be found almost exclusively within the provisions of the Sale of Goods Act 1979. It is the latest successor to an Act of the same name passed in 1893 which, in addition to codifying the law on the subject, also imposed upon the old Scots common law a set of statutory rules.

5.2 In those exceptional cases in which there is no appropriate provision made for a particular situation under the 1979 Act, then those old common law rules will still apply, as will the more general common law on matters such as misrepresentation and fraud.[1] In addition, other Acts of Parliament will be found dealing with specific trading phenomena encountered over the years,[2] but otherwise the study of the law relating to sale of goods is a study of the 1979 Act.

5.3 Put at its simplest, "sale of goods" encompasses all situations in which moveable property is exchanged for money, and governs countless thousands of everyday situations from the purchase of a newspaper from the corner shop to the acquisition of an ocean-going liner. While in many circumstances the parties would be well advised to record their contract in writing, it is not essential, since contracts for the sale of goods may be formed, and proved, in any form and by any legally admissible means,[3] except when a particular type of sale is governed by additional laws laid down by Parliament.[4]

---

[1] See s. 62(2). All section references are to the 1979 Act unless otherwise indicated.
[2] *e.g.* the Trade Descriptions Act 1968 and the Mock Auctions Act 1961.
[3] *i.e. prout de jure*; see s. 4. Such contracts may even be implied from the actions of the parties.
[4] As in the case of a ship sale.

DEFINITION OF SALE OF GOODS

5.4 Section 2 of the Act contains the following definition of the subject matter encompassed by the Act: "A contract of sale of goods is a contract by which the seller transfers or agrees to transfer the property in goods to the buyer for a money consideration, called the price."

5.5 This broad definition contains several elements which require closer examination.

Sale or Agreement to Sell

5.6 Since the objective of a contract for the sale of goods is to transfer the "property in" (*i.e.* the ownership of or the title to) the goods, this can only effectively take place when and if the seller is in a position to do so unconditionally. When this is the case, then a "sale" occurs; if for some reason he is not, then the contract between the parties can only be an "agreement to sell" which, while legally enforceable, will not give the intending buyer any legal right or title to the goods themselves.

5.7 If, for example, the contract is subject to some condition which has yet to be fulfilled[5] then there will be no "sale" until then, and in the meantime the parties are contractually bound only by an agreement to sell.[6] Equally, if the contract, or the operation of other sections of the Act, provide that the actual sale is to take place at some future time[7] then only an agreement to sell is created until the necessary time has elapsed.

5.8 The important point to keep in mind is that only a contract of *sale* gives the intending buyer a right to the goods themselves;

---

[5] *i.e.* a "suspensive" condition such as that encountered in a "sale or return" situation, for which see 5.36 below, as opposed to a "resolutive" condition such as that encountered in *Gavin's Tr.* v. *Fraser*, considered in 5.18 below.

[6] s. 2(6).

[7] As may be the case, for example, when the goods in question are "future" goods, or are "unascertained," both of which concepts are more fully explored in 5.22 below.

an agreement to sell simply entitles him to sue the defaulting seller for damages.

Price

5.9 It is essential to the creation of a contract for the sale of goods that the goods themselves be exchanged for a "price" expressed in money terms; an exchange of goods for goods is a "barter," dealt with in 5.16 below, and is excluded from the law governing sale of goods.

5.10 Section 8 of the Act allows this price to be fixed under the contract, or fixed in a manner agreed under the contract, or determined by the course of dealings between the parties. If all else fails, then the court will impose a "reasonable" price established by reference to all the circumstances of the case.[8]

5.11 For example, in *Glynwed Distribution Ltd. v. S. Koronka and Co.*[9] G. and K. entered into a contract for the sale of hot rolled steel, K. believing it to be British steel at £103.50 per tonne, while G. believed it to be foreign steel at £149 per tonne. After holding, on appeal, that the parties were *ad idem* on the sale of hot rolled steel, the Court of Session fixed a "reasonable" price per tonne at £135.

5.12 Section 9 even allows the price to be fixed by a third party. If he cannot or will not do so, then the agreement is avoided except to the extent that goods have already been delivered to, and accepted by, the buyer, in which case he must pay a "reasonable" price for those goods. Either party, by his own fault, preventing the third party from fixing the price will be liable to the other party in damages, but there will be no contract of sale.

---

[8] *N.B.* not necessarily the market price.
[9] 1977 S.C. 1; see also *Macdonald v. Clark* 1927 S.N. 6 when items for sale as part of an hotel were valued at a higher "reasonable" price than the sum of their total individual values because they were part of a going concern.

Goods

5.13 Section 61 of the Act defines goods as including "all corporeal moveables,"[10] which term "includes emblements, industrial growing crops, and things attached to or forming part of the land which are agreed to be severed under the contract of sale." Thus, trees are "goods" once there is an agreement to fell them,[11] as would be a portable garage sitting on a concrete base, or a crop of potatoes.[12]

5.14 As will emerge in 5.22 below, it is sometimes necessary to distinguish between "existing" and "future" goods, and between "specific" and "unascertained" goods, but such distinctions are only applicable once the "goods" in question have satisfied the definition laid down under section 61.

SALE OF GOODS DISTINGUISHED FROM OTHER COMMERCIAL TRANSACTIONS

5.15 For various reasons, it may become important to distinguish between contracts for the sale of goods (which are governed by the 1979 Act) and similar-looking commercial transactions (which are not). The following are among the more common in the latter category.

Barter

5.16 This is an agreement (which may be perfectly enforceable as a contract in its own right) whereby goods are exchanged for goods. Barter does not constitute sale of goods because there is no price in money form. Although rare in modern commerce, a contract of barter may still occasionally be encountered, as in *Widenmeyer* v. *Bain, Stewart and Co. Ltd.*,[13] in which it was important to establish whether or not the "risk" of destruction had

---

[10] Something which is "corporeal" is capable of being touched, while "moveable" property consists basically of anything which is capable of motion. N.B. money is excluded from the definition of "goods."

[11] See *Munro* v. *Belnagam Estates* in 5.31 below.

[12] *Paton's Trustee* v. *Finlayson* 1923 S.C. 872.

[13] 1967 S.C. 85.

passed to the buyer in an agreed exchange of a consignment of 1962 whisky for a consignment of 1964 whisky. It was held that in a "barter" situation such as this, the old common law rule[14] applied, and not the statutory rule.[15]

Pledge and other Forms of Security

5.17 Section 62(4) of the Act specifically excludes from the definition of sale of goods "any pretended . . . contract of sale which is intended to operate by way of mortgage, pledge, charge or other security." The contract in question may look like a contract of sale, but if its real purpose is to create a security over the goods in question then the transaction will not attract the special sale of goods provisions which allow title to pass without delivery.[16]

5.18 But there will still be a sale of goods when a genuine contract of sale is entered into which contains a "buy-back" clause. Thus, in *Gavin's Tr.* v. *Fraser*,[17] it was held that a contract of sale had been created under which a haulage contractor sold his plant to a timber merchant for £1,200, but continued to use it for an existing contract with the buyer, and had the option to repurchase it at the original sale price plus 6 per cent within the following 12 months.

Labour and Materials

5.19 A contract for the supply of labour and materials[18] is primarily a contract for services, and not a contract of sale, even though goods may change hands as part of its provisions.

---

[14] *i.e.* that the risk passed to the buyer before delivery.
[15] *i.e.* that risk passes with the transfer of the "property in" the goods. *N.B.* a contract involving a "trade-in," with a cash balance paid by the purchaser, will in most cases still be a contract for the sale of goods; see *Dawson* v. *Dutfield* [1936] 2 All E.R. 232.
[16] Which is one very good reason why a pawnbroker will always require physical possession before lending money on goods. Thus, in *Jones and Co.'s Tr.* v. *Allan* (1901) 4 F. 374 it was held that no true "sale" was created when J., a bicycle dealer, obtained a loan of £40 from A., and gave him a fictitious receipt for £72 worth of bicycles which then remained in J.'s possession.
[17] 1920 S.C. 674.
[18] As, *e.g.* in *Young and Moreten* v. *McManus Childs* [1969] 1 A.C. 454, where the contract was for the supply of a house roof.

Hire Purchase[19]

5.20 Under a hire-purchase agreement, the hirer does not commit himself to the purchase of the goods absolutely, but may do so by option at the end of the hiring period. Such an agreement does not, therefore, satisfy the basic requirement of a sale of goods contract, namely that it shall be one for the transfer of title to the goods.

Capacity

5.21 With one exception, contracts for the sale of goods are governed by the same rules of contractual capacity as other contracts.[20] The one exception concerns "necessaries"[21] which are supplied to a person under 16 or a person incompetent to contract by virtue of drunkenness or mental incapacity.[22] Such contracts are enforceable, but only to the extent that the person protected need only pay a "reasonable" price for the necessaries supplied, which may not of course be the contract price.[23]

TRANSFER OF PROPERTY IN GOODS

5.22 Since the primary objective of a contract of sale is to pass the "property in" the goods it is hardly surprising that the Act contains a set of precise rules determining how and when this is to happen, providing that the goods in question are "specific" or "ascertained" goods.

5.23 Section 61 of the Act defines "specific" goods as "goods identified and agreed on at the time a contract of sale is made," and any goods which do not come within this definition will be regarded as "unascertained" and incapable of being transferred so as to give the buyer an unchallengeable title to them.

---

[19] For which see generally chap. 6.
[20] For which see 2.91−2.112.
[21] *i.e.* "goods suitable to the condition in life . . ." of the person in question.
[22] And each of these conditions is considered more fully in 2.93−2.105.
[23] See generally s. 3 and *Nash* v. *Inman* [1908] 2 K.B. 1. (Court of Appeal).

5.24 Thus, in *Hayman* v. *McLintock*,[24] a firm of flour merchants owned a consignment of bags of flour which they kept at H.'s store. They sold 250 sacks to one purchaser and 100 to another, and notified H., who acknowledged to the purchasers that the sacks were being held pending their instructions. When the flour merchants went into liquidation it was held that the trustee had a prior claim over the sacks because the individual sacks within the store had not been separated out from the balance of the sacks held in the store.

5.25 Goods which are unascertained may be so for a variety of reasons. They may, for example, be "future" goods, *i.e.* "goods to be manufactured or acquired by the seller after the making of the contract of sale."[25] They may alternatively be "generic" goods (*e.g.* "twenty tons of coal" to be delivered in the future but without further identification, or they may, as in *Hayman's* case above, be an unsevered portion of a consignment which can be identified. Whatever the reason, when goods are unascertained, the effect of section 16 of the Act is that the "property" in them cannot be transferred.

5.26 In such cases, there may still be a binding "agreement to sell,"[26] but the buyer acquires no right to the goods themselves. This can be crucially important if the seller becomes insolvent or the goods are resold to an innocent third party.[27]

5.27 Assuming, then, that the goods in question are specific, the Act sets out to regulate the passing of the property in them. First and foremost, in section 17, it allows the intentions of the parties themselves to regulate the passing of the property, insofar as this may be deduced from the terms of the contract, their conduct or the circumstances of the case.

---

[24] 1907 S.C. 936.

[25] s. 5(1).

[26] For the distinction between such a contract and a full contract of sale, see 5.6 – 5.8 above. N.B. the buyer still, of course, has the right to sue for the breach of an agreement to sell.

[27] As in *Hayman's* case, above.

5.28 For example, in *Woodburn* v. *Andrew Motherwell Ltd.*[28] W. was a farmer who sold six haystacks to M. for an agreed price per ton. The terms of the agreement were that W. should leave the hay in his yard so that M. could bale it, and that W. would then transport it to the railhead to be weighed for pricing purposes. Some of the bales were destroyed by fire while they were still in W.'s yard, and it was held that the loss fell on M., since the terms of the contract clearly showed that it was the parties' intentions that the property[29] should pass once the hay was placed at M.'s disposal.

5.29 When, and only when, the parties' intentions regarding the passing of the property cannot be ascertained by reference to section 17, then section 18 takes over, and sets out five rules by means of which the parties' intentions may be construed. They are as follows:

Rule 1

5.30 "Where there is an unconditional contract for the sale of specific goods in a deliverable state[30] the property in the goods passes to the buyer when the contract is made, and it is immaterial whether the time of payment or the time of delivery, or both, be postponed."

5.31 Thus, in *Munro* v. *Liquidator of Balnagown Estates Co.*[31] it was held that the property in an estate of timber, which had been the subject of a contract of sale while the trees were still growing, passed to the buyer once they had been felled (since the timber was then in a deliverable state), regardless of the fact that it remained on the seller's land.

Rule 2

5.32 "Where there is a contract for the sale of specific goods and the seller is bound to do something to the goods for the purpose

---

[28] 1917 S.C. 533.
[29] And hence the risk of loss—see 5.43 below.
[30] *i.e.* in terms of s. 61(5), when they are in such a state that the buyer would under the contract be bound to take delivery of them.
[31] 1949 S.C. 49.

of putting them into a deliverable state, the property does not pass until the thing is done and the buyer has notice that it has been done."

5.33 For example, in *Brown Bros.* v. *Carron Co.*[32] it was held that the property had not passed in a contract which required B. to deliver, erect and modify a crane during the course of erection, while the crane remained in B.'s yard. In *Cockburn's Tr.v. Bowe*,[33] on the other hand, the fact that an entire crop of potatoes had yet to be delivered by the seller to the buyer, in terms of the contract, did not prevent the property in the potatoes passing to the buyer once the potatoes were placed in pits since they were then in a deliverable state, and the contractual term relating to delivery was a subsidiary matter to the main question of whether or not the property had passed.

Rule 3

5.34 "Where there is a contract for the sale of specific goods in a deliverable state but the seller is bound to weigh, measure, test, or do some other act or thing with reference to the goods for the purpose of ascertaining the price, the property does not pass until the act or thing is done and the buyer has notice that it has been done."

5.35 In *Woodburn* v. *Andrew Motherwell Ltd.* above, for example, the purchasers, M., sought to avoid the consequences of the loss by fire of the haystacks by arguing that Rule 3 should apply, since the goods had not been weighed at the time of the fire. For the decision above, s.17 took precedence but even had it not the court indicated that Rule 3 would not have applied because the contract did not oblige the seller to weigh the goods.

Rule 4

5.36 "When goods are delivered to the buyer on approval or on sale or on sale or return or other similar terms the property in the goods passes to the buyer:

---

[32] (1898) 6 S.L.T. 231.
[33] 1910 2 S.L.T. 17; a similar ruling was of course given in *Munro's* case above.

"(a) when he signifies his approval or acceptance to the seller
       or does any other act adopting the transaction;
"(b) if he does not signify his approval or acceptance to the
       seller but retains the goods without giving notice of rejec-
       tion, then, if a time has been fixed for the return of the
       goods, on the expiry of that time, and, if no time has
       been fixed, on the expiry of a reasonable time."

Rule 5

5.37

"(1) Where there is a contract for the sale of unascertained
      or future goods by description,[34] and goods of that
      description and in a deliverable state are unconditionally
      appropriated to the contract, either by the seller with the
      assent of the buyer or by the buyer with the assent of the
      seller, the property in the goods then passes to the buyer;
      and the assent may be express or implied, and may be
      given either before or after the appropriation is made.

"(2) Where, in pursuance of the contract, the seller delivers
      the goods to the buyer or to a carrier or other . . . custod-
      ier (whether named by the buyer or not) for the purpose
      of transmission to the buyer, and does not reserve the
      right of disposal, he is taken to have unconditionally
      appropriated the goods to the contract."

5.38 What is happening in the circumstances envisaged in Rule
5, of course, is that goods which were once "ascertained" have
become ascertained or specific, and it is in terms of Rule 5 that
most agreements to sell become contracts of sale, with the property
in the goods passing instantly to the buyer unless the seller
"reserves the right of disposal."

5.39 This ability of the seller to suspend the passing of the property in the goods,[35] and the general rule laid down in section 17
that the parties may stipulate in the contract when the property in

---

[34] For sales by description, see 5.68–5.70 below.
[35] Further confirmed by s. 19 of the Act.

the goods is to pass, have combined in recent years to create a common problem situation over "reservation of title" clauses, which may conveniently be examined next.

RESERVATION OF TITLE

5.40 Contracts under which the seller attempts, by means of a suitably drafted clause, to stipulate that the property in the goods will not pass to the buyer until some condition—usually the payment of the purchase price in full—has been met, were considered authoritatively in the case which gave rise to the generic name for such clauses—"Romalpa" clauses—namely *Aluminium Industrie Vaassen B.V. v. Romalpa Aluminium.*[36]

5.41 In this case, a Dutch company sold aluminium foil to an English company, which then sold some of it on to sub-purchasers. The contract between them contained a clause which stipulated that until the consignment had been paid for in full, the purchasers were to store it in such a way that it was clearly still the property of the sellers, and that any articles manufactured from the foil were to be held by the purchasers in guarantee of payment to the sellers. Further, it was stipulated that if the sellers sold on the property to third parties, then the purchasers were, if so required by the sellers, to hand over to the sellers any claims which they might have against the third parties. When a receiver was appointed to the purchasing company, it was held by the Court of Appeal that the original sellers were entitled to recover not only the foil still in the purchasers' possession, but also the proceeds of the sub-sales, since the purchaser had been acting at all times as the agents of the sellers.

5.42 While there is no difficulty in the use of a reservation of title clause in circumstances such as this, it has been held in subsequent cases limiting the effect of the *Romalpa* judgment[37] that such

---

[36] [1976] 1 W.L.R. 676. For cases upholding the *Romalpa* principle, see *Archivent Sales and Development Ltd. v. Strathclyde Regional Council*, 1985 S.L.T. 154, and *Zahnrad Fabrik Passau v. Terex Ltd.*, 1986 S.L.T. 84.

[37] *e.g. Bond Worth Ltd. Re* [1980] Ch. 228, and *Borden (U.K.) Ltd. v. Scottish Timber Products Ltd.* [1981] Ch. 25. However, in *Armour v. Thyssen Edelstahlwerke A.G.*, 1990 S.L.T. 891, the House of Lords held that since, in such cases, the purchaser does not own the goods in question, he cannot be said to be granting

clauses cannot be used so as to create any form of security without possession. Nor can such a clause create a form of trust over proceeds to be received by the purchaser at some future date.[38]

TRANSFER OF RISK

5.43   Section 20(1) of the Act lays down a general rule that unless otherwise agreed, the risk of the goods being damaged or destroyed remains with the seller until the property in them passes to the buyer, and that thereafter the risk is the buyer's, whether delivery has occurred or not.[39] In short, in the absence of a specific contractual term to the contrary, the risk passes with the title. To this rule there are four exceptions:

5.44   1. Under section 20(2) of the Act, when delivery has been delayed as the result of fault by either party, then the goods are at the risk of the party at fault if a loss occurs which might not have occurred at all but for his fault. If, for example, a car dealer fails to deliver a new car on the agreed date, and his showroom is destroyed by fire, then the loss is his, and not the buyer's, even though the property in the car will have passed to the buyer on the date when the purchase agreement was signed.

5.45   2. Under section 20(3) of the Act, when either party places himself in the position of custodier of the goods, he remains liable as custodier regardless of the provision of section 20(1). Thus, in the above example, if the car dealer agrees to look after the car until the buyer returns from holiday, and it is stolen and damaged through inadequate showroom security, the loss of the vehicle falls upon the seller.

5.46   3. If, without the knowledge of the seller, specific goods have perished at the time of the making of the contract, then the

---

a right in security over them anyway, and that a *Romalpa* clause could be used by the seller to secure payment, not only under the contract of sale, but in respect of any other sums owed by the purchaser to the seller, howsoever arising.

[38] See, *e.g. Clark Taylor and Co. Ltd.* v. *Quality Site Development (Edinburgh) Ltd.*, 1981 S.C. 111.

[39] An example of this process in action was, of course, the case of *Woodburn* v. *Andrew Motherwell*, considered in 5.28 above. It also follows from this rule that risk can only pass in respect of "specific" goods.

effect of section 6 of the Act is that the contract is void, even though, in terms of the contract, the property and the risk may already have passed before the true position is discovered.

5.47 4. If specific goods are accidentally destroyed before the risk has passed to the buyer, the contract is avoided. This is the effect of section 7, and the result is that neither party is under any liability. This is simply, of course, one example of the more general contractual principle of "frustration of contract" in action.

5.48 Problems can arise in the operation of the general rule when the goods are delivered to a carrier by the seller in order that they may be delivered to the buyer. When the seller has undertaken to deliver the goods, then the general rule is that the risk of loss or destruction passes to the buyer as soon as the goods are delivered to a carrier and placed at the buyer's disposal.[40] But if the terms of the contract are such that the seller reserves the right of disposal of the goods,[41] or if the contract is interpreted as imposing upon the seller an obligation actually to deliver the goods, then the risk remains with the seller until the goods actually arrive at the delivery point.

TRANSFER OF TITLE

General Rule

5.49 It has so far been assumed that the seller in a contract for the sale of goods has a valid title to the goods. If he does not, then although the disappointed buyer may well have good grounds for suing the purported seller,[42] he will in most cases not acquire a valid title to the goods themselves because of the operation of the maxim *nemo dat quod non habet*,[43] which finds expression in the general rule laid down in section 21(1) of the Act that where a person purports to sell goods to which he has no title, and without

---

[40] The combined effect of s. 18, rule 5(2), for which see 5.37 above, and s. 32.
[41] As he may under s. 19—see 5.40.
[42] *e.g.* for breach of implied warranty of title, dealt with in 5.62 below.
[43] "No one gives what he does not possess."

the authority or consent of the true owner, then the buyer acquires no better title to the goods than the seller had.

5.50 A good example of the general rule in operation was *Greenwood* v. *Bennett*,[44] in which B., the owner of a Jaguar car, left it with S. for certain repairs. S., having used it and damaged it, sold it to a garage proprietor, H., who believed S. to be the owner of it, and who repaired and resold it at a profit. It was held that the car still belonged to B. because S. had no valid title which he could transfer to H.

5.51 There are, however, exceptions to the general rule, of which the following are the most significant.

Exceptions

1. *The Proviso to section 21(1)*

5.52 Even the section itself acknowledges that in some circumstances his own conduct[45] may preclude the true owner of the goods from denying that the person who purported to sell them had title to do so. This form of personal bar will most clearly operate when the owner has placed the "seller" in a position in which a third party might reasonably conclude that the "seller" is genuine.

5.53 An obvious example arises when the seller is the employee or agent of the true owner,[46] but mere possession of the goods will not normally suffice to give the purported seller a valid title which he may transfer. Thus, in *Central Newbury Car Auctions* v. *Unity Finance*,[47] a car dealer unwisely allowed a purchaser to depart with the car and log book before the finance company approved the loan, which it in fact refused to do. In the meantime, the customer

---

[44] [1972] 3 W.L.R. 691.
[45] Which may consist simply of naïve trust.
[46] *e.g.* the shop manager who sells off shop fittings in an alleged "closing down sale."
[47] [1957] 1 Q.B. 371; this case also illustrates the important point that vehicle registration documents are not documents of title.

had sold the car to X, but it was held that X must hand the car back to the car dealer to whom it still belonged.

2. Sale under Voidable Title

5.54 A situation may arise in which A and B engage in a contract for the sale of goods which turns out to be "voidable"[48] by the seller, A, but before this happens, B, the purchaser, resells the goods to C. If, at the time of this second sale, C acts in good faith and has no notice of the defect in B's title, *and* A has not already "avoided" (*i.e.* set aside) the contract with B, then the effect of section 23 of the Act is that B acquires a valid title to pass on to C, who is free from any claim from A for the return of the goods.

5.55 Thus, in *MacLeod* v. *Kerr*,[49] G., a confidence trickster, purchased a car from K. using a stolen cheque. He then sold the car to X, using K.'s name. It was held that X had obtained a valid title to the car because he had acted innocently, and G.'s title, although voidable by K., had not been avoided at the time of the sale to X.

3. Sale by "Reputed Owner"

5.56 There are two situations in which the innocent purchaser of goods which have previously passed under a now disputed contract is allowed to retain title to them because at the time he purchased them the "seller" was the "reputed" owner as the result of the circumstances in which he came into possession of them.

5.57 Under section 24 of the Act, when A has sold goods to B, but remains in possession of either the goods themselves or the documents of title to them,[50] and he then delivers or transfers to C, either personally or via a "mercantile agent"[51] acting for him,

---

[48] *i.e.* capable in law of being set aside at the option of the injured party, in this case the original seller. One of the most common examples of this arises when B acquires the goods from A by fraud.

[49] 1965 S.C. 253. *N.B.* however that if the original contract is completely "void," then no title can ever pass to an innocent purchaser; see *Morrisson* v. *Robertson*, 1908 S.C. 332.

[50] *i.e.* he is what is known as the "seller in possession" of them.

[51] *i.e.* a person such as an auctioneer who normally acts as an agent in the transfer of goods or the raising of money on the security of goods; s. 26.

the goods themselves or the documents of title to them, and C acts in good faith without notice of the previous sale, then C obtains valid title to the goods, as if A had the authority of B to make the transfer.

5.58 The converse situation is provided for in section 25, when the person making the transfer to C is the "buyer in possession," and C has no notice of any continuing right which the original seller may still possess over the goods.[52] In such a case, the effect of section 25 is to place the buyer in possession in the same position as if he were a "mercantile agent" in possession of the goods or documents of title to them with the consent of the owner. The significance of this assumption will be considered below.

5.59 A good practical example of the sort of situation envisaged under section 25[53] arose in *Thomas Graham and Sons Ltd. v. Glenrothes Development Corporation*[54] in which T. had sold goods to X, a building contractor employed in the construction of what became Glenrothes, under a retention of title clause. The builders went into liquidation, and T. sought to recover the materials supplied by them from the site. It was held that G. might use section 25 in defence of that claim, since they had no knowledge of the existence of the clause in the contract between T. and X, and had acted in good faith.

4. Sale by Mercantile Agent

5.60 Under section 2 of the Factors Act 1889, when a "mercantile agent" is, with the consent of the owner, in possession of either goods or the documents of title to them, then any sale of the goods made in the ordinary course of business of a mercantile agent is valid, as if he had been expressly authorised by the owner of the goods, provided that the person buying the goods acts in good faith without knowledge of the agent's lack of authority.

---

[52] N.B. however that s. 25(2) specifically excludes from the operation of this provision goods which are the subject of a "conditional sale agreement," for which see 6.9 below.
[53] Although of course considered under an identical provision of the 1893 Act.
[54] 1967 S.C. 284. For an almost identical case, see *Archivent Sales and Development Ltd. v. Strathclyde Regional Council*, 1985 S.L.T. 154.

IMPLIED WARRANTIES

5.61 Sections 12 to 15 of the Act contain several "implied" warranties, that is, terms of contract which will be deemed to exist and which, if broken, will entitle the injured party either to treat the contract as having been repudiated by virtue of a "material breach" by the offending party, or proceed with the contract and claim damages in respect of the breach. Each of these implied warranties may be considered in turn.

Warranty of Title

5.62 Under section 12(1) of the Act, the seller is taken to have impliedly warranted that, in the case of a sale that he has the right to sell the goods, and that in the case of an agreement to sell he will have a right to sell the goods at the time when the property in them is to pass.

5.63 In addition, under section 12(1) he is taken to have impliedly warranted (a) that the goods are free, and will remain free, until the time when the property is to pass, from any charge or encumbrance not disclosed or known to the buyer before the contract was made *and* (b) that the buyer will enjoy "quiet possession" of the goods except so far as they may be disturbed by the owner or other person entitled to the benefit of any charge or encumbrance disclosed to or known of by the buyer.

5.64 An early example of both "legs" of what is now section 12 of the 1979 Act was the case of *Niblett Ltd.* v. *Confectioners' Materials Co.*,[55] in which the sellers agreed to sell tins of condensed milk, the labels of which infringed N.'s trademark. This entitled N. to injunction thereby preventing the sale of the tins as they then were, and requiring the removal of the offending labels. It was held that the sellers were in breach of both implied warranties, in that they had no right to sell the goods as they were, and that the buyers could not hope to enjoy quiet possession of them (*i.e.* without challenge by N.).

[55] [1921] 3 K.B. 387.

5.65 A more recent example of a breach of section 12(2) occurred in *Microbeads* v. *Vinhurst Road Markings*,[56] in which shortly after the sale of certain roadmarking machines by A to B, C claimed a patent on such machines which entitled C to prevent the unlicensed use of the machines by B. There had been no breach of section 12(1) in respect of title to sell, since the patent had not been in force at the time of sale, but there was a breach of section 12(2), which lays down an implied warranty that the buyer will enjoy quiet possession into the future.

5.66 There are exceptions to the general rule created by sections 12(1) and 12(2). These are found in sub-sections (3) to (5), and apply whenever the terms of the contract, or the circumstances of its making, indicate that the seller only intends to pass such limited title to the goods as he may possess, or may acquire from a third party. In such cases the implied warranty is to the effect that the seller has disclosed to the buyer all charges and encumbrances known by the seller and not known to the buyer, and that neither the seller nor any third party will disturb the buyer's quiet possession of the goods, nor anyone claiming through them otherwise than under a charge or encumbrance disclosed or made known before the contract was made.

5.67 The effect of the Unfair Contract Terms Act 1977, section 20(1) is that the parties cannot contract out of the implied warranties created by section 12.

Warranty of Description

5.68 Section 13 of the Act imports into contracts of sale an implied warranty that when goods are sold by "description," the goods delivered will comply with that description and that when sales are by sample, the goods delivered will not only comply with the sample, but also with the description.

5.69 "Description" for the purposes of section 13 has never been satisfactorily defined, but is generally taken to mean a statement of the "nature" or "kind" of goods which are being offered for

---

[56] [1975] 1 W.L.R. 218.

sale. Two good examples in practice were *Grant* v. *Australian Knitting Mills*[57] in which it was held that goods described as woollen underwear should meet that description in the sense that they should be fit for wearing next to the skin, and *Beale* v. *Taylor*,[58] in which it was held that a person seeking to buy a "1961 Triumph Herald" was entitled to one entire car, and not the front half of one 1961 Herald welded to the back half of another.

5.70 It is of course open to the parties themselves to describe the goods as closely as they wish, otherwise the "description" applied to the goods by section 13 will be kept broad. In section 13(3), however, the rule is laid down that when goods are simply displayed for sale (*e.g.* in a supermarket), the buyer may rely upon their implied description from appearance on purchasing them.[59]

5.71 The seller may not contract out of the implied warranty of description when the purchaser is a "consumer" (*i.e.* a non-business buyer), the seller is "dealing in the course of a business," and the goods are of a type normally supplied for domestic use or consumption.[60] In all other contracts (*i.e.* non-consumer contracts), the exclusion clause will only be enforceable if the court regards it as "fair and reasonable" at the time when the contract was made.[61] The factors which the court may take into account include the relative bargaining strengths of the parties, any inducement held out to the purchaser to accept the contract, the extent to which the purchaser should have been aware of the existence of the clause, and whether or not the goods were manufactured, processed or adapted to the purchaser's special requirements.[62]

---

[57] [1936] A.C. 85.
[58] [1967] 1 W.L.R. 1193. See also *McCallum* v. *Mason* in 5.80 below, in which it was held that "fertiliser" should not contain weedkiller.
[59] Thus, for example, a hot-water bottle exposed for sale on a shop counter must perform like one; see *Priest* v. *Last* in 5.82 below. What s. 13(3) establishes is that goods do not cease being sold by "description" simply because they are selected by the buyer from a silent display.
[60] Unfair Contract Terms Act 1977, s. 25.
[61] Unfair Contract Terms Act 1977, s. 24.
[62] For a recent example of these principles in operation, see *Denholm Fishselling* v. *Anderson*, 1991 S.L.T. (Sh.Ct.) 24.

5.72   The burden of proof of showing that the contract is not a consumer contract lies on the party asserting that it is not, while the burden of proof of showing that an exclusion clause is fair and reasonable lies on the party asserting that it is.

Warranty of Merchantable Quality

5.73   The general common law rule of *caveat emptor* ("let the buyer beware") is preserved under section 14(1), which imposes a general rule to the effect that in contracts of sale there is no overall implied warranty as to the quality of the goods being sold, or their suitability for the buyer's needs. Section 14(2) then creates an exception to this general rule in respect of goods being of "merchantable quality" (which is dealt with in this section), while section 14(3) creates a requirement for the goods to be "reasonably fit" for the purpose for which they are sold, which is considered in 5.79 below. In each case, however, the seller must be selling the goods "in the course of a business," although they need not necessarily be goods in which he normally deals.[63]

5.74   "Merchantable quality" for the purposes of section 14(2) is defined in section 14(6) of the Act in such a way as to require goods to be "as fit for the purpose or purposes for which goods of that kind are commonly bought as it is reasonable to expect having regard to any description applied to them, the price (if relevant) and all the other relevant circumstances."

5.75   It is important to bear in mind, in the context of section 14(2), that goods may be deemed to be of "merchantable quality" even though they are not fit for the purpose for which they were in fact purchased. Thus, in *Brown* v. *Craiks*,[64] a buyer purchased industrial fabric which he intended reselling as dress fabric. It was unsuitable for that purpose, and having failed to prove that the

[63] For example, a shopkeeper selling off surplus shelving from his display fittings would still be selling "in the course of a business." In *Buchanan-Jardine* v. *Hamilink*, 1983 S.L.T. 149, the definition was extended to include a liquidator selling a bankrupt business, and "business" is defined in s. 61 so as to include a professional practice and the activities of a central or local government authority.
[64] 1970 S.C. (H.L.) 51. *N.B.* that this case was based on the equivalent s. 14(1) of the 1893 Act.

seller knew of the purpose for which it had been supplied,[65] the buyer then attempted to sue for breach of the implied warranty that the goods be of merchantable quality. He failed in this objective because the fabric in question was reasonably capable of being used for other purposes, such as bag-making.

5.76 Similarly, after the passing of the 1979 Act, the same ruling was applied in *Millars Falkirk* v. *Turpie*,[66] in which a solicitor attempted to reject a new car on the basis that it had a persistent oil leak. In rejecting his submission that the car was not of merchantable quality, the court observed that the definition in section 14(6)[67] was "the best which has yet been devised."

5.77 The implied condition in respect of merchantable quality does not apply to defects specifically drawn to the purchaser's attention before the contract is made, or to defects which should have been revealed by an inspection made by the purchaser, when such an inspection actually occurs. There is, however, no obligation to inspect.

5.78 The rules relating to "contracting out" by the seller are the same for section 14(2) as they are for warranties of description, for which see 5.68 above.

Warranty of Fitness for Purpose

5.79 By virtue of section 14(3) of the Act there is, as a general rule, an implied term in every contract of sale that when the buyer, expressly or by implication, makes known to the seller a particular purpose for which goods are being purchased, then the goods will be "reasonably fit" for that purpose, even though the purpose in question is not one for which such goods are normally supplied.[68] The only exception to this rule applies when the circumstances

---

[65] Which is an important issue in the context of s. 14(3) — see below.
[66] 1976 S.L.T. (Notes) 66.
[67] Which apparently would have cost only £25 to fix.
[68] *N.B.* that the seller must be selling the goods in the course of business — see 5.71 above. *N.B.* also that different rules apply in respect of "credit sale agreements" which are considered in Chapter 6 below.

show that the buyer does not rely, or it would be unreasonable for him to rely, on the skill and judgment of the seller.

5.80 In *McCallum* v. *Mason*,[69] the buyer was a nurseryman whose tomatoes were going yellow, and the seller, a fertiliser dealer, recommended that he use a particular fertiliser sold by him to which the seller added a quantity of magnesium sulphate to correct a magnesium deficiency in the soil. The buyer lost all his crop as a result, and in the following year the buyer applied a second bag and lost not only all his healthy new tomato plants but also his chrysanthemums. When the fertiliser was analysed, it was found to contain the weedkiller sodium chlorate instead of magnesium sulphate. It was held that the buyer could recover in respect of the first-year crop, but not the second, since it was only in respect of the first that the buyer had specifically made known the purpose of purchase.

5.81 Similarly, in *Jacobs* v. *Scott*,[70] it was held that the seller was in breach of the implied condition of fitness for purpose when he failed to supply hay suitable for resale in the Glasgow market because of the market's conditions of sale, even though the hay was perfectly sound. This was because he was proved to have known of the resale intention of the buyer.[71]

5.82 Apart from any express notice given to the seller of the purpose for which goods are bought, such use may be implied from the circumstances, particularly if the purpose in question is one to which such goods are normally put. Thus, in *Frost* v. *Aylesbury Dairies*[72] it was held that a bottle of milk is impliedly sold as being fit for human consumption, while in *Priest* v. *Last*[73] it was held that an object sold for use as a hot-water bottle is impliedly held out as being fit to hold boiling water.

---

[69] 1956 S.C. 50, based on the equivalent section of the 1893 Act.

[70] (1899) 2 F.(H.L.) 70.

[71] Similarly, in *Brown* v. *Craiks* in 5.75 above, the buyer might have succeeded had he proved that the seller knew of his intended resale of the fabric in the clothing market.

[72] [1905] 1 K.B. 608.

[73] [1903] 2 K.B. 148.

5.83 However, any particular circumstances or requirements which take the purchaser out of the "normal" user category must be communicated to the seller before the implied term will be imported into the contract; thus, in *Griffiths* v. *Peter Conway*,[74] it was held that a purchaser who contracted dermatitis from wearing a tweed coat could not claim because of a specially sensitive skin condition which she had not made known to the seller.

5.84 Section 14(4) of the Act also allows "usage" to be relied upon in showing that fitness for a particular purpose was an implied term of a particular contract.

5.85 The rules relating to "contracting out" by the seller are the same in respect of section 14(3) as they are for warranties of description, for which see 5.68 above.

Warranties in Sale by Sample

5.86 When a sale is by "sample,"[75] then there is an implied term in the contract of sale, (a) that the bulk will correspond in quality with the sample; (b) that the buyer will have a reasonable opportunity of comparing the bulk with the sample, and (c) that the goods will be free of any defect making them "unmerchantable"[76] which would not be apparent upon reasonable examination of the sample. This is the effect of section 15(2) of the Act.

5.87 A good example of all these principles in action arose in *Godley* v. *Perry*,[77] in which a shopkeeper, P., bought a consignment of catapults from a supplier, having tested one for strength. A catapult was purchased from P. by a boy, G., who lost the use of an eye when it broke. G. successfully sued P. for breach of the implied terms regarding merchantability and fitness for purpose, and P. successfully sued the supplier under the provisions of section 15 because the goods had not been free from a defect rendering

---

[74] [1939] 1 All E.R. 685.
[75] *i.e.* when there is an express or implied term in the contract to that effect, and not simply because a so-called "sample" has been shown to the buyer and has influenced a sale; s. 15(1).
[76] Defined as per s. 14(6)—see 5.74 above.
[77] [1960] 1 W.L.R. 9, based upon an identical provision in the 1893 Act.

them unmerchantable which had not been apparent when he examined the sample.

5.88   The rules relating to "contracting out" of section 15 by the seller are the same as they are in respect of warranties of description, for which see 5.68 above.

PERFORMANCE OF THE CONTRACT

The General Rule

5.89   The general rule, subject to whatever may be stated to the contrary in the contract, is that the seller must deliver the goods and the buyer must accept and pay for them. This is the effect of section 27, and section 28 goes on to make these complementary obligations concurrent, in the sense that if, for example, the seller fails to deliver then the buyer is under no obligation to pay.

5.90   Modern commercial reality has, however, created many situations in which it has been necessary to supplement this simple arrangement with special rules, and these may now be considered.

The Seller's Duty to Deliver

5.91   It will depend upon the express or implied terms of the contract whether the seller is to send the goods to the purchaser or the latter is to take possession of them,[78] and in the absence of any special express or implied term the place of delivery is the seller's business premises, failing which his residence. Alternatively, in the case of specific goods which are known by the parties to be in a particular place at the time of the contract, the place of delivery is that particular place.[79]

5.92   When the obligation is on the seller to send the goods to the buyer, then in the absence of any specified time,[80] delivery must be

---

[78]   s. 29(1).
[79]   s. 29(2).
[80]   And time may be made "of the essence," and hence a material condition of the contract. Delivery or demand must be at a "reasonable" hour; s. 29(5).

within a "reasonable" time.[81] When the goods are in the possession of a third party at the time of sale, then there is no "delivery" by the seller until that third party acknowledges to the buyer that he holds the goods on his behalf.[82]

5.93 When goods have to be placed in a "deliverable" state, then in the absence of an agreement to the contrary, the cost of this process falls upon the seller.[83]

5.94 Unless the contract specifies otherwise, the seller is not entitled to deliver by instalment, but if instalment delivery is agreed upon, with separate payment per instalment, then a failure by the buyer to accept and pay for, or the seller to deliver, one particular instalment, may give rise to a repudiation of the entire contract. Whether or not it does have this effect, or is simply a severable but actionable breach, is a question of fact and interpretation in each case.[84]

5.95 When the seller opts to effect delivery as one of his contractual obligations, then the delivery of the goods to a carrier is deemed to be delivery to the buyer, and the carrier is regarded as the buyer's agent for the limited question of carriage.[85] In such a case, the seller must make a "reasonable" contract of carriage, failing which any loss or damage in transit will be the seller's responsibility.

5.96 But even when the seller agrees to effect delivery at his own risk, the normal rule in the absence of agreement to the contrary is that the buyer accepts the normal risks of deterioration incidental to a long journey.[86]

Remedies of the Buyer

5.97 The remedies available to an aggrieved buyer will depend upon the level of default by the seller. If the seller simply fails to

---

[81] s. 29(3).
[82] s. 29(4).
[83] s. 29(6).
[84] s. 31.
[85] But not acceptance of the goods; s. 32.
[86] s. 33.

deliver the goods without lawful excuse then the buyer may sue
for damages for non-delivery, the "measure" of such damages
being the difference in the contract price of the goods and their
"open market"[87] price at the time of the failed delivery. In suitable
cases the buyer may apply to the court for specific implement of
the contract,[88] but this will normally only be awarded when the
buyer can show that he has a particular reason[89] for requiring the
delivery of the goods.

5.98 When the seller delivers less than he was contractually
obliged to deliver, then the effect of section 30 of the Act is that
the buyer may either reject the entire delivery, or pay for it *pro
rata* at the contract rate. When the seller delivers *more* than contracted for, the buyer may accept what he contracted for, pay for
it and reject the rest, or he may reject the entire delivery. He is also
free to accept the entire delivery at the contract rate.

5.99 When the contract goods are delivered mixed up with other
goods not "conform to" the contract, the buyer may, if possible,
extract the contract goods and pay for them at the contract rate,
or reject the whole delivery. He may not, apparently, make such a
partial rejection where all the goods are of the one description,[90]
but of different quality. In such a case it is "all or nothing."

5.100 It will be a question of fact whether or not a breach by the
seller is so "material" as to entitle the buyer to reject the goods
and regard the contract as repudiated, or simply gives him a right
to retain the goods and sue for damages for "breach of warranty,"[91]
or use the breach as a lawful excuse for reducing the price payable
by him. When the breach *is* material, the buyer may elect either
course of action.[92]

---

[87] But only if a ready market exists; s. 51.
[88] s. 52.
[89] *Pretium affectionis, e.g.* where the item in question is a "one-off."
[90] For which see 5.68 above.
[91] As provided for under s. 53 of the Act, the "measure" of damages in normal
cases being the difference in the value of the goods occasioned by the breach.
[92] s. 11.

5.101 The buyer's right to reject the goods must, however, be exercised timeously in the circumstances. More specifically, section 35 of the Act states that he will be deemed to have accepted them[93] when either he intimates to the seller that he has done so, or the goods have been delivered to him, he has been allowed his right of examination (see below), and he thereafter either allows a reasonable period of time to elapse without intimating to the seller that he is rejecting the goods, or he performs some act which is inconsistent with the rights of the seller. However, it should be clearly kept in mind that the right of rejection is not lost until the final article is delivered, even though the "property" in it may have passed prior to physical delivery, as one of the terms of the contract.[94]

5.102 A buyer rejecting goods is not, in the absence of any contractual term, obliged to return them to the seller.[95]

5.103 Reference was made above to the buyer's right to examine the goods before deciding whether or not to accept them. Specifically, section 34 of the Act allows him a "reasonable" time to do so upon request to the seller. Time will not run while the seller is attempting to remedy any apparently remediable defect at the request of the buyer.

Buyer's Duty to Accept

5.104 Subject to his right to reasonable inspection and rejection of the goods, as described above, the buyer is obliged to take delivery within a reasonable time of any request to do so from the seller, failing which he will be liable to the seller for any loss occasioned by his failure and an additonal charge in respect of care and custody of the goods.[96] If the buyer's refusal amounts to a total repudiation of the contract (which is of course a question of fact) then the seller may also claim the remedies attendant upon that.[97]

---

[93] And thereby waived his right of rejection.
[94] For example, in an instalment contract in which the suitability of the final product cannot be properly ascertained until all the parts have been delivered and assembled.
[95] s. 36.
[96] s. 37(1).
[97] s. 37(2).

Unpaid Seller's Right to Damages

5.105 When the buyer fails in his duty to accept and pay for the goods, then the seller may sue for damages for non-acceptance, the measure of damages being, in the case of goods which have an available market, the difference between the stipulated contract price and the market price at the time of non-acceptance.[98] In other cases, the damages will be the estimated genuine loss to the seller occasioned by the buyer's breach.[99]

Unpaid Seller's Right to Price

5.106 When the buyer fails to pay the purchase price of the goods, the seller has two possible courses of action. In the following section are described the unpaid seller's rights against the goods themselves; his alternative, described in this section, is "an action for the price."

5.107 By virtue of section 49 of the Act, in cases in which the property in the goods has passed to the buyer, or the price was payable on a certain date,[1] the seller may sue for the purchase price. This is partly because the mere failure of the buyer to pay for the goods may not entitle the seller to rescind the contract and demand the return of the goods if the property has passed to the buyer, and the Act recognises that the seller in such a case requires a swift and simple remedy.

Unpaid Seller's Rights against the Goods Themselves

5.108 In order to be regarded as "unpaid" for the purpose of having rights against the goods themselves, the seller must be able to show that the whole of the purchase price has not been paid or tendered, or that some negotiable instrument which was received

---

[98] s. 50(3).

[99] N.B. that "special damages" may also be awardable in either case; see 4.84 above.

[1] Irrespective of whether or not delivery has occurred, and even if the property has not passed and the goods have not been appropriated to the contract.

as a conditional payment has been dishonoured.[2] In such cases, he has the following rights against the goods themselves.

1. *Right of Lien*

5.109 When the unpaid seller is still in physical possession of the goods[3] he may retain them until payment or tender of the price if the buyer has become insolvent if there was no stipulation as to credit or if an agreed credit period has expired.[4] The seller will not lose his right of lien simply because the buyer may have resold or pledged the goods,[5] but he will lose the right of lien if he waives it, if he delivers the goods to a carrier for transmission to the buyer without reserving his right of disposal, or if the buyer or his agent lawfully acquires possession of the goods.[6] Delivery of part of the consignment does not prevent the seller from exercising his lien over the remainder.[7]

2. *Stoppage in Transitu*

5.110 Under this right, the unpaid seller may, in a case in which the property has passed to a buyer who becomes insolvent,[8] and while the goods are still in transit to him, resume possession and retain the goods until the price is paid or tendered.[9] This right may be exercised either by taking actual possession of the goods or by notifying the carrier to return them at the seller's expense.[10]

5.111 "Transit" may end either at the place of intended delivery, or if the buyer or his agent obtain delivery before then. It will also

---

[2] s. 38.
[3] Whether or not the property in them has passed to the buyer.
[4] s. 41. "Insolvent" in this context means that the buyer cannot meet his debts as they fall due or in the ordinary course of business.
[5] s. 47.
[6] s. 43.
[7] s. 42.
[8] For which see note 3 above.
[9] s. 44. If the property has not passed, the seller has a similar right to withhold delivery subject to the same conditions; s. 39(2).
[10] s. 46.

end if the carrier acknowledges to the buyer that he holds the goods for him after they have arrived at their destination.[11]

5.112   Part delivery of a consignment does not affect stoppage of the remainder unless the part delivery may be construed as an agreement to part with possession of the whole.

5.113   There is, of course, no need for any exercise of a right of stoppage in transit until the seller has handed physical possession of the goods to a carrier, because until that time he has a right of lien over them.

3. Resale

5.114   An unpaid seller who has seized the goods either under his right of lien or by means of stoppage *in transitu* may resell them if (a) they are perishable, *or* (b) he has given notice to the buyer of his intention to resell, and the latter does not pay or tender payment within a reasonable time thereafter,[12] *or* (c) the contract contains a clause which preserves the seller's right to resell in the event of default by the buyer. The act of resale then acts as a rescission of the contract by the seller,[13] who is still entitled to sue the buyer for damage for non-acceptance.

---

[11] *e.g.* a railway goods holding yard.
[12] s. 48.
[13] *N.B.* that lien and stoppage in themselves do not have that effect.

6. CONSUMER PROTECTION

6.1   One of the major features of legislation in the past 30 years has been its increased protection of the domestic consumer. Examples of this have already been encountered in the Unfair Contract Terms Act 1977 (Chapters 3 and 5) and the Unsolicited Goods and Services Act 1971 (Chapter 2).

6.2   This chapter is devoted to a consideration of five of the most important areas of statutory consumer protection, namely:

1. Consumer credit.
2. Trade descriptions.
3. Fair trading.
4. Consumer safety.
5. Consumer protection.

CONSUMER CREDIT

Introduction

6.3   Consumer credit has grown phenomenally as a feature of modern commerce, since it is simple and attractive to the consumer. It is also potentially hazardous, and the abuses of the system which prior to 1974 led to untold social misery were not adequately controlled by the haphazard legislation which then existed. The Crowther Report of 1971 led to the passing of the Consumer Credit Act of 1974, which set out to achieve the following objectives:

1. The control of consumer credit under one single piece of legislation.
2. The licensing of all consumer credit businesses in an endeavour to rid the industry of those with a record of dishonesty and sharp practice. Consumer credit licences will only be granted by the Director General of Fair Trading to "fit and proper persons," and such licences may be revoked upon proof of malpractice.

3. The regulation of those agreements under which persons seeking credit commit themselves to repayment terms and conditions.
4. The supervision of the content and integrity of credit advertising.

6.4 The remainder of this section of the chapter concentrates on the last two of these objectives.

Regulated Agreements

6.5 Protection for those entering into credit agreements is provided by the Act only in respect of "regulated agreements." These consist of:

1. Consumer credit agreements.
2. Consumer hire agreements.

In each case, the agreement must not be one which falls into the category of an "exempt agreement." It is necessary to consider each of these categories separately.

Consumer Credit Agreements

6.6 A "consumer credit agreement" is defined under section 8 of the Act as "a personal credit agreement by which the creditor provides the debtor with credit not exceeding £15,000." A "personal credit agreement" is one under which the debtor is a natural person, a partnership or any other entity apart from a "body corporate,"[1] since these are not protected by the Act. "Credit" is defined as being either a cash loan or "any other form of financial accommodation," and is therefore broad enough to cover bank loans, hire-purchase agreements, overdrafts and department store credit cards.

6.7 The £15,000 limit referred to above applies only to the actual capital sum advanced, and does not include interest or any other "total charge for credit," such as an arrangement fee, interest or legal costs.

---

[1] For which see Chapter 7.

6.8 A consumer credit agreement is defined so as to include the older concept of the hire-purchase agreement, which is basically an agreement under which the debtor hires an item for a given period, making periodic payments, and then fulfils certain conditions at the end of that agreement[2] which allow the property in that item to pass to him. It is distinguished from a "consumer hire agreement" (considered below) primarily on the ground that it incorporates the possibility of purchase at the end.

6.9 Also incorporated within the definition of a consumer credit agreement are "conditional sale agreements" (under which it is agreed from the start that the debtor will buy the goods, but conditions[3] have to be met before the property will pass) and "credit sale agreements," which are agreements for the purchase of goods under which the purchase price is payable in five or more instalments, but which do not also constitute conditional sale agreements.

6.10 Because of the large number of different types of agreement encompassed within the definition of a consumer credit agreement, the Act further subdivides all such agreements into three different contrasting pairs, as follows.

1. Running-account Credit and Fixed-sum Credit

6.11 "Running-account credit" is an arrangement under which the debtor may keep borrowing up to an agreed limit. The more he pays off, the more he may borrow again, up to that limit. Obvious examples are bank overdrafts and department store credit cards.

6.12 "Fixed-sum" credit, on the other hand, is a fixed sum credit advance made available either in a lump sum or in instalments. Examples here are hire-purchase agreements, credit sale agreements and bank loans.

6.13 In an endeavour to prevent creditors from avoiding the provisions of the Act by extending credit in excess of £15,000 on the

---

[2] Such as exercising an option to purchase.
[3] *e.g.* the payment of all instalments.

face of the agreement,[4] but in reality limiting it below that, the Act itself states that an agreement will still be classed as a consumer credit agreement if the debtor cannot draw on more than £15,000 at a time, or if the credit terms alter in the creditor's favour over £15,000, or if at the time of the agreement it is "probable" that the debit balance on the agreement will not exceed £15,000.

2. Restricted-use Credit and Unrestricted-use Credit

6.14 This distinction is a fairly obvious one. Restricted-use credit is credit which is granted for a specified purpose (*e.g.* the purchase of a stereo from a department store or the purchase of a car from a motor dealer), while unrestricted-use credit is the grant of credit for any purpose desired by the creditor (*e.g.* a bank overdraft or a store credit card).

3. Debtor-creditor-supplier Agreements and Debtor-creditor Agreements

6.15 The distinction between these two categories is that in the first case the creditor in respect of the money is also the supplier of the goods (*e.g.* department store credit), whereas in the second case he is not (*e.g.* a bank loan). The debtor-creditor-supplier category is, however, extended to incorporate those situations in which there is a pre-existing agreement between the supplier and the creditor (as for example when a particular motor dealer always sells his vehicles through a particular finance company).

6.16 As will be seen below,[5] this distinction has crucial implications for the protection of the consumer/debtor should the supplier be in breach of contract.

6.17 It is important to appreciate that every consumer credit agreement will fall into one or other of *each* of the above contrasting categories. Thus, an unrestricted bank overdraft with a set amount limit is a running-account, unrestricted-use, debtor-creditor agreement, while a hire-purchase agreement for the

---

[4] Including open-ended agreements with no set limit.
[5] In 6.34.

purchase of a car for £7,000 is a fixed-sum, restricted-use, debtor-creditor-supplier agreement, assuming that the finance company is one normally used by the motor dealer/supplier.

Consumer Hire Agreements

6.18 The Act defines a consumer hire agreement (in section 15) as an agreement which is not a hire-purchase agreement, but under which the debtor agrees to hire goods from the hirer, which is capable of subsisting for more than three months, and does not require the hirer to pay more than £15,000.

Exempt Agreements

6.19 Agreements which would otherwise qualify as regulated agreements will lose that protection if they come within one of the categories of "exempt agreement." If they do, then only those provisions of the Act which relate to "extortionate credit bargains" will apply.

6.20 Exempt agreements include the following:

1. Agreements which involve the use of land as security,[6] when the creditor is a local authority, or any other body such as a building society, insurance company, friendly society, trade union or charity specified in a statutory instrument.
2. Agreements which do not involve more than four payments.
3. Credit card agreements which require the debtor to clear in one payment the amount shown in each statement.
4. Agreements in which the rate of interest does not exceed the rate specified by statutory instrument at any given time.
5. Agreements which have a connection with a country outside the United Kingdom.

Special Forms of Regulated Agreement

6.21 In addition to those consumer credit agreements which are virtually exempt from all the provisions of the Act, certain forms

---

[6] *e.g.* mortgages.

of partly regulated agreements have special rules applicable to them, which emerge below.

6.22   1. *Credit token agreements.* These are consumer credit agreements in which the creditor supplies the debtor with some form of credit card. Automatic cash dispenser cards[7] issued by banks, and department store credit cards are clear examples.

6.23   2. *Small agreements.* These are consumer credit agreements other than hire-purchase and conditional-sale agreements in which the amount of credit provided does not exceed £50. Anti-avoidance provisions apply.

6.24   3. *Non-commercial agreements.* These are agreements in which the creditor does not lend money or otherwise supply credit in the course of a business.

Control of Regulated Agreements

6.25   Once a particular type of agreement is designated as a "regulated agreement," its formation, contents and termination are closely controlled by the 1974 Act. Each of these elements of statutory control may be considered separately.

Formation of Regulated Agreements

6.26   Even before the parties enter into a regulated agreement, the Act protects the debtor by ensuring that any "antecedent negotiations" entered into by a "negotiator"[8] are deemed to be as agent for the creditor, so that any misrepresentation by the negotiator will be actionable by the debtor against the creditor. These "ante-

---

[7] *N.B.* not mere cheque cards.
[8] Defined as including a credit-broker or the supplier of goods under a debtor-creditor-supplier agreement.

cedent negotiations" are deemed to begin as soon as the debtor and negotiator first begin communicating.[9]

6.27 Like all other contracts, a regulated agreement is formed by means of offer and acceptance, although, as will be seen below, it requires to be executed in terms of section 61 of the Act. Normally, the offer will be the debtor's application for credit, and this may be revoked at any time until the acceptance by the creditor is posted. Section 57 of the Act allows this revocation to be made verbally, and if necessary to the supplier instead of the creditor. When effective revocation is made, any "linked transaction" with a supplier is also cancelled if the agreement is a debtor-creditor-supplier agreement.

6.28 The form and content of a regulated agreement are controlled by section 60 of the Act, which allows for the creation of regulations to ensure that the debtor is fully advised in advance of what he is entering into. The document must clearly identify (on the first page) the type of regulated agreement being executed, and in addition must specify the names and addresses of the parties, the cash price in a "restricted-use debtor-creditor-supplier" agreement, the amount of any deposit, the amount and timing of each payment, the amount of the "total charge for credit," the annual percentage rate of the total charge for credit, the total amount payable, details of any security to be supplied by the debtor, and details of any default charges payable by the debtor.

6.29 Section 61 sets out the requirements of the execution of the agreement, which are again governed by regulations. The agreement is only "executed" when both parties have signed it, and the debtor must always receive one copy for himself, and a second copy within seven days of the creditor signing if, at the time of the debtor signing, the creditor has not done so.

6.30 Certain agreements are exempted from the formation regulations, but not the antecedent negotiation rules. These are "non-commercial agreements" (see 6.24 above), and certain

---

[9] s. 56.

debtor-creditor agreements relating to overdrafts and certain payments on a person's death.[10]

Cooling-off Period

6.31   In addition to giving the debtor the opportunity of revoking his application for credit before the agreement is even entered into, the Act[11] extends to the debtor the opportunity, in the case of certain forms of regulated agreement, to cancel during a "cooling-off" period immediately following the execution of the agreement. The only regulated agreements which attract this right are those in which verbal representations were made by the creditor[12] and the agreement was signed by the debtor off trade premises.[13]

6.32   When agreements are cancellable, the copy or copies of the agreement given to the debtor must say so. The notice must advise him of the person to whom cancellation may be communicated, and the debtor must cancel within five days of receiving either notice of his right to cancel, or his second copy of the agreement, where applicable. The notice must be in writing, and if posted, must be posted within five days.

6.33   The effect of cancellation is to terminate both the credit agreement and any "linked transaction."[14] Any sums already paid by the debtor (including deposits) are returnable, and any goods supplied are also returnable.

Statutory Controls during Currency of Agreement

6.34   There are various ways in which the interests of the debtor are guarded by the provisions of the Act while the agreement is in force. For example, if it transpires that the supplier in a debtor-creditor-supplier agreement has been guilty of misrepresentation or

---

[10] *e.g.* loans and credit for funeral expenses.
[11] In s. 67.
[12] Or the supplier in a debtor-creditor-supplier agreement.
[13] *e.g.* in the debtor's own home. The provisions are aimed at "hard sell" techniques practised, *inter alia*, on customer doorsteps.
[14] *e.g.* with the supplier in a debtor-credior-supplier agreement.

breach of contract, then the creditor will be equally liable, jointly and severally, with him.[15]

6.35 Section 76 of the Act requires the creditor to give seven days' notice in the prescribed form before demanding earlier payment of any sum, recovering possession of any goods or land, or terminating, restricting or deferring any of the debtor's or hirer's rights. The debtor may then apply to the court for protection. Default notices (considered below) do not come within this section.

6.36 Section 77 requires the creditor, upon written request from the debtor, to supply certain information to him, including information relating to the state of his account and the amount remaining payable. This section does not apply to non-commercial agreements.

Default and Termination

6.37 When it is alleged by the creditor that the debtor is in breach of a regulated agreement, the creditor cannot take any action on that breach without serving on the debtor a "default notice." This is required[16] before the creditor may terminate the agreement, demand earlier payment of any sum, recover possession of goods or land, enforce any security, or treat the debtor's rights as in any way terminated, restricted or deferred. The creditor may, however, without such a notice, refuse to extend credit any further.

6.38 The notice must give at least seven days' warning to the debtor, who may, within that period, remedy his fault[17] and thereby prevent the threatened action. After the seven days have expired without remedy, the creditor may proceed to enforcement action, but even this is controlled under the Act.

---

[15] s. 75. Exceptions to this rule are non-commercial agremeents and agreements involving a cash price of between £50 and £30,000. For a successful use of s. 75 in a case involving the sale of a car under finance, see *U.D.T.* v. *Taylor*, 1980 S.L.T. (Sh.Ct.) 28.

[16] *Per* s. 87.

[17] If it may be remedied. s. 88 requires the notice to specify any action which the debtor may take in order to retrieve the situation.

6.39 For example, in those cases in which the property in the goods has not yet passed to the debtor,[18] the effect of sections 90 and 91 of the Act is that the creditor cannot, without a court order, take physical repossession of the goods if the debtor has paid one-third or more of the total price of the goods. Such goods are said to be "protected goods," and instead of granting the creditor a "return order," the court may grant the debtor a "time order" which in effect reschedules his repayments in accordance with his ability to pay. None of this applies if the debtor himself voluntarily terminates the agreement, or if the goods themselves are in the possession of a third party.

6.40 Section 93 of the Act prevents the creditor from increasing the interest payable in cases in which the debtor is in default of any regulated agreement.

6.41 When a debtor finds that he is in a position to make early repayment in full, section 94 of the Act gives him the right to do so after calling upon the creditor to give him a payout quotation, which must incorporate a rebate of charges calculated in accordance with regulations in force at the time.

6.42 Equally, if a debtor finds that he is no longer able to keep up payments, he may apply to the creditor for termination of the agreement, if that agreement is a hire-purchase or conditional-sale agreement which is regulated under the Act.[19] The goods must be returned, arrears of payment must be made good, and the debtor must normally make a further payment which will bring total payments up to one-half of the total price he was obliged to pay under the agreement.

6.43 Section 101 of the Act grants to the debtor under a regulated consumer hire agreement the right to terminate the agreement by notice to the creditor to take effect no earlier than three months hence, or the payment period itself, if shorter.[20] Normally this right

[18] *e.g.* hire-purchase or conditional-sale agreement.
[19] *N.B.* this option is not exercisable in respect of any other form of regulated agreement; s. 99.
[20] *e.g.* one month if payments are made monthly.

cannot be exercised until the agreement is at least 18 months old,[21] and all arrears of payment must be made good. Agreements involving rental payments of £900 per year or more are excluded from section 101.

Control of Credit Agreement Advertising and Promotion

6.44 Because of the popular appeal of credit in all its forms, and the potential for abuse of modern sales techniques, the 1974 Act sets out to promote "truth in lending" by ensuring that the public are not misled by information fed to them in any form, by any medium, by anyone in the credit or hiring business. Although some types of agreement[22] are not covered by this section of the Act, it covers most forms of consumer credit, and is applicable beyond the normal categories of "regulated agreement."

6.45 Regulations cover the form and content of advertisements, and any false or misleading advertising will constitute a criminal offence. It is also a criminal offence for anyone to "cold canvass"[23] credit facilities off trade premises (*e.g.* on a doorstep-selling basis) when the facilities are for personal loans or other forms of debtor-creditor agreements.[24]

6.46 Further criminal offences established by the Act involve sending invitations to persons under 18 to borrow money, obtain goods or services on credit, or even apply for further credit information. An apparent loophole in the Act overlooks handing out such information, as opposed to sending it. It is also an offence to send an unsolicited credit card to anyone.

TRADE DESCRIPTIONS

6.47 One of the earliest methods devised by Parliament to protect the ordinary consumer was to make criminal offences out of unacceptable business practices. One of the first singled out for punish-

---

[21] Including the notice period.
[22] *e.g.* for credit in excess of £15,000.
[23] *i.e.* without prior invitation from the canvasser.
[24] *N.B.* that debtor-creditor-supplier agreements may be canvassed in this way.

ment was the false trade description, and the Trade Descriptions Act of 1968 seeks to prevent consumers from being misled by this type of behaviour.[25]

False Trade Description

6.48 A "trade description" is defined under section 2 of the Act as being any indication, direct or indirect, and by whatever means, of size, quality, composition, method of manufacture, fitness for purpose, physical characteristics, testing and its results, approval by any person or body, date or place of manufacture and previous ownership or use.

6.49 Obvious examples of false descriptions from the above list would be margarine described as butter, the size label on an item of clothing, the allegation of "one previous owner" in the case of a second-hand car, and "Safety Council approved" in the case of a child's cot. Even the packaging of a product can be indirectly misleading, as in the use of a picture of Edinburgh on a tin of shortbread made in Reading. Other examples of silent deception are the milometer reading on a car,[26] and the display of a reconditioned washing machine in a section of a store devoted to new products.

6.50 The application of a false trade description to goods, or the making of false or misleading statements about services, is a criminal offence which will be pursued by inspectors appointed for this purpose. The aggrieved buyer loses none of his or her civil remedies.[27]

False Trade Descriptions as to Goods

6.51 Anyone who in the course of a trade or business[28] applies a false trade description to any goods, or supplies or offers to supply

---

[25] All references which follow are to this Act. N.B. representations regarding price are now dealt with under the Consumer Protection Act of 1987, considered below.

[26] *MacNab* v. *Alexanders of Greenock Ltd.*, 1971 S.L.T. 121.

[27] *e.g.* under the Sale of Goods Act 1979; see Chapter 5.

[28] N.B. that private sales are not covered by the Act.

any goods to which a false trade description has been applied, is guilty of a criminal offence under section 1 of the Act. One may apply a false trade description to goods by any means, direct or indirect, and such a description may be oral or written. It may even include actions such as the physical concealment of faults, as in the case of body rot on a car being covered by fresh underseal.

6.52 Provided that the offender is operating a trade or business, it does not matter whether he is the seller or the buyer. A striking example of the latter situation was *Fletcher* v. *Budgen*,[29] in which a car dealer, having told a seller that his car was fit only for scrap and purchased it from him for £2, subsequently repaired it for £56 and advertised it for sale for £135.

False and Misleading Statements Relating to Services

6.53 Section 14 of the Act protects consumers against false statements relating to services offered or supplied in the course of any trade or business. It is an offence for anyone in that capacity to make, in connection with the services covered by the section, either a statement which he knows to be false, or a reckless statement which turns out to be false. The "services" include all the usual ones,[30] and all forms of accommodation and other facilities (*e.g.* storage). Some of the most frequent offenders in this area, to judge by the case law, have been tour operators, but it would cover, for example, work done badly by an unqualified builder who claimed to be qualified.

6.54 There have been difficulties encountered in distinguishing between false statements (which are criminal offences) and optimistic promises (which if genuinely believed at the time, and not made recklessly, will not be). Thus in *R.* v. *Sunair Holidays*,[31] it was held that a tour promoter was not liable for what was promised in a 1970 tour brochure printed in 1969, when at the time of printing it was genuinely believed that the facilities advertised had been

---

[29] [1974] 2 All E.R. 1234.
[30] *e.g.* repair, transport, professional work, etc.
[31] [1973] 1 W.L.R. 1105.

booked. Whereas in *British Airways Board* v. *Taylor*,[32] it was held that a firm flight booking confirmation issued by an airline was a positive statement that a seat had been reserved, and that the failure to produce the seat in due course was a criminal offence.

Defences

6.55 When a person or body is charged with an offence under either section 1 or section 14 of the Act, it is a defence for him to prove:

> "(a) that the commission of the offence was due to a mistake, or due to reliance on information supplied to him, or to the act or default of another person, or to an accident, or due to some other cause beyond his control; and
> (b) that he took all reasonable precautions and exercised all due diligence to avoid the commission of such an offence by himself or any person under his control."

6.56 Anyone seeking to rely on this defence, however, must identify the person he claims was responsible, and it is possible in law for that person to be an employee of the original defendant. The Act has come in for much criticism for the ease with which large organisations can acquire immunity from prosecution by pointing the finger at an employee who failed to comply with instructions issued by management.[33]

6.57 A good example of a person clearing the hurdle of reliance on information supplied, but falling down on lack of "due diligence," was *Costello* v. *Lowe*,[34] in which a car sales yard bought in a second-hand taxi showing the suspiciously low mileage of 35,000. It had, in fact, been wound back from 135,000, and the

---

[32] [1976] 1 All E.R. 65.

[33] As in *Tesco Supermarkets* v. *Nattrass* [1972] A.C. 153, in which an advertised "special" on washing powder was incorrectly labelled at the full price; and in *Beckett* v. *Kingston Bros.* [1970] 1 Q.B. 606, in which so-called "Norfolk King Turkeys" had in fact travelled from Denmark. In each case the company escaped conviction by blaming the store manager for ignoring instruction circulars from head office.

[34] 1990 S.L.T. 760; see also *Ford* v. *Guild*, 1990 S.L.T. 502.

dealer had not even bothered to check with police records kept of taxi mileage.

6.58 A further defence under section 25 of the Act covers the innocent publication of an advertisement which contains a false trade description.

FAIR TRADING

6.59 The Fair Trading Act of 1973 was primarily an "enabling" Act which established the Office of the Director-General of Fair Trading, and empowered him to keep all manner of consumer-related activities under review, if necessary recommending new legislation in the form of orders[35] made by the Secretary of State for Trade and Industry, breaches of which will be a criminal offence.

6.60 The "consumer trade practices" which come within the remit of the Director-General include all supplies of goods and services, including related issues such as terms and conditions of supply and methods of salesmanship,[36] and debt-enforcement techniques. Among the current protections available to the consumer thanks to the Director-General are the publication on all "guarantee" forms of a statement clearly advising the consumer that his "statutory rights"[37] are not affected, and the requirement that all mail order advertisements carry the true name and address of the seller.

6.61 Whenever the Director-General is satisfied that someone in the course of a trade or business has "persisted"[38] in a course of conduct which is both unfair to consumers and detrimental to their interests, he may seek a written assurance that it will cease, failing which the Director-General may commence court proceedings in either the Restrictive Practices Court or in some cases the local

---

[35] Issued as "statutory instruments"; see 1.15.
[36] *e.g.* "pyramid selling," covered by regulations issued in 1973, and price-fixing dealt with under the Restrictive Trade Practices legislation under which the Director-General of Fair Trading may refer matters to court; see also 3.61.
[37] *e.g.* under the Sale of Goods Act 1979; see Chapter 5.
[38] Which may consist of nothing more than ignoring "warning shots" from local Fair Trading officers.

sheriff court, seeking an interdict against that behaviour or course of conduct.

6.62 The Director-General also exercises a considerable amount of informal power and influence which is reflected in the number of professional and trade organisations which have, in recent years, become more stringently self-regulating under Codes of Practice governing them which have originated from the Director-General's mandate to encourage such non-statutory regulation of consumer-orientated businesses.

CONSUMER SAFETY

6.63 Like the Fair Trading Act, the Consumer Safety Act of 1978 was an enabling Act designed to give to the Secretary of State for Trade and Industry a wide power to draft delegated legislation which would ensure that consumers were assured physical safety in the use of products supplied to them in the course of trade or business. The safety regulations issued under the Act have also covered related items such as packaging and consumer information on product use. From wiring instructions on electric plugs to warnings on plastic bags, the influence of the 1978 Act may be seen in hundreds of contexts every day of the week.

6.64 Enforcement methods follow a now familiar formula. In one of its mildest manifestations, enforcement may take the form of a "notice to warn," requiring manufacturers, distributors, etc., to publish to the consumer, at their own expense, warnings regarding dangers inherent in the use of specified items. The notice to warn is normally preceded by advance notification.

6.65 The next stage may well be a "prohibition order," which ultimately has the effect of taking a product off the market for a limited period. A proposal to issue such a notice must be published in advance, representations from the trade must be considered, and such a notice will last for only 12 months; by then, the ultimate step of issuing a safety regulation via the statutory instrument procedure should have been taken.

6.66 A "prohibition notice" takes the process a final step further in those cases in which warnings to the consumer and temporary bans simply will not do, and the product must be taken off the market, or its supply made subject to conditions. Before the notice is actually served, and therefore becomes effective, the trade must be given an opportunity to make representations, unless the danger is such that the Secretary of State decides to override this requirement.

6.67   Failure to observe prohibition notices, prohibition orders or notices to warn is in itself a criminal offence.

CONSUMER PROTECTION ACT 1987

6.68   This Act had several purposes, one of which was to improve and consolidate the law relating to price indications associated with products, which had previously been the province of the Trade Descriptions Act. The Act came into force on various dates set for it, and its main provisions relating to price indication control are as follows:

6.69   By virtue of section 20 of the Act, it is a criminal offence, in the course of a trade or business, to give what is referred to as a "misleading" statement to a consumer concerning the price upon which goods, services, accommodation or facilities are offered. The "misleading" test is an objective one, in that the court may form its own opinion of what the consumer at whom it was directed might "reasonably" infer from the statement[39] which was made.

6.70   The "services and facilities" referred to above cover not only the most obvious ones, but also activities such as credit, banking and insurance services, electricity supply, currency transactions, off-road parking facilities and caravan parks. It will also be an offence to allow consumers to believe that a certain price is applicable when it is no longer (*e.g.* a "special offer" which has expired), or may not be when application is made (hence the usual caveat "while stocks last"). Limited applications (*e.g.* half price for the first 20 customers) must be clearly spelt out, and considerable care

---

[39] Which may of course be oral or written, or communicated via television, radio or other advertisement.

must be taken when comparing the price of one's own product with that of rivals.

6.71 There is a Code of Practice in force designed to give practical guidance on how to avoid misleading price statements. Like all Codes of Practice,[40] it does not have the force of law, but may well be referred to as a benchmark in any prosecution.

6.72 Among the available defences are the fact that the offender took all reasonable steps and exercised all due diligence,[41] that the offender was obliged to comply with a statutory regulation, that the offender was simply a publisher who innocently published an offending advert, and that in the case of a supplier, the product was advertised in the belief that the ultimate retailer would comply with a resale price recommended by him.

---

[40] *e.g.* on disciplinary procedures at work; see Chapter 12.
[41] Similar to the Trade Descriptions Act defence; see 6.55.

7. AGENCY

The Nature of Agency

7.1 Agency is an arrangement whereby a person (A) acts on behalf of another person (B) in order to bring him into contractual relations with a third party (C). In such an arrangement, B is known as the "principal," and as a general rule he is legally bound by whatever the agent has negotiated on his behalf. The main contract is between B and C, the principal and the third party, and while the agent will normally have his own contract with his principal, he will not in the normal course of things become a party to the contract with C.

7.2 The agent will normally earn a commission or salary for his efforts, but he may not necessarily refer to himself as an agent, and for most legal purposes there is no reason why he need do so. The payment of a fee is the main distinction between agency and "mandate," in which the "mandatory"[1] is not paid for his services. Many employees are agents for their employers,[2] as will be seen below, and normally they are paid by way of agreed salary, or salary and commission. But by no means is every employee an agent; see generally below.

7.3 Equally, the law regards one partner as the agent of the others,[3] and a director is the agent of his company. In neither case is the term "agent" normally used, although the legal effect is the same.

7.4 A distinction must also be drawn carefully between agency and sub-contract. Whereas an agent remains in the picture for as long as it takes to bring his principal into contractual relations with the third party, and then bows out, the sub-contractor is some-

---

[1] The equivalent of the agent, the "principal" being known as the "mandant."
[2] See, *e.g. International Sponge Importers* v. *Watt*, referred to in 7.11 below.
[3] See 8.14 below.

one who is employed by a party to the main contract to perform a certain portion of it. The sub-contractor does not normally negotiate directly with the other party.

7.5   A clearer picture of the agency relationship emerges when one considers the contractual capacity[4] required by agent and principal respectively. Since the contract which is being made with the third party is being made by the principal, it is *his* contractual capacity which is important. Provided that the principal has the contractual capacity for what is being negotiated, it does not matter that the agent has not, provided of course that he has the contractual capacity to be an agent. By the same token, a principal who lacks the requisite contractual capacity to contract with the third party[5] cannot extend his capacity by employing an agent who has that capacity. In fact, if he has no contractual capacity, he cannot even employ an agent.

Formation of Agency

7.6   The relationship between agent and principal may be established in one of the following ways:

1. Express appointment.
2. Implied appointment.
3. Holding out.
4. Ratification.
5. Necessity.

Express Appointment

7.7   The most straightforward way in which a person can become the agent of another is for him to be expressly so appointed, orally or in writing. There is no legal requirement for appointment in any particular form, but commercial caution normally dictates that any form of business agency[6] be carefully recorded in writing, incorporating agreement on such vital matters as how the agency may be

---

[4] For the definition of which, see 2.91 above.
[5] *e.g.* someone under 16.
[6] *e.g.* estate agency, commercial factoring, sales commissioning.

terminated, and when the agency fee will be deemed to have been earned.

Implied Appointment

7.8 In some cases, the relationship of agent and principal is implied from the existing relationship of the parties to each other,[7] or from the appointment of a person into a position such as manager of a business, in which it can hardly be denied that his actions bind his principal. This process can often extend far down the management chain so that, for example, a sales assistant is an agent for a department store.

Holding Out

7.9 In addition to those routine cases in which the very existing relationship between the parties implies agency, there are situations in which B will be regarded as having "held out" A as being his agent, by allowing him to occupy a position in which third parties could reasonably assume that he was. It does not matter what the precise relationship between A and B actually is, if third parties are led into reasonably believing that A is B's agent.

7.10 This principle extends to the situation in which A used to have authority to act for B, but it was withdrawn without potential third parties being advised. In such cases, the "ostensible authority" of A lives on until adequate communication is made to third parties of the termination of actual authority.[8]

7.11 A simple example of the "holding out" principle was *International Sponge Importers* v. *Watt and Sons*,[9] in which C., a com-

---

[7] *e.g.* under section 5 of the Partnership Act 1890, for which see 8.14 below. The master of a ship is the implied agent of the owner of the vessel; see *Barnetson* v. *Peterson Brothers* (1902) 5 F. 86.

[8] Thus, *e.g.* under s. 36 of the Partnership Act 1890, a retiring partner remains liable for the debts of the firm until such time as his retirement is suitably publicised, and the remaining partners therefore cease to be his agents.

[9] 1911 S.C. (H.L.) 57. For a case which went the other way because the employer was not aware of the arrangement, far less approved of it, see *British Bata Shoe Co. Ltd.* v. *Double M. Shah Ltd.*, 1981 S.L.T. (Notes) 14.

mercial traveller for I., was authorised to collect payment of customers' accounts, provided that it was by crossed cheque. Occasionally W. made payment by cheque payable directly to C., and I. allowed it to pass unchallenged. C. eventually fell prey to temptation, and it was held that since payment had been made to I.'s agent in a manner within his ostensible authority, the payment had in law been made to I.

Ratification

7.12   On occasions, A may act on B's behalf without any authority whatsoever, and B, after finding out what has happened, decides to adopt or "ratify" the agreement, so that he replaces the agent as the person on the other end of the contract with the third party. The legal effect of such ratification is as if the principal always was the party contracting via the agent.

7.13   Before this may validly occur, the principal must have been in existence not only at the time of the ratification but also at the time when the unauthorised act was performed. Thus, for example, a contract made by an agent for a company in its pre-incorporation stage cannot be ratified by the company even once it is incorporated.[10] Also, the act being ratified must be one which the principal was originally capable of authorising,[11] and the agent must at the time have professed to be acting for an identifiable principal who is the one who subsequently ratifies what he has done.

7.14   An illustration of this last rule was the case of *Keighley Maxted and Co.* v. *Durant*,[12] in which R., an agent for K., purchased wheat from D. at a higher than authorised price, using his own name without reference to K. When the contract was dishonoured, it was held that D., who knew nothing of K.'s existence, could sue R. for the purchase price, because R. had not professed to be acting for K.

---

[10] See, *e.g. Cumming* v. *Quartzag Ltd.*, 1980 S.C. 276.
[11] *e.g.* he must have the appropriate legal capacity at the time.
[12] [1901] A.C. 240.

7.15 When the validity of an act requires that it be performed within a certain time,[13] then the ratification must be complete within that time.

Necessity

7.16 An "agency of necessity" arises in the occasional, and unusual, case in which B has been left in a situation in which he has to take urgent action on behalf of A when he has been given no authority to do so. The theory is that the urgency of the situation gives B that authority, which A must then honour, but the case law revolves around horses left unstabled at lonely railway stations, perishable cargoes rotting away on sailing ships in mid-ocean, and other quaint features of a bygone age before satellite communications, and modern examples of the principle in action will be rare indeed.

Types of Agency

7.17 Agencies may be either "general" (in which A acts for B in all, or most, of his business dealings, as in the case of a business manager), or "special" (where the purpose of the agency is limited to one transaction such as an estate agent selling a house). A general agent may also act for his principal in one area of his affairs.[14]

7.18 A special form of agency is the *del credere* agency, in which the agent, by way of exception to the general rule, indemnifies his principal from any default by the third party he has introduced, normally for an additional, or higher, commission.

Authority of Agent

7.19 When considering the scope of an agent's authority, one is obliged to examine the position from the point of view of both the principal and the third party. While the former may reasonably be expected to know what authority he has given to the agent, the

---

[13] *e.g.* as in *Goodall* v. *Bilsland*, 1909 S.C. 1152, the lodging of an appeal.
[14] Hence the somewhat old-fashioned term "law agent" to describe a solicitor.

third party can only be guided by the information he has been given, usually by the agent.

As between the Agent and the Principal

7.20 The actual authority devolved upon an agent by his principal can normally only be assessed by reference to the actual agreement between them, be it written or verbal, express or implied. If the agent has acted within his authority, the principal is contractually bound with the third party. If the agent has exceeded his authority, he will be liable in damages to the principal for breach of contract, but whether or not the principal will be contractually bound with the third party will depend upon a range of factors which may now be considered.

As between the Principal and the Third Party

7.21 The principal will always be bound by the contract negotiated for him by the agent in those cases in which the agent had what may be referred to as "actual" authority, *i.e.* express authority or authority implied from the position which the agent occupied (see 7.7 and 7.8 above).

7.22 In many cases, reference must be made to normal commercial or professional practice in order to ascertain whether or not an agent in a particular position has the implied authority to commit his principal to a particular transaction. Among the decided cases may be found rulings to the effect that a general agent has no implied authority to borrow money for his principal,[15] that while an agent may operate a bank account for his principal he may not create an overdraft thereon,[16] and that a salesman may take orders for his principal.[17]

7.23 However, apart from the "actual" authority enjoyed by an agent, there are some situations in which the courts will hold that

[15] *Sinclair, Moorhead and Co.* v. *Wallace and Co.* (1880) 7 R.874.
[16] *Royal Bank of Scotland* v. *Skinner*, 1931 S.L.T. 382 (O.H.).
[17] *Barry, Ostlere and Shepherd Ltd.* v. *Edinburgh Cork Importing Co.*, 1909 S.C. 1113.

he possessed "ostensible" or apparent authority to do what he did, in order to protect the interests of a third party who was led to believe that actual authority existed. This normally arises when the principal has "held out" the agent as possessing such authority, and is now personally barred from denying it. A good example of this process in action was *International Sponge Importers Ltd.* v. *Watt and Sons*, encountered in 7.11 above.

7.24 In such cases, the principal will be bound by what the agent has done; it is up to the principal to ensure that the limits of the agent's authority are carefully spelt out to third parties.

Rights and Duties of Agent and Principal to Each Other

7.25 These may conveniently be considered under two simple headings, since the rights of an agent are clearly the duties of his principal, and vice versa.

Duties of Agent to Principal

7.26 1. *To follow his instructions.* Clearly, an agent is employed to perform a particular task or set of tasks, and if he fails to do so, then he is liable to the principal for breach of contract. Thus, when the agent in *Gilmour* v. *Clark*,[18] who had been instructed to load goods on to the *Earl of Zetland* in fact loaded them on to the *Magnet*, he was liable to the owner of the goods when the *Magnet* went down.

7.27 An agent failing to do what he is told will also lose his right to any commission he might otherwise have earned; see *Graham and Co.* v. *United Turkey Red Co. Ltd.*[19] considered more fully in 4.72 above.

---

[18] (1853) 15 D.478.
[19] 1922 S.C. 533. Contrast this case, however, with *Lothian* v. *Jenolite Ltd.*, 1969 S.C. 111, in which the agency contract did not require the agent to deal exclusively with his principal's product, and it was held that he was not in breach by selling a rival product.

7.28 Whether or not the agent has the authority to delegate the performance of his duties will depend upon the circumstances,[20] but as a general rule he may not.

7.29 2. *To exercise care and skill.* In performing his duties, the agent must display the reasonable care and skill of a person normally appointed to perform such duties; if he is a professional man, then of course the level of care and skill required will be the professional level. Even if he is performing the duties for nothing, as a favour or for a friend, he is bound by the duty to exercise reasonable care and skill, and may be sued for negligence if he fails in that duty.

7.30 3. *To account to his principal.* Every agent must "account" to his principal for money and goods entrusted to him either by his principal or on his principal's behalf. Any deficiencies must be made good by the agent even if no fault on his part can be proved. Added to this is the duty to "relieve" his principal of the consequences of any excess of actual authority on his part.

7.31 4. *To act in good faith in his principal's best interests.* Every agent owes a "fiduciary" duty to his principal,[21] which ensures that he never allows his own interests to conflict with those of his principal, never makes any secret profit from his position, and never makes unauthorised use of information or resources supplied to him by his principal.

7.32 Among the many manifestations of this general principle is the general rule against agents selling their own products to their principals, or buying their principals' property, without the knowledge of the principal. Thus, in *McPherson's Trustees* v. *Watt*,[22] the court set aside a contract under which the solicitor for a trust arranged to sell four houses owned by the trust to his brother,

---

[20] *e.g.* whereas in *Black* v. *Cornelius* (1879) 6 R.581 it was held that an architect might lawfully delegate the measurement of final plans to a surveyor, in *Knox and Robb* v. *Scottish Garden Suburb Ltd.*, 1913 S.C. 872 it was held that he might not when the final plans had not been approved.

[21] *i.e.* he occupies a position of trust; see 3.34 above.

[22] (1877) 5 R. (H.L.).

under an arrangement whereby the brother would then give him a favourable price on the resale of two of them.

7.33 Equally, the agent must not use his position in order to benefit personally beyond his normal commission. Secret profits are not only an actionable breach of contract by the agent, but they will also normally result in the loss of any commission payable, the loss of the secret profit earned[23] and the termination of the agency. When a bribe is involved, the person offering it may be sued by the principal, and in certain cases the agent and third party may face criminal prosecution.[24]

7.34 Any agent who receives a discount or donation from the third party must also give the principal the benefit thereof, as part of his general duty to account to his principal. To fail to do so will constitute a breach of the fiduciary duty.

The Rights of an Agent against his Principal

7.35 1. *To receive remuneration.* If the agent has performed those duties which he was contracted to perform, then he is entitled to receive his commission, although it will depend upon the precise terms and conditions of the agreement when this payment is due. In the absence of any agreed sum, a *quantum meruit*[25] payment will be awarded by the court.

7.36 2. *To be relieved from liability.* An agent performing his duties properly and loyally is entitled to be indemnified by his principal against any liability he has thereby incurred, as in *Stevenson* v. *Duncan*,[26] in which S., a firm of stockbrokers, obtained relief from a client, D., against an action brought against them by an irate "purchaser" of shares which S. had been commissioned by D. to sell, but which D. did not own.

---

[23] Which may be claimed by the principal. The principal may also claim the benefit of any discount which the agent is able to secure when acting on the principal's behalf; see *Solicitors' Estate Agency (Glasgow)* v. *MacIver*, 1993 S.L.T. 23.

[24] Under the Prevention of Corruption Acts of 1906 and 1916.

[25] "As much as he has earned."

[26] (1842) 5 D.167.

7.37 3. *Lien.* An agent who is a "factor" or mercantile agent has a right of lien[27] over any of his principal's property within his physical possession until such time as his commission has been paid and he has been relieved of all and any liability incurred. However, a right of sale does not necessarily follow; this depends upon the type of agency.

Rights and Liabilities of Third Parties

7.38 The position of the third party in an agency situation depends considerably upon what took place when the agent negotiated the contract, and specifically whether or not he disclosed to the third party that he was in fact acting on behalf of a principal. At the one extreme, if C is led by A to believe that he is contracting with A, then he is entitled to insist on A fulfilling the contract and will then have no contractual redress against B, the principal. At the other end of the scale, if C always believed that he was entering into a contract with B, then he may insist on doing so. There are, of course, shades of factual situations in between these two extremes, and it is traditional to analyse this area of the law under four distinct headings.

Agent Contracting for a Named Principal

7.39 This is the second of the two extremes considered above, and the two parties to the contract negotiated by A are B and C, the principal and the third party respectively. The agent drops out of the picture completely once the contract is finalised, and has no rights or duties under it. This rule applies equally when the principal is not actually named, but may be ascertained by the third party.[28]

7.40 Exceptions to the general rule are recognised when the agent volunteers personal liability, when a trade custom imposes it on him anyway, when the agent has an interest of his own in the

---

[27] *i.e.* a right to retain physically.
[28] As in *Armour* v. *Duff*, 1912 S.C. 120, in which suppliers of goods to a vessel at the request of the vessel's agent could have identified the owners of the vessel from the shipping register.

contract negotiated with the third party,[29] and when the principal has no legal "persona," or existence in the eyes of the law.[30]

Agent Contracting for an Unnamed Principal

7.41   When the agent, at the time of contracting, makes it clear to the third party that he is acting for a principal, then the general rule is as if the agent had named him, since the third party is clearly aware that the agent is not the other party to the contract. However, in such a situation, the agent is liable in damages to the third party if he does not name his principal when called upon by the third party to do so.

7.42   The same exceptions exist to the general rule as above.

Agent Contracting Ostensibly as Principal

7.43   When, at the time of negotiating the contract, the third party is unaware that the real party with whom he is contracting is intended to be not the agent but his principal, then he may insist on continuing with the agent as the other party to his contract, even though he becomes aware of the existence of the principal.

7.44   Alternatively, he may "elect" to hold the principal liable under the contract, but once he has done so, he may no longer hold the agent liable. Equally, having "elected" for the agent, he will have no contractual right against the principal.

7.45   Thus, in *Ferrier* v. *Dods*,[31] F. purchased a warranted horse from an auctioneer, D., and complained shortly afterwards that the horse was not sound. D. invited him to return the horse to its

---

[29] In which case he may sue the third party under that contract, as in *Mackenzie* v. *Cormack*, 1950 S.C. 183, in which an auctioneer sued the successful bidder for a carpet sold by his client, in order to preserve his commission entitlement, when the bidder refused to honour his bid.

[30] As in the case of a church congregation (*McMeakin* v. *Easton* (1889) 16 R. 363), an unincorporated club (*Thomson and Gillespie* v. *Victoria Eighty Club* (1905) 43 S.L.R. 628) or a company which is not yet registered (European Communities Act 1972, s. 9(2)).

[31] (1865) 3 M.561.

original owner, B., who had not been named at the time of the
sale. F. did so, and later attempted to sue both F. and B. It was
held that, having returned the horse to B., he had "elected" him,
and could no longer sue F.

7.46 In *James Laidlaw & Sons Ltd.* v. *Griffin*,[32] J. contracted
with G. to perform work on the latter's hotel, which unknown to
J. at that time was owned by G.'s company, G. Ltd. After J. became
aware that G. had only been acting as agent for the company, they
sued G. personally for non-payment, and it was held that G., as
agent for G. Ltd, could counterclaim for damage to the hotel.

7.47 If the principal in an "undisclosed principal" situation
chooses to announce his existence, he may sue the third party.[33]

Breach of Warranty of Authority

7.48 As has already been seen, an agent who exceeds both his
actual and his ostensible authority does not bind his principal in
any contract with the third party unless the principal chooses to
ratify what the agent has done, and the rules relating to ratification
are satisfied. However, this does not leave the third party without
remedy, since he may sue the agent for breach of the implied warranty which the law will recognise as having been given by the
agent at the time of contracting, to the effect that he had the principal's authority to make the contract.

7.49 The "measure," or quantum, of damages in such a case will
normally be the loss suffered by the third party as the result of not
having the contract he thought he had with the principal.[34] How-

---

[32] 1968 S.L.T. 278.
[33] As in *Bennett* v. *Inveresk Paper Co.* (1891) 18 R.975, in which an Australian
newspaper proprietor was held entitled to sue for the damage to a consignment of
paper shipped to Australia on the order of a London agent who had never disclosed
his existence to I.
[34] See, *e.g. Anderson* v. *Croall* (1903) 6 F. 153, in which the awarded damages
through an auctioneer's innocent, but mistaken, belief that he had authority to
auction a horse was the difference between the agreed price at the auction in October
1902 and the horse's eventual sale price in May 1903. For a more recent case
involving damages for breach of warranty of authority, see *Scott* v. *J.B. Livingston
and Nicol*, 1990 S.L.T. 305.

ever, if the agent acted fraudulently, the third party may seek damages for fraud, which will normally be higher.

Termination of Agency

7.50 The relationship of agent and principal may come to an end in one of the following ways.

Completion of Contract

7.51 This may occur either when a defined task is completed (*e.g.* goods are sold by auction, or a house is sold to a buyer by an estate agent) or on the expiry of an agreed period of time (*e.g.* a three-year sales commission).

Mutual Agreement

7.52 This is self-explanatory. *N.B.* that in some situations,[35] the agency will not be terminated effectively until third parties are advised.

Revocation by Principal

7.53 It will depend upon the terms of the agency agreement if, when and how the principal may revoke his agent's authority. If he chooses to do so, he must give adequate notice to third parties, in order to avoid "ostensible" agency continuing (see 7.23 above), and the agent must be given reasonable time to conclude matters already in the pipeline. In certain rare cases,[36] agencies are irrevocable without the agent's consent. The discontinuance of the principal's business will normally constitute an implied revocation by the principal.

Renunciation by Agent

7.54 An agent may of course renounce his agency, but if he does so contrary to the terms of the agency agreement, he will be liable in damages to his principal.

---

[35] *e.g.* the retirement of a partner; see 7.10 and note 8 above.

[36] When the agent has been given authority to pursue a personal interest (a procuratory *in rem suam*—for his own benefit).

Frustration of Agency

7.55   An agency agreement, like any other contract, may be "frustrated" by the occurrence of some event beyond the parties' control.[37] The death of the principal or agent will normally have this
effect, as will the bankruptcy of either party. The insanity of the
agent will normally frustrate the contract, but not apparently the
insanity of the principal until it is known of by the third party.

---

[37] For which, generally, see 4.33 above.

8. PARTNERSHIP

Definition of Partnership

8.1 The modern law of partnership is largely controlled by the Partnership Act of 1890, section 1 of which defines a partnership as "the relation which subsists between persons carrying on a business in common with a view of profit."

8.2 The term "business" includes trades and professions, and partnership is still the most popular form of business association for professionals such as solicitors and accountants. Specifically excluded from the definition of a partnership are companies, whether registered[1] or formed under statute or charter. The minimum number of partners is obviously two, and the maximum is normally 20,[2] although firms of solicitors, accountants and Stock Exchange members may exceed this number, as may individual partnerships granted exemption by the Department of Trade.

8.3 The requirement that the enterprise be formed with a view to making a profit will exclude from partnership status such non-profitmaking organisations as members' clubs and church congregations. Partnerships may also be formed for limited enterprises,[3] in which case they are normally referred to as "joint ventures."

8.4 Section 2 of the Act establishes certain tests to be applied in determining whether or not a given enterprise is a partnership in law. Each of the tests may be combined with the others, since none of them is conclusive. Clearly, however, if a given organisation satisfies all three of the tests, it will be hard to argue against the existence of a partnership.[4]

---

[1] For which see Chapter 9 below.

[2] By virtue of the Companies Act 1967, s. 120.

[3] *e.g.* gold exploration or concert promotion.

[4] Which, as will be seen below, can have important implications for the liability of each of the individuals within the organisation for debts incurred by one of the others in connection with the business.

1. Joint or Common Tenancy or Ownership of Property

8.5   The fact that the individuals within the firm own or lease property jointly or in common will not of itself create a partnership, but it is one indication that a partnership exists. Thus, in *Sharpe* v. *Carswell*,[5] the fact that the salaried master of a ship held shares in the ship he commanded did not prevent him from being an employee so as to permit his widow to claim for workmen's compensation when he died in an accident on board.

2. Sharing of Gross Returns

8.6   Once again, this does not of itself create a partnership, but it assists in showing that a partnership exists. In *Clark* v. *G.R. and W. Jamieson*,[6] a case almost identical to *Sharpe*'s case above, it was held that the fact that C. was paid entirely by a share in the gross earnings of the vessel did not prevent him from being an employee.

3. Sharing of Net Profits

8.7   A person who shares in the net profits of a business is prima facie a partner in it, but even this test is not conclusive, and obvious exceptions are salaries paid on a calculation from profits, annuities paid to former partners' widows out of profits, or the repayment of bona fide loans from an agreed share of profits.

Formation of Partnership

8.8   A partnership requires no formal document for its formation, although clearly it is preferable from a legal point of view for the partners to record such essential matters as the share of the profits between the partners, the management rights of each of them, the capital which each of them is to contribute, and so on. When they do so, it is customary to draw up a full deed for signature by each of the partners, formally known as a "contract of co-partnery."

---

[5]   1910 S.C. 391.
[6]   1909 S.C. 132.

However, a partnership can exist purely on an unwritten understanding between the partners.

Separate Persona of Firm

8.9 By virtue of section 4 of the Act, the "firm,"[7] is a separate legal person from the individual partners who make it up, unlike the position under English law. However, it is not a full "corporation" like a company, and in particular the partners cannot all[8] avoid liability for the firm's debts, as the members of a company may.

8.10 However, certain important legal implications flow from the separate existence of the firm from the individual partners. For example, the firm can sue an individual partner, and vice versa, and each may be the debtor or creditor of the other. Equally, the individual partner can act as agent for the firm,[9] and the firm may be the principal in any contract thereby negotiated with a third party.

8.11 The firm may also be liable in its own right for "delicts"[10] committed by it, and may sue for delicts committed against it. However, the firm will not be liable to partner A for a delict committed upon him by partner B, so that in *Mair* v. *Wood*,[11] the court refused to award damages against a fishing firm for injuries suffered by one of the partner crew members as the result of personal negligence by another who removed an engine-room floorboard through which the victim fell.

8.12 The firm may own property, both heritable and moveable,[12] which is not owned directly by the partners themselves, since they have the right only to a share in the surplus of any such assets when the firm is wound up and all liabilities are met.

---

[7] The collective name for the business formed by the partners.
[8] *N.B.* some may in a "limited partnership," considered below.
[9] And, at the same time, the other partners if the firm fails to pay the debt.
[10] For which see Chapter 10.
[11] 1948 S.C. 83.
[12] For the definition of which see 13.5 below.

8.13 Another important implication of the separate existence of
the firm is that a partner is not a creditor in any debt owed to the
firm, although by virtue of the separate rule which makes partners
liable for firm debts, he will always be a debtor to any debt due
by the firm. By the same rule of separate debts, a firm may become
bankrupt without any of the individual partners becoming bankrupt.

Authority of Partner

8.14 The effect of section 5 of the Act is to make every partner
an agent of the firm, and of his partners, for all actions carried out
by him which might be said to constitute the carrying on of the
business for which the partnership was formed. The only exception
to this rule arises when the authority of a particular partner has
been limited by the other partners, and the third party dealing with
him is aware of the limitation, or does not even believe him to be
a partner.

8.15 It will be noted that in the normal course of things, the
partner's authority extends only to matters relating to the normal
business of the partnership. However, this may extend to other
actions if the partners ratify[13] what he has done, or if he acquires
"ostensible authority"[14] because the rest of the partners hold him
out as having authority to do what he has done. This is true even
if the partner exceeds the actual authority he had at the time.

8.16 The authority of a partner does not simply extend to incurring debts on behalf of the firm, but to incurring other forms of
civil liability as well. Thus, in *Kirkintilloch Equitable Co-operative
Society Ltd.* v. *Livingstone*,[15] when one of the partners in a firm
of accountants who was acting as auditor to the Society made
errors in his work, it was held that the Society could sue not only
him but also the firm, on the basis that section 12 of the Act renders
all partners in a firm jointly and severally liable for the firm's

---

[13] For which see 7.12.
[14] For which see 7.10.
[15] 1972 S.C. 111.

wrongs, and that by virtue of section 10 of the Act, a firm is just as liable as the partners for any financial penalty imposed.

8.17 The effect of section 11 is that when a partner misappropriates money or property belonging to a third party, the firm is liable to the third party if the partner was acting within the scope of his apparent authority, the money or property is received by the firm in the course of its business and it is misapplied while in the firm's custody.

Liability of Partner

8.18 It is a necessary corollary of the above that each partner of the firm will be liable for the actions of the others, by virtue of the joint and several liability which flows from the agency of each partner for the firm and its partners. The creditor must sue the firm first, but if he does not receive payment, he may then proceed against the partners, each of whom may call upon the others to bear an equal share of the liability, depending upon the terms of the partnership contract.

8.19 However, the incoming partner does not normally incur any liability for debts incurred prior to his entry into the firm,[16] unless this is agreed between the new firm and the creditor, or unless the new firm takes over the liabilities of the old firm. An example of the latter situation was the case of *Miller* v. *MacLeod*,[17] in which M., then in practice on his own, undertook the winding-up of an estate in 1955, which was still being done, badly, in 1958, when P. became his partner. The firm continued to act for the original client without fresh instructions, M. died in 1958, and P. took X into partnership with him in 1959. When sued by an irate executrix in 1962, it was held that the firm and its partners in 1962 were liable for events prior to 1958 because the facts gave rise to the implication that the new firm(s) had on each occasion taken over the liabilities which existed at the time.

---

[16] The general rule laid down by s. 17 of the Act.
[17] 1973 S.C. 172. But see *Thomson and Balfour* v. *Boag and Son*, 1936 S.C. 2 in which the court refused to apply the same rule to a situation in which the former sole trader, when taking in a partner, agreed to settle all his debts, and wipe the slate clean for the new partnership.

8.20 When a partner retires, it is[18] his responsibility to ensure that third parties are adequately advised of this fact if he wishes to avoid liability for debts incurred after his retirement. This is normally done by means of an advertisement in the *Edinburgh Gazette*. Once a partner dies or becomes bankrupt, however, notice of his automatic retirement is deemed to have been given to the whole world.

8.21 Liability as a partner may even extend, via the "holding out" principle[19] to a person who is not in fact a partner, but who has been held out as such by the firm.

8.22 Mention should be made of "limited partnerships," which are a form of partnership permitted under the Limited Partnerships Act of 1907, under which some (but not all) of the partners enjoy a fixed liability for the firm's debts. This fixed amount is the amount contributed by the limited partner on his entry into the firm, which must not thereafter be removed by him until he retires.

8.23 Such partnerships must be registered with the Registrar of Companies, with whom certain particulars must be lodged prior to registration, rather in the nature of a company's memorandum of incorporation.[20] The firm must contain at least one "general partner" whose liability is not limited in any way. The limited partner(s) must not take part in the management of the firm, and have no power to bind the firm as general partners have. Any limited partner taking part in management automatically becomes liable in the normal way for any liabilities incurred during that period.

8.24 Limited partnerships are neither popular nor numerous, because of the easy alternative of company formation.

---

[18] As noted in 7.10. *N.B.* that he will retain liability for debts incurred *during* his period as a partner unless there is an express agreement between the firm and its creditors, or one may be implied; see s. 17.
[19] For which see 7.9.
[20] For which see 9.42 et seq.

Relations between Partners

8.25 A partnership contract is one involving *delectus personae*,[21] and also one in which each of the partners owes a "fiduciary" duty[22] to the others. These two principles underlie the detailed rules which govern the relationship of the partners as between each other (*inter se*), which will be largely governed by the provisions of any contract of co-partnery drawn up between them.

8.26 Sections 28 to 30 of the Act reflect the two general principles outlined above by requiring that the partners disclose all relevant information to each other, give a true accounting of the firm's financial position, account for all benefits derived by them in the course of the partnership business, and yield up all profits from competing businesses conducted by them without the consent of the other partners.

8.27 Section 24 lays down the financial rules which govern the partnership in the absence of anything to the contrary in the agreement. All partners are entitled to share equally in the capital and profits of the business, and must contribute equally to the losses, and the firm must indemnify every partner for payments made or liabilities incurred in the ordinary business of the firm or for the preservation of the business. Each partner has an equal right in the management of the firm, and no partner is entitled to a wage as opposed to a share in the profits. No new partners may be introduced without the consent of all existing partners, and whereas most normal partnership business decisions may be made by majority vote, no change may be made in the nature of the partnership business without the consent of all existing partners.

8.28 No partner may assign his share of the partnership without the consent of the remaining partners, and even then the "cedent"[23] will not in law become a partner.

---

[21] See 4.31.
[22] *i.e.* a position of utmost trust.
[23] See 4.33.

Termination of Partnership

8.29 A partnership may terminate either by being "rescinded" or "dissolved." Rescission involves putting the parties back into the position they were in beforehand,[24] and is in effect a cancellation of the original contract of co-partnery, as if it had never happened. It may only occur in one of those limited situations in which the normal law of contract permits rescission.

8.30 All other forms of termination of a partnership involve dissolution, either by the partners or the court, or by the automatic operation of law. It may arise on the expiry of a fixed term agreed in advance, or at the end of an agreed joint venture (in both cases, the dissolution being automatic unless extended by agreement between the partners). When no fixed date or purpose is specified, a partner may dissolve the firm by giving notice to the others of his desire to terminate the partnership. Alternatively, dissolution may be by mutual consent. All these possible methods of dissolution are covered by section 32 of the Act.

8.31 Additionally, dissolution may occur automatically on the death or bankruptcy of one of the partners, subject to agreement to the contrary (section 33), or by the partnership becoming an illegal one (section 34).

8.32 A final alternative exists under section 35 of the Act, which allows any of the partners to apply to the court for a dissolution when:

1. a partner is shown to be a lunatic, or of permanently unsound mind;
2. a partner becomes permanently incapable of performing his partnership duties;
3. a partner commits conduct prejudicial to the carrying on of the business;
4. a partner persistently breaches the partnership agreement or behaves in such a way that it is unreasonable to expect the remaining partners to continue working with him.

---

[24] See 4.92. For an example of rescission of a partnership on the grounds of misrepresentation, see *Ferguson* v. *Wilson* (1904) 6 F.779.

5. the business can only be carried out at a loss;
6. circumstances have arisen in which the court reaches the
    conclusion that it is just and equitable that the firm be dis-
    solved.

8.33 In all cases, the court has a complete discretion as to whether
or not to grant the dissolution order. In cases 2, 3 and 4 above,
the petitioning partner must not be the partner incapable, or at
fault.

8.34 Even after the order is given, the partners must continue in
business for as long as it takes to complete existing business obligations and wind up the firm's affairs. If the partners run into difficulties in this regard, the court may appoint a judicial factor to
perform the task for them (section 39).

8.35 On dissolution, the partnership assets are realised, and in
the absence of any agreement to the contrary, are used to meet the
debts and liabilities of the firm, and then, in order of priority, to
repay contributions by partners over and above the agreed amount,
to repay the partners their capital, and then finally to share the
remainder between the partners in the same proportion as they
shared the profits.

8.36 Any losses are paid first of all from the partnership capital,
and if this is not sufficient, by the partners personally in the proportion in which they shared profits.

Business Names

8.37 It is convenient to deal here with the provisions of the Business Names Act 1985, even though it applies to all forms of business association,[25] and not just partnership. Its primary purpose is
to ensure that when a business is conducted under a business name
(*e.g.* "Acme Cycle Repairs") the true identity of the proprietors
(*i.e.* the people to sue, should the need arise) is made known to its
customers.

---

[25] *e.g.* sole trader, partnership or company.

8.38 Accordingly, section 28 of the Act requires anyone conducting a business in any name other than his or her name (or, in the case of a partnership, the names of the partners) to register that name as a business name. There are certain permitted minor deviations from this general rule, such as, in the case of partnership, the use of the forenames of the individual partners, or their initials, or the use of the plural "s" at the end of the name if two or more partners have the same surname. An individual may also use his forename or initial, and in both cases, it may be indicated that the business is being conducted in succession to a former proprietor.

8.39 In all other cases, section 29 of the Act requires the proprietor to display legibly on all business correspondence the true name(s) of the proprietor(s), or in the case of a company its corporate name, and an address in the United Kingdom for the service of documents on *each* of the individuals thus identified. All business premises must display a notice in a prominent position containing all the above information, while a document containing the same information must be given on request to anyone with whom business discussions are conducted.

8.40 Failure to comply with the Act is not only a criminal offence, but the court has a discretion to dismiss any legal action by the business as pursuer if the defender can show that as a result of the breach he has been unable to pursue a claim against the pursuer, or has suffered some financial loss.

8.41 In addition, the Act prohibits the use of certain names either specified in the Act itself (*e.g.* a name suggesting a government connection) or specified in Regulations passed from time to time which require prior approval from the Secretary of State (*e.g.* "Scottish" or "trade union").

9. REGISTERED COMPANY FORMATION

9.1 This chapter concentrates on the procedures and legal consequences of forming a registered company under the Companies Act of 1985, which is the main codifying statute which now governs company law in Scotland. Companies registered under this Act may be contrasted with corporations formed under royal charter or under private Act of Parliament, which were briefly considered in 2.51 above. They are all forms of corporation, but 1985 Act registered companies are by far the most numerous in practice, and the most commercially important.

9.2 Other areas of company law—such as statutory rules for company management, procedural requirements and dissolution provisions—are outside the scope of this chapter, the primary function of which is to introduce the registered company as a legal entity.

Types of Registered Company

9.3 There are two main ways in which companies registered under the 1985 Act may be classified, namely:

(a) public and private companies;
(b) unlimited companies and companies limited by shares or guarantee.

Public and Private Companies

9.4 Historically, the difference between public and private companies was more important than it is now, since it carried implications for the size of the membership and the transferability of the shares. Since 1980, however, the main differences have been as follows:

9.5 1. *Company name.* A public company must conclude its name with the words "public limited company," or simply "plc."[1] A private company, on the other hand, must end its name with "limited," or "ltd." In the case of a private unlimited company,[2] no such words may be used.

9.6 2. *Form of memorandum.* When completing its Memorandum of Association (for which see 9.42 below), a public company must state that it is public. If no such declaration is made, then the company will in law be regarded as a private one.

9.7 3. *Transfer of shares.* Members of a public company must be free to transfer their shares to whomsoever they wish; a private company, on the other hand, may if it chooses include in its Articles of Association (for which see 9.55 below) a "pre-emption" clause which requires the transferor to offer the shares first to the existing members.

9.8 4. *Share capital.* A public company must have a minimum share capital[3] of £50,000, whereas private companies need have none at all.[4]

9.9 5. *Share dealings.* The shares of a public company may be (but need not be) traded on the Stock Exchange, whereas those of a private company may not be. Equally, only public companies may offer shares and debentures[5] to the public.

9.10 6. *Directors.* A public company must have at least two directors, whereas a private company need have only one. Only public company directors need retire at 70. Only public company secretaries require to be members of certain specified professional bodies.

9.11 7. *Publishing of audited accounts.* A public company must publish audited accounts within seven months of the end of its

---

[1] N.B. there is a special alternative for Welsh companies.
[2] N.B. that no public company may be unlimited.
[3] *i.e.* the "nominal" capital, not necessarily the amount fully subscribed.
[4] And will not, of course, if they are limited by guarantee; see 9.18.
[5] In effect, loans.

financial year. The period for private companies is 10 months, and partial exemption is available from publication.

9.12 8. *Trading certificate.* Only a public company requires a trading certificate before it may begin trading. This is only issued by the Registrar of Companies to those public companies which can show that no less than 25 per cent of the nominal value of the issued shares has been received,[6] and that the nominal value of those issued shares[7] exceeds £50,000. Thus, for example, a company which has a nominal share capital of £100,000 (being 100,000 shares of £1 each) which issues £60,000 of them at "par" (*i.e.* £1 per share) and has received £15,000 will qualify for a trading certificate.

9.13 A private company, on the other hand, may begin trading as soon as it receives its "certificate of incorporation" (for which see 9.38 below).

9.14 Companies may transfer from private to public status, and vice versa, by following a fairly complex procedure and satisfying the necessary tests outlined above.

Companies Limited by Shares or Guarantee and Unlimited Companies

Companies Limited by Shares

9.15 This is by far the most common type of registered company, and its name must always include the word "limited," although it need not necessarily be a public company.

9.16 In a company of this type, the liability of the members (*i.e.* the shareholders) for the debts of the company is limited by the amount which remains "on call" by the company for the purchase

---

[6] Plus any "premium" which is the "above par" value which the shares have attracted. For example, if shares of a nominal value of £1 sell for £1.25, then 25p. is the "premium" over and above the nominal value.

[7] *i.e.* actually sold and allocated to shareholders, who may not be required to pay the full price at once, but may do so in instalments "called" by the company as and when it requires the money. The amount unpaid is said to be "on call."

price of their shares. If, for example, a member holds 1,000 shares issued at £1 per share, and was only required to pay 50p. on "allotment and first call," then if the company becomes insolvent he is liable to pay a total of £500 (and no more) to the creditors. If the shares are fully paid, then he owes nothing.

9.17   A company limited by shares must publish its Memorandum of Association in a certain form laid down under the Act, but need not by law register Articles if it does not wish, since in such a case it will be deemed to be governed by the model Articles laid down under the Act.

Companies Limited by Guarantee

9.18   In this type of company, the liability of the members for the debts of the company is limited to the amount which each of them has guaranteed to pay in the event of the company being wound up; this guarantee is to be found in the Memorandum of Association. By virtue of a 1980 Act, all guarantee companies must be private companies.

9.19   Once again, the Memorandum of Association of a guarantee company must be in a form prescribed by the Act, but unlike share capital companies, a guarantee company must always publish Articles of Association, which must be in a particular statutory form. Certain educational, charitable and artistic guarantee companies may dispense with the word "limited" in their name, if the profits from their activities are devoted to their objects, and their members are not entitled to receive dividends.

Unlimited Companies

9.20   An unlimited company is one in which the liability of the members for the company's debts is not limited in any way. Such companies are something of a paradox, and must always be private companies. The only advantage gained by forming such a company is that of keeping the balance sheet secret from the public.

The Nature of a Registered Company

9.21   Ironically, in view of all the complex legislation which now governs company law, the most important principle of that law—

that the company exists in its own right as a legal entity distinct from its members—is a common law principle which is based on the leading case of *Salomon* v. *Salomon*.[8] However, through increased sophistication, convenience and sheer necessity, the "corporate veil" which is said to exist so as to hide the individual members within the company has on numerous occasions been lifted, by way of exception to the *Salomon* principle.

9.22   Accordingly, any consideration of the general rule and its applications must be immediately followed by an appreciation of its limitations.

The General Rule

9.23   The facts of *Salomon* itself are a perfect illustration of the corporate veil in operation. S., after years of successful sole trading,[9] as a leather merchant and boot manufacturer, decided to form a company with himself holding 20,000 shares and his family members (six in number) holding one each. S. also transferred the assets of his business to the company by way of a loan secured over the company's capital.

9.24   The business fell upon hard times and was wound up, and it was held that S.'s charge over the company's assets, being preferential to the claims of other trade creditors, must be met first. Although in practical terms S. was the company, in law he was at "arm's length" from it, and in his separate capacity as a creditor had a higher claim on the assets because of his "floating charge."[10]

9.25   This principle was applied again and again in succeeding years, in circumstances just as bizarre. Thus, in *Lee* v. *Lee's Air Farming*,[11] a crop sprayer formed a company out of his successful business, with 2,999 shares allocated to himself and one to his wife. He employed himself as a pilot, and when he was killed during the course of his work, his widow (herself of course a

---

[8] [1897] A.C. 22.
[9] No pun is intended.
[10] A form of mortgage of company assets.
[11] [1961] A.C. 12.

shareholder) obtained compensation from the government because her husband had been an employee (of the company) killed in the course of his employment.

9.26   By the same principle, of course, a "mere employee" or shareholder may lose out if he seeks compensation which is only payable to the company, as in *Woolfson v. Strathclyde Regional Council*,[12] in which the sole director/manager of a company shop which he had established failed to obtain compensation from the Council in respect of a compulsory purchase for road-widening. In *Macaura v. Northern Assurance Co. Ltd.*,[13] it was also held that a shareholder in a company (virtually the only shareholder, and its main creditor) could not claim under an insurance policy he had taken out over the timber stock which was the company's main asset because he had no "insurable interest" in it. It was a company asset, and he was legally distinct from the company.

Exceptions to the General Rule

9.27   As indicated above, circumstances have arisen in the past in which either Parliament (by way of statute) or the common law have intervened to prevent the principle of the corporate veil being utilised in order to perpetrate an injustice. Some leading examples are as follows.

1. *Trading with the Enemy*

9.28   When the real owner of a company (as distinct from the company itself) is an enemy alien,[14] the corporate veil will be lifted[15] so as to regard the leading shareholder(s) as the true parties to the contract, which will then be deemed to be illegal.[16]

---

[12]   1978 S.C. (H.L.) 90; 1977 S.C. 84.
[13]   [1925] A.C. 619.
[14]   For which see 2.106 above.
[15]   Under emergency legislation.
[16]   And in *Daimler Co. Ltd. v. Continental Tyre and Rubber Co. (Great Britain) Ltd.* [1916] 2 A.C. 307, this principle was applied so as to prevent C. (which despite its name was almost entirely German owned) enforcing an alleged debt against D.

2. Taxation

9.29   For the purposes of tax law, a company is held to be resident in the country in which its main management is conducted, which may not be the same country in which it is incorporated and has its registered office. In establishing these facts, it is sometimes necessary to lift the corporate veil.

3. Membership below Two

9.30   Every company must have a minimum of two members in order to continue in existence legally for more than six months. Thereafter, full responsibility for the business's debts falls on the remaining member as a sole trader. In such a case, the company's debts are then being enforced against an individual member, as an exception to the general rule of separate personae, and separate debts.

4. "Sham" Companies

9.31   When it is suspected that a company has been formed as a "front" or sham to hide the activities of what is in reality a sole trader situation, the corporate veil will be lifted and the proprietor made liable for the "company's" actions. This principle was applied in *Gilford Motor Co. Ltd.* v. *Horne,*[17] in which H. attempted to sidestep a restrictive covenant[18] against his future employment in the motor trade in competition with his former employers by forming a company to trade for him. The covenant was enforced against both H. and his company.

Formation of a Registered Company

9.32   A registered company is entirely a creature of statute,[19] and in order for a company to be "born," it is necessary for those promoting it to observe many formalities. These formalities may

---

[17] [1933] Ch. 935 (C.A.).
[18] For which see 3.58 above.
[19] Currently the 1985 Act, the last in a long and confusing line of company law statutes.

first be considered in outline before more detailed consideration is given to some of the more important aspects of company registration.

Formation Procedures in Outline

9.33 The procedure for forming a registered company consists primarily of lodging certain documents with the Registrar of Companies. These documents are as follows.

    1. A Memorandum of Association.
    2. Articles of Association.

9.34 These are the two most important documents to be lodged, and form the basis of the "constitution" in line with which the company must be run. Each of these must be "subscribed" (signed) by the founder members of the company (a minimum of two). In addition to these primary documents, the following must also be lodged with the Registrar:

9.35 3. A statement by or on behalf of the subscribers to the Memorandum which contains the names and particulars of the first directors and secretary, and a consent signed by each of them to confirm that they are prepared to act in that capacity. The statement must also specify the intended location of the company's registered office.

9.36 4. A statutory declaration by a director or the secretary of the company, or a solicitor retained for the formation procedure, to the effect that the requirements of the Act have been complied with.

9.37 5. A statement of capital for those companies which are to have share capital.

9.38 If all the procedural requirements are met, then the Registrar will issue the company with a Certificate of Incorporation, which is in effect its official birth certificate as a body corporate. A private company may begin trading immediately, but a public company must also acquire a "trading certificate," for which see 9.12 above.

Promoters and Pre-Incorporation Contracts

9.39 Those who undertake to form a company, acquire share-holders and backing capital, etc., are referred to in law as the "promoters" of the company, a term which does not normally include the professionals (solicitors, accountants, etc.) who advise them. But promoters are not agents for the company in a strict sense because the company at that stage does not exist, and it follows from this that the company, even when formed, cannot in law "ratify" what the promoter has done,[20] and the result is that promoters can be held personally liable for any contracts made at the pre-incorporation stage.

9.40 But a promoter, although he cannot necessarily call upon the company, after its subsequent formation, to honour his actions, does owe a "fiduciary" duty (*i.e.* one of utmost good faith) to that company, which means among other things that he may not allow his interests to conflict with the company's and must account to it fully for his actions. Most promoters are shareholders in the proposed company anyway.

9.41 Just as important is the duty which the promoter has to the subscribing public, and civil and criminal action for fraud can be brought against any company promoter who crosses the line of honesty in his enthusiasm.

Memorandum of Association

9.42 As indicated above, the Memorandum of Association is the first of the two most important documents to be lodged with the Registrar when a company applies for registration. It constitutes what may best be termed the "public face" of the company, and from the Memorandum (which is a document of public record which may be examined by anyone interested) may be gleaned all the formal information such as its name, registered office, share-

---

[20] See 7.12 above. *N.B.* however that a company which is awaiting a new Certificate of Incorporation necessitated by a change of name is still in existence for the purpose of ratifying an obligation entered into on its behalf, and the agent will not therefore become personally liable; see *Vic Spence Associates* v. *Balchin*, 1990 S.L.T. 10.

holders, main business objects, etc. The Memorandum may be altered from time to time if the necessary statutory formalities are observed.

9.43 The following are the main contents of a company Memorandum of Association.

1. *Name Clause*

9.44 Reference has already been made (in 9.5) to the use of words such as "plc" and "ltd." in the company name. Care is also taken by the Registrar to ensure that a company does not become registered with a name which is so close to the name of an existing company as to cause confusion in the public mind. By the same token, a company will not be allowed to register with a name which is offensive, which suggests a connection with a central or local government body, or which infringes any regulation currently in force.

9.45 The company must have its name clearly displayed on the outside of every business premises which it uses, must have a company seal with its name on, and must use its registered name in all business correspondence, publications, etc. If it wishes to trade under a "business name" which is not its registered name, then it must comply with the provisions of the Business Names Act of 1981.[21]

9.46 A company may change its name by special resolution of the members; the Memorandum must then be amended, and of course the principles outlined above apply equally to the new name clause.

2. *Registered Office Clause*

9.47 The Memorandum must state whether the registered office of the company is to be located in England and Wales or in Scotland. This is sufficient to "fix the domicile" of the company, which is important for legal purposes. The actual address of the company

---

[21] For which see 8.37 above.

is usually not quoted in this formal clause of the Memorandum, but elsewhere in it.

9.48   At all times, a registered company must have a registered address to which all formal communications may be sent, legal documents served, etc., and any change in address must be communicated within 14 days to the Registrar, who will then cause it to be publicised. No special resolution of the members is required for a change of address. There may be no change of address which constitutes a change of "domicile" (*e.g.* from London to Glasgow).

9.49   At its registered office, the company must keep certain important documents for inspection by members, including minutes of general meetings and a register of members.

3. *Objects Clause*

9.50   When compiling its Memorandum of Association, the company must complete a clause which indicates the "objects" (*i.e.* purposes) for which it was formed. It was formerly the case that a company could not make a binding contract for any object which was outside those objects,[22] but a gradual erosion of this principle, by both statute and creative drafting, led to final official acknowledgment that such a rule could not be enforced, and since 1989 companies have been able to adopt a form of objects clause which allows them to pursue any line of legal activity which they wish. By the same statute,[23] no company may use the *ultra vires* argument to avoid a binding contract with an outsider.

9.51   The objects clause of a Memorandum may now be amended by a special resolution of the members.

4. *Limitation of Liability Clause*

9.52   In this clause, a company enjoying limited liability states that the liability of the members is limited. This clause itself does not reveal *how* such liability is limited (*i.e.* by shares or by

---

[22] And therefore *ultra vires* — beyond the powers of the company.
[23] Companies Act 1989.

guarantee) and that information is contained in the next succeeding clause.

5. *Share Capital Clause*

9.53 In the case of a company whose members' liability is limited by shares, the share capital clause states the amount of the "nominal" or authorised share capital, and how it is divided (*e.g.* "£10,000 dividend in 100,000 shares of £1 each"). The company may not issue any more capital than this, but the "par" value of each share may rise, so that, for example, the final £20,000 to be issued may fetch £1.75 each.

9.54 The only maximum share capital is that fixed by the company; the only minimum requirements are that all public companies must have a minimum authorised share capital of £50,000.

Articles of Association

9.55 The Articles of Association of a registered company may best be described as the company's "internal face," since they govern the relationship between the members and the company. They also deal with such matters as the issue and transfer of shares, the appointment and powers of the directors and company secretary, the holding of meetings (including notice, quorum, types of resolution required for certain types of decision, etc.) and the means by which company dividends are to be determined.

9.56 A company may go to the trouble of drafting its own articles, or it may adopt the "model" articles laid down in Table A of the Companies Regulations of 1985. Each of the "subscribers" to the company must sign the Articles before they may be registered, and the signatures must be witnessed.

9.57 A company may always alter its Articles, by means of a special resolution in general meeting. By virtue of the Companies Act of 1989, a private company may even alter its Articles by means of the written consent of all the shareholders, without recourse to any meeting at all. No company may bind itself never to amend its Articles, but the Articles may not be altered so as to conflict with the Memorandum or to compel a member to accept increased liability (although he may consent to do so in writing).

Legal Effect of Memorandum and Articles

9.58 A person subscribing to a company as a shareholder is entitled to protection by the law, and section 14(1) of the Companies Act of 1985 states that the Memorandum and Articles of a company are to be regarded in law as a contract between the company and each of its members, thus allowing either party to sue if the other breaches the terms of the Memorandum or Articles as they stand at any given time.

9.59 This clarifies what was always believed to be the law prior to 1985, and in cases decided before that date it has been held that a member may enforce a provision in the Articles which requires the company to pay dividends in cash,[24] that disputes between members and the company are to go to arbitration because the Articles required this prior to any court action,[25] and that members of the company can enforce the Articles against each other.[26]

---

[24] *Wood* v. *Odessa Waterworks Co.* (1889) 2 Ch.D. 636.
[25] *Hickman* v. *Kent and Romney Marsh Sheep Breeders Association* [1915] 1 Ch.881.
[26] As in *Rayfield* v. *Hands* [1960] Ch.1, in which a member successfully enforced a provision in the Articles requiring the directors to buy his shares when he decided to sell them.

10. DELICT

THE NATURE OF DELICTUAL LIABILITY

10.1 A delict is a wrong committed by one individual or entity against another and which is recognised by the law as giving rise to a right to "reparation," or compensation. It may be distinguished from a crime, which is a wrong committed against society as a whole, even though the immediate victim may be an individual. Whereas a crime leads to a prosecution, a delict gives rise to an action in the civil courts by the victim/pursuer against the perpetrator/defender. Some delicts (*e.g.* assault) can also be crimes, and victims of crime can now receive compensation from the courts which operates as a form of reparation, and may be taken into account when assessing delictual liability.

10.2 Reparation for delict is always expressed in terms of damages, although a threat of delict may be averted by means of interdict.[1]

10.3 The elements of delictual liability may first be examined, before some of the more important examples of delict are considered.

ELEMENTS OF DELICTUAL LIABILITY

10.4 The basic principle underlying the law of delict is the performance of a harmful act which gives rise to a legal wrong.[2] A delict therefore requires that all of the following elements be present.

    1. Wrongful conduct by the defender (*injuria*).
    2. Loss or injury suffered by the pursuer (*damnum*).

---

[1] A court order prohibiting a proposed course of action, for example a nuisance such as that suffered by the pursuer in *Webster* v. *Lord Advocate* considered in 10.53 below.

[2] *Damnum injuria datum.*

3. Causation, or put another way, a link between 1 and 2.

10.5 A legal wrong which does not give rise to provable injury on the part of the pursuer[3] is not an actionable delict, nor can the pursuer recover damages for a proved loss which cannot be shown to have arisen from any wrongful act on the part of the defender.[4]

10.6 Each of the above elements may be considered in more detail.

✳ Injuria

10.7 It is of course a matter of substantive law which particular actions on the part of a defender will constitute *injuria*, and much of the remainder of this chapter is devoted to consideration of individual delicts such as negligence and nuisance. Not all actions by a potential defender, even if harmful to the pursuer, will however be classed as delicts,[5] and it comes down to a question of which harmful actions are made actionable in law, and which are not.

10.8 Sometimes the delictual liability will be declared by statute, as in the case of the Occupiers Liability (Scotland) Act of 1960, and sometimes it is derived from case law, when a court of sufficient authority rules that a particular piece of behaviour ought to give the victim a right to compensation.[6]

10.9 The leading case in the law of negligence, *Donoghue* v. *Stevenson*,[7] was a classic example of a delict being created by a court decision, in that particular instance a ruling by the House of Lords that a manufacturer owed a "duty of care" to the ultimate consumer of his product.

---

[3] *Injuria sine damno.*
[4] *Damnum absque injuria.*
[5] *e.g.* lawful competition by one trader against another, or involuntary behaviour such as a heart attack whilst behind the wheel of a car which leads to a collision.
[6] Sometimes delictual liability may arise both ways, as in the case of occupiers' liability, which is recognised both under statute and under common law.
[7] 1932 S.C.(H.L.) 31, for which see 10.31.

10.10 Before an action will be classed as *injuria*, however, it must be a conscious act or omission on the part of the defender which may be intentional, careless, or in some cases[8] totally without fault on his part.

⋇ Damnum

10.11 The loss or injury suffered by a pursuer need not be purely physical, since the law recognises liability for nervous shock, mental anguish, lost reputation and economic loss, as some of the cases examined elsewhere in this chapter illustrate. Even dented pride can be compensated, while *solatium* also takes account of the pain and suffering resulting from a physical injury.

10.12 But unless the pursuer can point to a recognised form of loss arising directly from the behaviour of the defender, there can be no delictual claim.

⋇ Causation

10.13 Even though the pursuer may have suffered *damnum*, and the defender may at the same time have committed *injuria*, there will still be no delict unless the two are linked, in the sense that the *injuria* has caused the *damnum*. This link is known as "causation," and has given rise to some interesting borderline cases over the years, of which two examples will suffice.

10.14 In *McWilliams v. Arrol (Sir William) and Co.*[9] a steel erector was killed when he fell from a tower being erected in a Port Glasgow shipyard. In an action by his widow for damages for negligence on the part of the employer, in which it was proved in evidence that a safety harness would have prevented the accident if supplied, the final verdict went to the employers when they in turn proved that the deceased would not have worn it anyway. The *injuria* (the failure to supply the harness) could not be shown to have led directly to the *damnum* (the death).

---

[8] Referred to as cases of "strict liability."
[9] 1962 S.C. (H.L.) 70.

10.15 In *Kay's Tutor* v. *Ayrshire and Arran Health Board*,[10] in a well-publicised challenge by the parents of a deaf child who claimed that his deafness had been caused by a negligent overdose of penicillin, the Health Board defended by claiming that the real cause of the deafness had been an underlying meningitis condition for which the penicillin had been prescribed. Because the parents could not show that penicillin overdoses had in the past caused deafness (and in the face of evidence that meningitis often had), the court was obliged to find in favour of the Health Board, on the grounds of lack of proven causation.

10.16 Sometimes the link between *damnum* and *injuria* is confused and obscured by the presence of *novus actus interveniens*, or an intervening factor. For example, in *McKew* v. *Holland and Hannen and Cubitts (Scotland) Ltd.*,[11] M. claimed damages for an injury to his left leg as the result of an injury at work. Three weeks after the accident at work, he had a second accident at a friend's house when he experienced a weakness in his left leg and jumped down several steps, severely injuring his right leg. It was held that while he might claim for the left leg, the injuries to the right leg had been as the sole result of a deliberate action on his part which broke the "chain of causation."

10.17 More recently, in *Knightly* v. *Johns*,[12] J. negligently overturned his car at the entrance to a tunnel, and a police officer negligently ordered a police motorcyclist to ride down the tunnel against the normal traffic flow in order to close it. In doing so, the motorcyclist, K., was hit by an oncoming car. It was held that J.'s original negligence was not the cause of K.'s injuries, because of the intervening negligence of the police officer in charge.

10.18 But once it is demonstrated that the ultimate injury to the pursuer was the "reasonably foreseeable" and direct result of the wrongful act of the defender, then he is liable for the full extent of the injury. Applying what is sometimes called the "thin skull rule," the law requires the defender to take his victim as he finds him.

[10] 1987 S.L.T. 577.
[11] 1970 S.C.(H.L.) 20.
[12] [1982] 1 All E.R. 851.

Thus, in *Smith* v. *Leach Brain and Co. Ltd.*,[13] the defendants were
held liable for the death of a former employee arising from a relatively minor burn which activated a pre-existing proneness to
cancer.

IMPOSITION OF DELICTUAL LIABILITY

General Rule

10.19 The general rule is that delictual liability is incurred by
whoever commits the *injuria* which causes the *damnum* suffered
by the pursuer. By the same token, A cannot be held liable for
the delicts of B. To this general rule there are, however, certain
exceptions.

Joint and Several Liability

10.20 In cases in which it is held that two or more persons have
contributed to the loss suffered by the pursuer, they will be liable
"jointly and severally," *i.e.* each one is fully liable to the pursuer,
who may choose to sue only one of them.[14] The one thus chosen
may, however, bring an action against the other wrongdoer in
order to recover his share. Under procedural rules which govern
the civil courts, the court of trial must allocate the proportions of
liability between the two defenders, failing which it will fall equally
between them if apportionment is impossible.

10.21 In *Drew* v. *Western S.M.T.*,[15] for example, liability was
applied jointly and severally between a delivery van owner whose
tail lights were obscured and a bus company whose driver drove
into the back of the van, killing the van boy. In a similar case,
Davies v. *Swan Motor Co.*,[16] a collision between a dustbin lorry
and a bus led to an apportionment of liability of two-thirds to the
bus company and one-third to the refuse company, reduced in each

---

[13] [1961] 3 All E.R. 1159.
[14] Usually the one with the money.
[15] 1947 S.C. 222.
[16] [1949] 2 K.B. 291.

case by one-fifth to take account of the "contributory negligence"[17] of the deceased dustman for standing on the running board at the time.

Vicarious Liability

10.22 "Vicarious"[18] liability arises when A is, in law, held responsible for the delicts of B. This can clearly only happen in cases in which there is something in the relationship between A and B which justifies it. The following are among the main examples of such relationships.

Employer/Employee

10.23 An employer is liable for the delicts of an employee committed in the course of his employment, and within the normal scope of his duties. It is of course very common for the injured party to sue the employer (who may have the resources or the insurance policy) rather than the employee (who may well have neither), and in practice the employer rarely seeks a contribution from the employee.[19]

10.24 Most of the difficulties encountered in such cases revolve around whether or not the employee was acting in the normal course of his employment at the time of the delict. For example, in *Rose v. Plenty*,[20] a milk-float driver who disobeyed his employer's instructions and allowed a child to help him on his milk round was held to be acting within the scope of his employment (hence making his employers vicariously liable) when the boy was injured. Similarly, the court in *Bell v. Blackwood Morton & Sons*[21] held that workers rushing down factory stairs when the end of work hooter sounded were acting within the scope of their employment, and

---

[17] For which see 10.75.
[18] Literally interpreted as "in place of."
[19] An exception being the case of *Lister v. Romford Ice and Cold Storage Co.* [1957] A.C. 555, in which an employer of a lorry driver recovered from the driver all the damages they had paid to the fellow employee he had knocked down, who happened to be his father!
[20] [1976] 1 All E.R. 97.
[21] 1960 S.C. 18.

that the employers were therefore liable to a female employee injured in the rush.[22]

Partnership

10.25 Under the Partnership Act of 1890, a firm is liable vicariously for any wrongful act or omission performed by a partner in the normal course of the firm's business; see 8.16 above.

Agency

10.26 Similarly, a principal will be held liable for actions, etc., performed by an agent carrying out his instructions, or acting within the actual or implied scope of his authority; see generally 7.21.

Liability of the Crown

10.27 Under the Crown Proceedings Act 1947, the Crown, as an employer, is held liable for delicts committed by its servants or agents; it will not, however, be liable for wrongs committed by an independent contractor,[23] unless the Crown has been negligent in its choice of contractor in the first place, the work in question is inherently dangerous (*e.g.* building operations) or the Crown has retained control over the method of work. It will also be liable to employees injured at work either under the normal rules of employment law,[24] or "vicariously," as the result of negligence, etc., by other Crown employees.

10.28 The Crown will also incur delictual liability under statute when the statute in question "binds" the Crown.[25]

---

[22] See also *Williams* v. *Hemphill*, 1966 S.C.(H.L.) 31, in which it was held that a charter bus driver who deviated from the normal route at the request of some of his passengers was still acting within the scope of his employment when he crashed during the deviation.

[23] Nor for that matter will an ordinary employer, apart from the exceptions indicated.

[24] For which see 12.92 et seq. below.

[25] As does, for example, the Occupiers' Liability (Scotland) Act 1960.

✄ NEGLIGENCE

10.29 Negligence is the most important of the modern delicts, and the one which gives rise to the greatest number of delictual claims. It results from what may broadly be described as the defender's failure to take "reasonable care" for the safety and interests of the pursuer, in circumstances in which the law decides that he has a "duty" to do so. Not all acts of carelessness by the defender will give the pursuer a right of action in negligence, and before they will do so, the following factors must be considered.

The Duty of Care

10.30 For the delict of negligence to arise, the defender must owe a "duty of care" to the pursuer. Whether or not D. owes a duty of care to P. is a matter of law, and can only be established by reference to decided cases or, increasingly, statute. The classic example of a duty of care being established by case precedent, and the most influential "watershed" case in the law of negligence, was *Donoghue* v. *Stevenson*.[26]

10.31 The facts were simple enough. P. entered a café in Paisley with a friend, and her friend purchased a ginger beer for P. Having consumed half the drink, P. poured the remaining half into her glass, only to watch horrified as the remains of a decomposed snail swam into view from the bottle, which was dark enough in colour to have concealed its contents. P. suffered both nervous shock and gastroenteritis, and wanted to sue someone. She could not sue the café proprietor, since she had not purchased the ginger beer. She therefore sued the manufacturer, and the case went all the way to the House of Lords. From the House of Lords emanated the famous ruling that everyone owes a duty of care not to injure one's "neighbour," the latter being anyone sufficiently close to one's actions as to be foreseeably injured by them.

10.32 In the specific context of this case, the principle was applied so as to make manufacturers of products liable to ultimate consumers in situations in which there is no prior opportunity to exam-

---

[26] 1932 A.C. 562; 1932 S.C.(H.L.) 31.

ine the product, but the "neighbour" principle has been applied extensively in a whole host of contexts.

10.33 In *Bourhill* v. *Young*,[27] for example, it was applied in a claim by a lady standing on the platform of an Edinburgh tramcar when a motorcyclist was involved in a collision with a car and died. It was held that she could not recover, from the deceased's estate, damages for the nervous shock sustained from hearing the accident, since it was not "foreseeable" by the deceased as he rode his motorcycle negligently. Had she been in the area of foreseeable physical impact (as were the passengers in the car), and had she suffered physical injuries, it would have been another story altogether. The law in this area, however, has since moved on, as will be seen below.

10.34 In *Muir* v. *Glasgow Corporation*[28] it was held that the manageress of a tearoom in a park who allowed a picnic party to use the tearoom in order to shelter from the rain was not negligent when a tea urn being carried in was dropped by one of the party, and several children using the tearoom were scalded. It was held that the accident was not a "foreseeable" consequence of her action.

10.35 In neither of these cases was the ultimate victim of the accident a "foreseeable" victim, and hence the "neighbour" of the person negligent. It was a different matter in *Hughes* v. *Lord Advocate*,[29] however, when the court held that it was foreseeable, when workmen left a hole in the ground covered by a canvas shelter and surrounded by paraffin lamps, that one of the lamps might fall into the hole and cause an explosion. The fact that this happened via the agency of two inquisitive boys was irrelevant. It was likely to happen, and it did.

10.36 In the years since *Donoghue* v. *Stevenson*, the courts have grown more confident and generous in their application of the

[27] 1942 S.C.(H.L.) 78.
[28] 1943 S.C.(H.L.) 3.
[29] 1963 S.C.(H.L.) 31.

neighbour principle of the duty of care. It has, for example, been extended beyond the context of straight physical injury and into the arena of economic loss caused either by negligent mis-statement or negligent acts. Liability for economic loss for negligent mis-statement was finally confirmed in *Hedley Byrne and Co.* v. *Heller and Partners*,[30] in which a merchant bank was held to owe a duty of care to a firm of advertising agents who relied on their credit reference when extending credit to a mutual client; only the existence of an exemption clause in the letter of advice[31] saved the defenders from having to compensate the pursuers for their financial loss.

10.37   An example of a physical action leading to liability for economic loss was *Junior Books* v. *The Veitchi Co. Ltd.*,[32] in which the sub-contractors laying a floor in business premises, under contract with X, the main contractor, were held to owe a duty of care to the customer who employed the main contractor (with whom the sub-contractors had no direct contract) to lay it properly because of the "proximity" of their work to the economic interests of the customer. The same might apply, for example, if a contractor digging up a roadway severed a power cable to a nearby factory.

10.38   Liability for negligent actions has now extended to reasonably foreseeable nervous shock. It will be recalled that in *Bourhill* v. *Young*, above, the court was not prepared to recognise this as a foreseeable consequence of an accident unless the victim was in the immediate firing line. However, in *Chadwick* v. *BTC*,[33] it was held that those responsible for a rail disaster were liable for the nervous shock suffered by a volunteer rescuer. In *McLaughlin* v. *O'Brien*,[34] damages were awarded to a lady for the nervous shock sustained when seeing her family (one of whom died) undergoing casualty treatment in the hospital as the result of a road accident she had not witnessed.

---

[30]   1964 A.C. 465, recently applied in *Bank of Scotland* v. *3i plc*, 1990 S.C. 215.
[31]   For which see 10.64 below.
[32]   1982 S.L.T. 492.
[33]   [1967] 2 All E.R. 945.
[34]   1983 A.C. 410.

✳Breach of the Duty of Care

10.39 It is not enough for P. simply to show that D. owes him a duty of care; he must also show that by his actions D. has been in breach of that duty. In order to be in breach, the defender must have failed to take "reasonable care" for the pursuer, and what is "reasonable" care will depend upon the facts of each individual case. It is still traditional to ask what the "reasonable man" would have done in those circumstances. The seriousness of the consequences must be countered with increased care, and the ease of precautions will dictate how "reasonable" it is to expect them to be taken.

10.40 In *Bolton* v. *Stone*,[35] for example, it was held to be unreasonable to expect a local cricket club to improve on its existing seven-foot fence to guard against an event (namely a ball going over that fence) which had only occurred six times in 30 years, and even then without injury. In *Paris* v. *Stepney Borough Council*,[36] on the other hand, it was held not to be unreasonable to require an employer to supply safety goggles to P. in circumstances in which they were not issued to other employees (reasonably, said the court) because he was already blind in one eye.

10.41 By the same token, greater care must be taken in respect of children, the elderly and the infirm. The nature of the work undertaken will also dictate its own standard of care. Delicate brain surgery requires more skill and sensitivity than cutting hair, and those who set themselves up as professional persons must perform according to the reasonable standards of competence of that profession.

Causation and Remoteness

10.42 Having established both the existence and the breach of the duty of care, the pursuer must also show that the loss or injury for which he is claiming arose directly from the breach, without

[35] 1951 A.C. 850.
[36] 1951 A.C. 367.

any intervening cause. This concept has been adequately considered in 10.13 above.

✳ Burden of Proof

10.43 As a general rule, it is for the pursuer to prove that the defender has been guilty of negligence, but he need only do so "on a balance of probabilities."[37] However, as the result of the operation of a presumption of fact known by the Latin phrase *res ipsa loquitur*,[38] the burden of proof may be transferred to the defender.

10.44 In *res ipsa loquitur* situations, once the pursuer is able to show that the immediate cause of injury to him was something within the exclusive control of the defender, and the accident would not have happened had proper management care been exercised, then it is for the defender to show that the cause of the accident might have been something for which he cannot be held responsible. If he succeeds, then the onus passes back to the pursuer to show that the actual cause of the loss was in fact the defender's negligence.

10.45 A few illustrative cases may assist in assessing the relevance of *res ipsa loquitur*. In *O'Hara* v. *Central SMT*,[39] a passenger standing on the platform of a bus was thrown off and injured when the bus swerved for no apparent reason. It was held that in these circumstances it was for the defender to prove, as alleged, that a pedestrian had run in front of the bus, or lose the case. In *Cassidy* v. *Minister of Health*,[40] it was held that it was for a hospital board to explain away (which they could not) how a patient who went in for corrective surgery on two fingers came out with four useless ones.

10.46 The true effect of *res ipsa loquitur* is well illustrated by *Devine* v. *Colvilles*,[41] in which D., a workman, was injured when he jumped 15 feet from a platform following an explosion. It was

---

[37] The "quantum" of proof required in all civil cases.
[38] Which is perhaps most helpfully translated as "matters speak for themselves."
[39] 1941 S.C. 363.
[40] [1951] 2 K.B. 343.
[41] 1969 S.C.(H.L.) 67. For a more modern example involving yoghurt on a supermarket floor, see *Ward* v. *Tesco Stores* [1976] 1 W.L.R. 810.

shown that the cause was a blocked hose under the defender's management, and the court held that in the absence of an explanation inconsistent with the defender's negligence, and given that the burden of proof lay on them, the pursuer must succeed.

Occupier's Liability

10.47 A specific application of the delict of negligence—namely the duty of care owed by occupiers of premises—is now dealt with by the Occupiers' Liability (Scotland) Act 1960, which requires the occupiers of all premises to exercise reasonable care for the safety of all persons who venture on their land. This duty extends, not only to the state of the land or premises themselves, but also to the activities conducted on and within them. It also extends to vehicles and aircraft, and the liable "occupier" need not be the owner (*e.g.* he could be a tenant or licensee). The liability also extends not just to injury to the person but also injury to property.

10.48 The amount of care which the occupier is required to exercise will depend upon the type of person who comes on to the premises, and the purpose of their being there. One can readily appreciate that the occupier of dangerous premises which are also a lure to children (*e.g.* a fairground) must be shown to have exercised a high degree of care, not only in protecting them while on the premises lawfully, but also in preventing them from entering unlawfully and unsupervised. At the other extreme, the owner of an empty field owes little duty to a trespasser, even though trespassers are protected by the Act.

10.49 A good illustration of the Act in use was *McGlone v. British Railways Board*,[42] in which a 12-year-old boy climbed up a transformer in a Glasgow railway yard and was severely burned. In order to do so, he had passed a "danger" notice and climbed through a barbed-wire barrier. The court held that the Board had done all that might reasonably be expected of them.

[42] 1966 S.C.(H.L.) 1.

Nuisance

10.50 The delict of nuisance occurs when the defender performs some unauthorised act which interferes with the quiet enjoyment of someone's land. The classic example is the noisy neighbour, but nuisance can consist of smells, vibration and other forms of distressful or unacceptable disturbance.

10.51 In order to be a nuisance, the behaviour complained of must be substantial and more than just occasional; for example, there is a world of difference between an occasional noisy party and a commercial disco. The normal remedy is an interdict to prevent the behaviour complained of continuing, although damages for past discomfort may also be appropriate.

10.52 In order to succeed, the pursuer must show that the defender has been at least negligent in his behaviour; however, it is no defence to show that the pursuer must have been alerted to the possibility of disturbance when he moved into the property.[43]

10.53 A fairly recent — and well-publicised — nuisance action was *Webster* v. *Lord Advocate*,[44] in which a flat owner overlooking the Edinburgh Castle Esplanade raised an interdict action in the Court of Session to prevent the Edinburgh Military Tattoo, on the grounds of the noise it created, both from the performances and from the erection of stands and from rehearsals. Having rejected the argument that the Tattoo had been there longer than the pursuer, the court awarded interdict against the limited nuisance of clanging metal during the erection stage.

Strict Liability under Statute

10.54 Whereas the general rule at common law is that no one may be held liable in respect of a delict unless he is in some way at fault, there are under statute an increasing number of situations in which fault (*culpa*) is not required, and one may be held liable for injury or loss however much care was taken, and however

---

[43] *e.g.* at the end of an airport runway.
[44] 1985 S.C. 173.

blameless one is. These are said to be examples of "strict liability," and the following are among the main examples.

1. Factories Acts

10.55 Successive Factories Acts[45] have imposed strict duties upon employers designed to ensure the maintenance of a safe work environment. In most cases it does not matter how much care is taken; the premises must be safe, and if anyone is injured there is a strong presumption that the premises are unsafe, rebutted only perhaps by evidence of very stupid behaviour by the injured employee. Since breach of the legislation gives the injured person a right to civil action, the Factories Acts are an example of delictual liability which does not require fault on the part of the defender, as in *Millar* v. *Galashiels Gas Co. Ltd.*,[46] in which a workman was killed when the brakes failed on a factory hoist. The employers had taken every precaution they could, and the cause of the failure was never proved. The employers were nevertheless held liable.

2. Hotel Proprietors Act 1956

10.56 Under this Act, the proprietor of an "hotel" within the definition supplied by the Act is liable to guests staying at the hotel for any loss or damage to their property during their stay.[47] The liability does not apply if the guest is himself totally to blame for the loss, but in all other cases the hotelier is in effect the insurer of the guest's property. However, by displaying a notice in the prescribed form, the hotelier may limit his liability in financial terms.

3. Animals (Scotland) Act 1987

10.57 This Act imposes upon the "keeper" of any animal which has the propensity to kill or injure other animals or damage prop-

---

[45] Now in many ways overshadowed by the Health and Safety at Work Act, for which see 12.92 et seq. below.
[46] 1949 S.C.(H.L.) 31.
[47] But not vehicles or property left in vehicles.

erty a duty to ensure that none of this happens. If it does, the keeper is liable, however much care he takes.

4. *Consumer Protection Act 1987*

10.58 *Donoghue* v. *Stevenson* was taken to its logical statutory conclusion in the 1987 Act, which imposes strict liability on the manufacturer of any product[48] which injures any consumer either physically or via his property, although economic loss is not recoverable.

10.59 The producer or manufacturer may escape liability by showing that he did not supply it in the course of a trade or business, or that the injured party was himself guilty of contributory negligence (see below). No claim may be made beyond 10 years from the supply of the product, and no claim may be brought for less than £275 in damages.

10.60 These exceptions apart, if someone is injured, or suffers property loss or damage, through the supply of a defective product, the defender may not escape liability merely by showing that he took reasonable care. His liability is strict.

10.61 At common law, there are only two remaining examples of strict liability, namely liability for the alteration of the course of a natural stream, and unintentional slander, both of which are outside the realistic scope of this book.

LIMITATION OF DELICTUAL LIABILITY

10.62 There are basically three ways in which delictual liability which might otherwise have arisen in respect of a particular act or omission may be prevented from arising in the first place, as opposed to being avoided by way of defence, exclusion, etc., once it has arisen. These are 1. under statute, 2. under contract, and 3. by way of immunity.

---

[48] Including gas, water or electricity.

Statutory Limitation of Delictual Liability

10.63 Occasionally (and only for very good reason), a statute may declare that actions which would otherwise be delictual will not be if they are performed by designated persons for designated reasons, or in specified circumstances. Examples are few and far between, but one clear example is section 13 of the Trade Union and Labour Relations Act 1974, which extends to actions taken by trade union members "in contemplation or furtherance of a trade dispute," immunity from the delictual consequences of inducing a breach of contract.

Contractual Limitation of Delictual Liability

10.64 At common law, there is nothing to prevent the parties from agreeing, as a term of a contract, that in the event of some misconduct by one of them, he will not be held delictually liable to the other. All that was written in 4.11 above concerning the extinction of delictual liability by means of contractual clauses (including the effect of the Unfair Contract Terms Act 1977) is applicable here.

Immunity

10.65 In certain well-defined situations, certain persons are granted immunity from being sued for delict. The best-known examples are as follows.

1. *The Crown*

The Queen in her personal capacity is immune from delictual liability. However, as explained in 10.27 above, this does not necessarily mean that all officers of the Crown will be so immune, even when acting in lawful furtherance of Crown interests. Nor do other members of the Royal Family enjoy the Queen's immunity.

2. *Foreign Sovereigns and Diplomatic Staff*

10.66 These enjoy diplomatic immunity from delictual liability, as do formal heads of foreign states (*e.g.* presidents).

3. *M.P.s and Judges*

10.67 Judges of the Court of Session, the High Court and the sheriff courts enjoy immunity from liability in the performance of judicial acts. M.P.s enjoy limited immunity from actions for defamation of character in respect of things said in the House under "parliamentary privilege." This extends to statements made outside the House in the course of their duties, but there must be no suggestion of malicious motivation.

4. *Trade Unions*

10.68 As indicated above, immunity from some delicts (conspiracy, inducing breach of contract and intimidation) is granted to trade unions acting "in contemplation or furtherance of a trade dispute." This is of course also an example of statutory limitation of delictual liability.

DEFENCES TO DELICTUAL LIABILITY

10.69 There are basically four defences open to a defender facing civil action for an alleged delict.

Damnum Fatale

10.70 This is another term for "Act of God," which apart from being a haven of refuge for insurance companies is also a defence to an action in delict. If the defender can show that God (and not he) was the author of the pursuer's misfortunes (in the form, *e.g.* of earthquake, tempest or presumably a plague of boils), then this is a complete defence. An Act of God is basically some natural catastrophe beyond the cause or control of man.[49]

Lawful Justification

10.71 In some cases, otherwise delictual behaviour is lawful, either because of an Act of Parliament, or because of the develop-

---

[49] Thus, for example, if another Biblical flood destroyed a house, no one would be held liable, but if the same damage were caused by a burst dam, *damnum fatale* would not apply.

ment of the common law. Into the latter category fall assaults performed in self-defence (when the defence is proportional to the initial assault) and "necessity" (*e.g.* trespass over property in order to capture a dangerous criminal or to escape a wild animal). Members of the armed forces and police officers possess statutory authority to restrain other persons in the lawful furtherance of their duties. The defence is a total one, and may also be used in mitigation of damages if an originally lawful action went "over the score."

Volenti Non Fit Injuria

[One who volunteers no harm can be done]

10.72 A pursuer may be barred from recovering delictual damages at all if the defender can show that he volunteered for the risk which led to his injury. Two obvious examples are consent to the known risks of surgery (hence the prior requirement to sign the consent form) and participation or spectating in a dangerous sport (*e.g.* motor racing). However, such consent is only in respect of the normal risks, and will not cover, *e.g.* surgical negligence or excessive violence in a rugby scrum.

10.73 The courts also lean against the *volenti* defence in employment situations, even when men are paid a higher wage because of the inherent risk (*e.g.* on oil rigs). Employers are still required to keep workplaces safe within "reasonable" limits (see 12.92 below), and injured employees may sue if they do not. Only exceptionally will a court accept a *volenti* defence in the workplace.

10.74 The courts will *never* accept *volenti* when a rescuer puts himself at risk to preserve life or property in a dangerous situation created by the defender. Thus, in *Baker* v. *Hopkins*,[50] the widow of a doctor recovered damages in respect of his death when he had lowered himself down a well in an effort to save the lives of two men overcome by noxious fumes which were the result of the defender's negligence. The defence of *volenti* was raised, but rejected by the court.

[50] [1959] 1 W.L.R. 966; 2 All E.R. 225.

✳ Contributory Negligence

10.75 Even though the defender may not have a total defence to an action for delict, he may prevail upon the court to reduce the damages awarded by the proportion to which it may be said that the pursuer himself was "contributorily negligent," *i.e.* partly to blame for what happened. A clear example would be a two-car collision in which, on the facts, the court is persuaded that the pursuer was 30 per cent to blame.[51] If the "head" damages assessment is £10,000, the pursuer in such a case will receive £7,000.

10.76 The burden of proof is on the defender to show contributory negligence on the part of the pursuer, and the court will be less inclined to find it in cases involving the very young, the elderly and the infirm. Again, the courts will be less sympathetic to a contributory negligence defence in those cases in which the pursuer has reacted instinctively (to his detriment) in a dangerous situation created by the defender in the first place.[52]

EXTINCTION OF DELICTUAL LIABILITY

10.77 There are two ways in which delictual liability may be extinguished after it has arisen and without the matter being litigated.

Personal Bar

10.78 The behaviour of the pursuer may result in him being unable to exert his rights. For example, he may have consented to the action in the first place ("acquiescence," akin to *volenti*), he

---

[51] As in *Joliffe v. Hay*, 1991 S.L.T. 151. In *Hill v. Chivers*, 1987 S.L.T. 323, for example, the court held that a passenger in a car driven by a man he knew was drunk, and who failed to wear a seat-belt, was one-third to blame for his injuries. In *Feeney v. Lyall*, 1991 S.L.T. 156, the court found 25 per cent liability on the part of a golfer who moved into the line of another fairway in order to collect his own stray ball, and was struck by a driving shot.
[52] As in *Wallace v. Bergius*, 1915 S.C. 205, in which A saw a car coming towards him on the other side of the road, driven by B, he changed sides (so as to be on his wrong side of the road) and so did B! It was held that B's claim of contributory negligence must fail.

may have delayed too long with his claim ("mora and taciturnity," largely overtaken in modern litigation by prescription and limitation, below), or he may have "waived" his claim in some way.

Prescription and Limitation

10.79 Under the Prescription and Limitation (Scotland) Act of 1973, an action in respect of personal injury or death must be commenced within three years of the incident giving rise to the claim. This period may be extended when the pursuer is under a legal disability (*e.g.* under 16 or insane) and has no custodial parent or grandparent,[53] or where "material facts of a decisive character" were not known to him until a certain date,[54] or it seems "just and equitable" to the court to allow an extension.

10.80 Since 1985, a similar rule has applied in defamation cases. In all other cases, the limitation period is five years, extended by any period during which the pursuer was not aware of the loss or damage which he had suffered, and could not with reasonable diligence have been so aware.

10.81 The effect of overrunning a limitation period is that court action may no longer be raised; although the liability is not theoretically extinguished, it is unenforceable in practical terms.

---

[53] In which case the time runs from the end of the disability.
[54] In which case the time runs from that date.

11. CONTRACTS OF EMPLOYMENT

Introduction

11.1 Nowhere is the recent swing from common law to statute referred to in Chapter 1 better illustrated than in the transformation which has overtaken the law of employment since 1960 or thereabouts. Chapter 12 examines some of the more important pieces of modern legislation which now govern the employer/employee relationship, but that relationship is still essentially a contractual one, and this chapter explores the basic rules of law which remain the "ground rules" of the law of employment.

11.2 These rules have their origin in the old "master and servant" days of the nineteenth century, and technically it is still correct to describe the relationship of employer and employee as one of contract, governed by the laws of contract considered in Chapters 2, 3 and 4. What has changed dramatically in the past thirty years is the freedom of the parties to negotiate whatever terms they wish. This transformation is due in varying degrees to the vastly increased complexity of the business organisation, the influence of trade unions negotiating for their members en masse, and the increasing interference of successive governments in the fight against employee exploitation.[1]

11.3 Notwithstanding this rapid movement in "industrial law," as it is now more commonly termed, a thorough grasp of the law of employment can only be achieved by a preliminary examination of the contractual base upon which it rests.

THE RELATIONSHIP BETWEEN EMPLOYER AND EMPLOYEE

The Importance of Employee Status

11.4 Not everyone who performs a service for another is necessarily an employee; many such persons are independent con-

---

[1] Prompted in no small measure by the requirements of EC Regulations and Directives imposed upon the United Kingdom by its membership of the EC.

tractors, while others may be agents, partners or simply friends. It is vitally important, therefore, to understand the methods and tests utilised in order to identify employees, because of the legal implications of the employer/employee relationship. The following are among the most important of these implications:

11.5 1. An employer is "vicariously" liable for delicts and other wrongful actions performed on his behalf by an employee, but not normally for anyone else. Vicarious liability in a delictual context was considered in 10.23 – 10.24.

2. An employer owes a range of common law duties to an employee, and vice-versa. Different duties are owed in other relationships and the employer/employee duties are considered in 11.32 onwards.

3. Modern employment statutes (e.g. relating to redundancy payment and unfair dismissal) govern only employees, and no-one else who may be performing services for the "employer."

4. Employers are required to act as unpaid revenue harvesters for the government in matters such as PAYE tax and social security contributions. Different rules apply, for example, in the case of independent contractors.

11.6 Paradoxically, despite the importance of defining precisely who is, and who is not, an employee, the law provides no clear-cut rules, perhaps because of the varied nature of employment in modern industrial society. Several tests exist, of course, but none of them is exclusive, as will emerge below.

11.7 The following are the most common "non employees" to be mistaken for such:

✴ Independent Contractors

11.8 It is often said that the distinction between an employee and an independent contractor is that the former has a contract of service while the latter works under a contract for services. This distinction even found its way into the Employment Protection (Consolidation) Act of 1978 (EPCA), but it takes one no further when making fine distinctions in borderline cases. While it may be obvious that a chauffeur is an employee while a taxi driver is an independent contractor, there are problems surrounding those who sell specialist skills, such as doctors under the NHS and entertainers working on long-term television contracts. Over the years, the courts have developed the following tests in an attempt to distinguish between the two:

The Control Test

11.9   Under this test, a man is said to be the employee of another if that other can tell him not only what job to do, but also how to do it. Otherwise, he is an independent contractor. This was the earliest of the tests, and perhaps worked well in the simple nineteenth century world of domestic servants and shop assistants.[2] However, it is hardly a realistic test in modern industrial society, with its technical specialisms. An airline pilot can be told which route to fly, but no managing director of any airline would attempt to tell him *how* to fly. He is, however, almost always an employee.

The Integration Test / Organisation Test

11.10   Sometimes also referred to as the organisation test, this distinguishes between an employee and an independent contractor on the basis that an employee is an integral and permanent part of the organisation which employs him. There are surprisingly few cases which illustrate the test in practice, but the most frequently quoted is *Stevenson, Jordan and Harrison Ltd.* v. *MacDonald and Evans*,[3] in which it was held that part of a book written by an accountant employed by a firm of business managers as part of an assignment for which he received a salary was the "intellectual property" of the firm, since he was an "employee" of theirs on a full-time basis.

---

[2] Among the leading "control test" cases were *Stephen* v. *Thurso Police Commissioners* (1876) 3 R. 535, which held that a contract street cleaner was an employee of the Commissioners, and *Scottish Insurance Commissioner* v. *Church of Scotland*, 1914 S.C. 16, in which it was decided that an assistant church minister was not an employee of the church, since his divine orders came from higher up.
[3] [1952] 1 T.L.R. 101.

11.11   The integration tests breaks down, however, when it comes down to undoubtedly "integrated" members of an organisation such as partners and directors of companies, who are not employees in the eyes of the law, as will be seen below.

✳ *The Multiple Test*

11.12   This is not really a test at all, but simply recognition of the fact that in the modern industrial world, all relevant factors must be considered in each individual case, and there can be no general rule. It first saw the light of day in *Ready Mixed Concrete (South East) Ltd.* v. *Minister of Pensions and National Insurance*,[4] in which a fleet of lorry drivers were required to wear the company's uniforms, use their lorries only on company business, obey the instructions of a foreman, and sell the lorries back to the company at market prices. On the other hand, they paid their own tax and national insurance, maintained and fuelled the lorries at their own expense, and negotiated their own rate and times with management. They were also permitted to employ substitute drivers. It was held that they were self-employed.

11.13   As can be seen from this case, the important factors to take into account will be who makes the tax and social security contributions to the Revenue, whether or not the "employer" can hire and fire, the supply of tools and equipment, the organisation of the workplace and the bearing of the financial risks should the business fail.

11.14   Not even the labels put upon themselves by the parties will be conclusive. In *Young and Woods* v. *West*,[5] for example, even though W., a skilled sheet metal worker, paid his own tax and national insurance, never received paid holidays or sickness benefits, and described himself as self-employed in his contract with the company, it was held that he was an employee, and therefore entitled to claim for unfair dismissal.

11.15   The most recent prevailing test seems to be one of whether or not the so-called "employee" is in business on his own account,

---

[4] [1968] 1 Q.B. 497.
[5] [1980] I.R.L.R. 201.

as a separate commercial entity, or simply part of someone else's business. In *Lee* v. *Chung*,[6] for example, the Privy Council held that a skilled stonemason, paid by the job and working unsupervised, was nevertheless an employee, since he had no management control over the work done or the price charged to the client, and worked on sites selected for him, and with equipment supplied to him, by the employer.

Agents

11.16 In many cases, as explained in 7.2 above, an employee will be regarded in law as the agent of his employer. However, it by no means follows that an agent is an employee, and a clear distinction is made in law between an employee working for wages, and an agent working for a commission which he may or may not earn. See generally Chapter 7.

Partners

11.17 A partner is not regarded in law as an employee of his partnership; see 8.5 and the case of *Sharpe* v. *Carswell* referred to therein. So-called "salaried partners" of firms, however, retain their employee status unless and until they enjoy the profit-sharing status which distinguishes partners from employees. See generally Chapter 8.

Directors

11.18 A company director is regarded as an "officer" of that company, and in that capacity cannot be an employee of it. A director may, however, at one and the same time, be both an employee of the company (for which he is remunerated in the normal way) and a director (for which he may not necessarily be). The two identities will, however, be regarded as distinct and separate in law.

---

[6] [1990] I.R.L.R. 237 (PC).

FORMATION OF THE CONTRACT OF EMPLOYMENT

Introduction

11.19 All contracts of employment for a period of more than a year require to be in "probative" form.[7] Contracts for a shorter period may be made orally, but as will be seen below, after the first thirteen weeks the employee will still be entitled to have certain basic terms of his employment handed to him in written form.

11.20 So far as concerns the actual content of a contract of employment, the basic rule is still the common law principle applicable to all contracts, namely that the parties are free to negotiate their own terms. This apparent freedom is, however, considerably restricted in practice, not only by the fact that trade unions frequently negotiate the terms on behalf of thousands of their members at a time, but also by the intervention of statutory protections for employees which require, for example, that the employer grant minimum periods of notice, that he refrain from discriminating against employees on the grounds of sex or race, and that he pay wages in the form only of money. These statutory restrictions are considered in this and the following chapter.

11.21 In addition to those terms and conditions which the parties expressly negotiate, certain terms are implied by law, and these are considered in 11.27 below. A contract of employment is therefore a mixture of express and implied terms, some of which are non-negotiable and simply imposed upon the parties by the operation of statute.

Written Terms and Conditions

11.22 By virtue of section 1 of EPCA, most employees are entitled, after the first thirteen weeks of their employment, to a written statement from the employer which sets out certain essential details concerning his or her contract. Any changes in these terms and conditions must thereafter be communicated to the

---

[7] For which see 2.60 above. This means, in effect, that they must be in writing and signed by the parties.

employee within four weeks of the change taking effect. The main exception to the requirements of section 1 cover crown employees, employees located mainly outside the United Kingdom and employees who already have written contracts which contain all the provisions required under the Act to be communicated to the employee.

11.23 These are:
the identities of the parties, the date upon which the employment began, the date of expiry in the case of a fixed-term contract, whether or not any period of employment with a previous employer will count towards "continuous employment" with the current employer (for which see 11.82 below), and if so from what date, the employee's job title, the scale of remuneration or the method of calculating it and the intervals at which it is to be paid, hours of work (including any provisions as to "normal working hours"), any entitlement to holidays, holiday pay, sickness leave and sickness pay, any provisions relating to pension schemes, the length of notice which the employee is required to give and entitled to receive (for which see 11.75 below), rules of disciplinary procedure to which the employee will be subject, any grievance procedures which are observed in the workplace, and whether or not a "contracting out" certificate is in force for that employment.

11.24 If there are no provisions relating to holidays, holiday pay, sickness and sick pay, or pensions, then the section 1 statement must say so. When it is deemed more convenient, the employer may refer the employee to another, more comprehensive, document in which he will find further detail on a particular point (*e.g.* a pension scheme or a collective agreement with the union), and this document will thereby be deemed to be incorporated into the contract.

11.25 It is also important to keep in mind that the section 1 statement is not itself a contract, but is merely some evidence of what the contract contains. It can be overridden by other more cogent evidence (*e.g.* a letter of appointment which contains a different job title). When the employee signs for his copy of the statement, he is not thereby signing a contract, but merely acknowledging the fact that he has received it.

11.26 Reference was briefly made above to the possibility that many of the terms and conditions which find their way into a section 1 statement will have been negotiated between management and union in the form of a collective agreement. These are not legally binding in themselves unless and until each individual agreement contains a declaration to that effect, or unless and until they become incorporated into the contracts of employment of individual employees. As indicated above, their appearance in a section 1 statement is some evidence that they are part of such a contract, but not conclusive.

Implied Terms and Conditions

11.27 In addition to those terms and conditions which are expressly agreed between the parties, either orally or in writing, there are some which find their way into the relationship between the parties by implication. They may be implied by statute, by custom or by common law.

Implied by Statute

11.28 In some very important instances which are considered elsewhere (*e.g.* the Equal Pay Act, 1970, which ensures equal pay between the sexes for equal work performed), Parliament has forced employers to grant certain safeguards or benefits to employees by enacting statutory provisions under which these safeguards or benefits are contained within a clause which is "deemed" to be in the individual's contract of employment.

Implied by Custom

11.29 It is still theoretically possible (but in practice increasingly unlikely) for a term or condition to be incorporated into a contract of employment by means of the operation of a trade custom which is certain in its scope, reasonable and well recognised. It can disappear as the result of statutory change, or "negotiation out" between management and unions, as in the case some years ago in which refuse collectors traded in what they regarded as their traditional right to sell valuable items consigned to the refuse (so-called "totting rights").

✳ Implied by Common Law

11.30 By far the most common of the implied terms of a contract of employment are those which have been created by the courts, using their common law powers to fill gaps in the employment relationship left by the parties' failure to negotiate everything. They are in theory capable of being overridden by the parties' own clear written terms to the contrary, and some have been eroded by statute, as will be seen.

11.31 It is convenient to classify these into duties owed by the employee to the employer, and duties owed by the employer to the employee.

(A) *Duties Owed by the Employee to the Employer*

11.32 The following are the implied duties of an employee towards his employer:

11.33 1. *To act in person.* Contracts of employment are contracts involving "delectus personae,"[8] and an employee cannot therefore, without the agreement of the employer, substitute someone else in his place.

11.34 2. *Obedience.* An employee is bound by an implied duty to obey all lawful, reasonable and authorised instructions from his employer concerning his work, and he will be in breach of contract if he does not. Obviously each case will stand or fall on its individual facts, but in *Chakarion v. The Ottoman Bank,*[9] it was held not to be unreasonable for a bank employee to transfer to a foreign branch in which he might run the risk of being assassinated, while in the landmark case of *Secretary of State for Employment v. ASLEF*[10] it was held to be in breach of contract for an employee to "work to rule." As Lord Denning so aptly put it, "Wages are to be paid for services rendered, not for producing deliberate chaos."

---

[8] For which see 4.31 above.
[9] [1930] A.C. 277.
[10] [1972] 2 Q.B. 455.

11.35 3. *Good faith.* An employee must in all ways act in good faith towards his employer, and must not let his own interests conflict with his employer's. This covers the obvious requirement of acting honestly, and in *Sinclair* v. *Neighbour*[11] it was held that the manager of a betting shop, who contrary to a well-established company rule, borrowed £15 from the till, leaving an IOU, had been validly dismissed even though he replaced the money the next day, and there was no suggestion of direct dishonesty.

11.36 What an employee does after hours can be a breach of good faith if it has the effect of injuring his employer's interests. Thus, in *Hivac* v. *Park Royal Scientific Instruments*[12] it was held to be in breach of the implied duty of good faith for a group of skilled engineers to work for a trade rival in their spare time. The same rule was applied in *IDC* v. *Cooley*[13] in a case in which a former employee of a company which had failed to win a contract later successfully bid for it himself. The duty clearly lives on after the contract has ended, as in *Sanders* v. *Parry*,[14] in which a former employee was successfully sued for leaving his former employer and taking his secretary and his best client with him.

11.37 The disclosure of confidential information will normally fall foul of the requirement of good faith only if the information in question is the sort which may be restrained under contract.[15] Even then, the former employee may be able to defend his actions on some "public interest" ground, as in *Initial Services* v. *Putterill*,[16] in which the information in question concerned price-fixing in the laundry industry.

11.38 The old common law rule whereby the employer was automatically entitled to the fruits of any invention created during the course of the employment has now been diluted by the Patents Act 1977, which preserves this rule only when the invention in question

---

[11] [1966] 3 All E.R. 988.
[12] [1946] 1 Ch. 169.
[13] [1972] 2 All E.R. 162.
[14] [1967] 1 W.L.R. 753.
[15] For which see 3.67 above. See also *Harben Pumps (Scotland)* v. *Lafferty*, 1989 S.L.T. 752.
[16] [1968] 1 Q.B. 396.

was devised by the employee in the normal course of his duties in circumstances in which an invention was a reasonably likely outcome of the work being performed, or in which the employee had a special obligation to further his employer's interests. Even then, in some cases of "outstanding benefit" to the employer, the employee may be entitled to financial compensation for any patent taken out by the employer. In all other cases, the invention remains the employee's.

11.39 4. *Reasonable care.* The employee must carry out his duties to his employer with reasonable care, particularly since the employer may be vicariously liable to others if he does not (as explained elsewhere). If he does not, then in theory not only may he be dismissed but the employer may seek compensation from him and an indemnity against any damages the employer is obliged to pay to third parties. Thus, in *Janata Bank* v. *Ahmed*[17] a bank successfully sued a former employee for his negligence in granting overdraft facilities to customers of insufficient credit worthiness.

(B) *Duties Owed by the Employer to the Employee*

11.40 To a significant extent, those duties of an employer towards an employee which were formerly implied into the contract of employment by the common law have now been superseded by statutes such as the Health and Safety at Work Act 1974 and the Wages Act 1986. Nevertheless, it is important to understand the common law base from which those statutes proceed, particularly since they may leave gaps which the common law may still fill.

11.41 1. *Remuneration.* Although the amount to be paid to the employee is an item which must in most cases be specified either in the contract of employment or in the section 1 statement under EPCA, in the absence of any such stated amount the courts will imply a duty to pay a "quantum meruit" amount (*i.e.* a reasonable

---

[17] [1981] I.C.R. 791; see also *Lister* v. *Romford Ice and Cold Storage Co.* at 10.23 above.

amount in the circumstances, based on prevailing rates in equivalent jobs).

11.42 The employer is also regarded as having undertaken to make payment to any worker who makes himself available for work, even though no work may be available. This duty may, however, be circumvented when the employer gives prior notice of the unavailability of work in terms of "guarantee payment" provisions negotiated with workers, collective agreements, redundancy provisions, etc.

11.43 Under the Wages Act 1986, which replaced and modernised a series of former statutes known as the Truck Acts, restrictions are placed on the method of payment of wages, which must be in cash unless the worker makes written request for payment by cheque or other money order, paid directly into his account or otherwise. In addition, no deductions may be made "at source" from the net wage paid to the worker other than those authorised by statute (*e.g.* income tax) or by means of the original contract of employment or some written document subsequently signed by the employee.

11.44 This final provision was intended to prevent the recurrence of former exploitation of employees by virtue of excessive deductions for alleged transgressions such as lateness, breakages, negligence, etc. Only those previously agreed to in writing will be lawful, and in the case of workers in the retail trade, there are special rules governing deductions for stock or money shortages, the most important of which is that no fine or deduction may exceed ten per cent of the employee's gross wage on each pay day. In serious cases, of course, the employee may well be dismissed, for which see 11.93.

11.45 Other statutory provisions which have eroded the employer's freedom to exploit his workforce financially are the Equal Pay Act 1970 (for which see 12.3 below), and section 8 of EPCA, which entitles every employee, after thirteen weeks of employment, to insist on the provision of an itemised pay statement showing the gross wage, the amount of the fixed and variable deductions and the reasons therefor, and the corresponding net wage. As will be seen in Chapter 12, an employee also has preserved wage rights in respect of guarantee payments for workless days, time off for maternity and other natal reasons, and time off as a union official.

11.46　2. *Provision of work*. As a general rule, an employer is under no obligation to supply the employee with actual work to do, provided that he pays him his due wage in terms of "guarantee payment" under statute, the provisions of the contract of employment, etc. Only when the employee has a special interest in actually performing the work (*e.g.* publicity in the case of an entertainer) or is in fact paid by the amount of work produced (*e.g.* piece-rate or commission work) will the common law imply a duty to provide the actual work itself, as opposed to simply paying wages.

✶ **11.47　3. *References*.** No employer is legally obliged to provide an outgoing employee with a reference, unless he has been unwise enough to oblige himself contractually to do so. If he chooses to supply a reference, he is required to steer a narrow course between an action for the delict of fraud by any subsequent employer who acts upon a reference which is deliberately or recklessly favourable to the employee, and which causes loss to the new employer when it is proved to be false, and the delict of defamation or negligence which may be committed against the former employee if the information given is falsely derogatory.

11.48　Any employee who can show that in giving him a reference his employer blackened his character unjustly so far as concerned his suitability as an employee, may sue that employer for negligence (for which see 10.29) or for defamation of character.

11.49　However, so far as concerns defamation, the employer has two possible defences. The first ("veritas") arises when the employer can show that what he said or wrote was substantially true. Not every word has to be justified, but the material substance must be.

11.50　The second defence is more subtle, and is known as "qualified privilege." It covers the situation in which the employer cannot necessarily prove what he alleged, but can show that he acted in good faith in order to give the most honest assessment he could of the employee in question, in circumstances which were "privileged," in the sense that the employer owed a moral responsibility to anyone relying on the statement and that the person for whom it was intended had a legitimate interest in receiving as candid a report as possible. The privilege will be lost by the employer if it can be shown that he was motivated in any way by malice.

11.51 4. *Indemnity.* Any employee who is acting lawfully within the authorised instructions given to him by his employer is entitled to be indemnified by him against the consequences of his actions. When he acts negligently, however, in circumstances in which his employer becomes vicariously liable for his actions, he is not acting lawfully, and the employer may in theory seek an indemnity from him.[18]

11.52 5. *Integrity.* It is now common to hear lawyers referring to a duty of "respect" or "trust" which an employer owes to his employee. This amounts to another way of expressing the modern legal view that any employer who treats his employee shabbily, or in circumstances which amount to humiliation or demotion, may find that his employee is entitled to resign and claim "constructive dismissal" as if he or she had been unfairly dismissed. This is considered more fully in 11.124 below.

11.53 6. *Safety.* To a material extent, the common law duty of an employer to take reasonable care for the safety of his employees has been overtaken by the duties which he owes to them in terms of the Health and Safety at Work Act, considered in Chapter 12. However, this is only the case so far as concerns the *prevention* of injury; when it comes to compensation, it is the duty of care which the law imposes on the employer for the safety of his employees which forms the basis of the delictual action by the employee which follows his injury.[19] For that reason, the old common law rules remain important.

11.54 The duty is a *personal* one, in the sense that however many safety experts or consultants the employer may employ, his is the ultimate responsibility for the safety of the employee. Thus, in

[18] See 10.23 and 11.40.
[19] See generally Chapter 10.

Wilsons and Clyde Coal Co. Ltd. v. *English*,[20] the court rejected an argument raised in defence by the employers of an injured miner that they had, as required by law, delegated the technical management of the mine to a qualified manager. It was firmly pointed out that no employer could delegate his legal duty in this fashion.

11.55 The duty, as in all negligence matters, is to take "reasonable" care, with the result that no court will, with the benefit of hindsight, retrospectively impose upon any employer a duty to prevent an accident which would have required disproportionate effort on his part. For example, in *Latimer* v. *AEC Ltd.*,[21] employers had reacted to a flash flood in a factory which caused oil to run from drainage channels by spreading three tons of sawdust on the floor. Nevertheless, the pursuer slipped and was injured. It was held that the employers had done all that might reasonably have been required of them.

11.56 However, once it is shown that a particular employee was more vulnerable to injury, or its consequences, then the duty of care increases proportionately. Reference may be made to *Paris* v. *Stepney Borough Council* in 10.40 above for a perfect illustration of this principle in action.

11.57 The duty of safety extends to competent fellow employees, safe plant and materials and a safe system of work, each of which may be considered in turn.

11.58 Reference was made in 10.23 above to the fact that an employer is vicariously liable for the actions of his employees, including their negligent actions, and this is the case even if the person injured is a fellow employee. Put another way, the employer is legally liable to supply his employees with competent colleagues. This duty extends not only to ensuring that employees who are hired are sufficiently experienced, or subsequently trained, in their duties, but also that adequate steps are taken in response to shop-floor complaints about incompetence, attitude, etc.

---

[20] [1938] A.C. 57.
[21] [1953] 2 All E.R. 449.

11.59   Thus, in *Hudson* v. *Ridge Manufacturing Co. Ltd.*,[22] a workman who was injured when he was tripped by a practical joker colleague about whom unanswered and unremedied complaints had been sent to the management for the previous four years was awarded damages against his employers.

11.60   So far as concerns the provision of safe plant and materials, this duty extends to entrances and exits, working surfaces, ventilation, fire security, sanitary facilities, tools and machinery and just about anything else which employees come into contact with during their working lives. Maintenance and inspection are obviously important, as is training of machine operatives and the guarding of dangerous equipment.

11.61   Cases in this area can sometimes border on the bizarre, as in *Bradford* v. *Robinson Rentals*,[23] in which a radio engineer sent on a 400 mile round trip in an unheated van in the middle of winter successfully sued his employer for damages in respect of his resulting frostbite!

11.62   At common law, it was sufficient for an employer to show, in respect of defective equipment, that he had purchased it from a reputable source, and had no reasonable cause for being suspicious of it. This left the employee with the daunting task of identifying and suing the manufacturer, and so in the Employer's Liability (Defective Equipment) Act of 1969, Parliament passed the onus back on the employer, who must now compensate the employee in such circumstances, and seek recompense from the manufacturer.

11.63   The requirement for a "safe system" of work is intended to cover the situation in which an employee, although properly equipped and assisted by colleagues, is ordered to do something which is unnecessarily dangerous, such as the window cleaner in *General Cleaning Contractors Ltd.* v. *Christmas*,[24] who was required to stand on the outside of a window ledge, hanging onto the window frame, in order to clean a window. When the

---

[22] [1957] Q.B. 348.
[23] [1967] 1 W.L.R. 337.
[24] [1953] A.C. 180.

unstopped sash fell from the upper window and hit his fingers, he fell off and was injured. His damages claim was successful.

11.64 In many cases such as this, it is the predictable response of the sued employer to argue that the employee was disobeying orders, taking short cuts, ignoring the availability of safety equipment, or paid to take the risk. In short, the employer sets up *volenti non fit injuria* and/or contributory negligence as his defence. These concepts were considered in 10.72−10.76 above, and the principles explained therein apply equally to the employer/employee situation.

✳ TERMINATION OF THE CONTRACT OF EMPLOYMENT

11.65 A contract of employment may terminate in one of the following ways, each of which requires separate consideration.

1. Frustration.
2. Breach of contract.
3. Under notice.
4. Dismissal.

✳ Frustration

11.66 The concept of frustration of contract was considered in 4.53, and in theory a contract of employment is just as capable of being frustrated as any other contract.[25] However, in recent years, industrial tribunals considering unfair dismissal cases (about which see below) have become increasingly reluctant to allow employers to dismiss staff, for example, on the grounds of the latter's serious illness, and simply write it down to "frustration." Instead, employers are required to demonstrate why such dismissal should not be classed as "unfair."[26]

11.67 But one may readily imagine a contract of employment being frustrated by some other event which would have the same effect on any other type of contract. The accidental destruction of

---

[25] See in particular 4.62 and the case of *Condor* v. *The Barron Knights* considered therein.
[26] The "watershed" case was *Harman* v. *Flexible Lamps Ltd.* [1980] I.R.L.R. 418.

the workplace, or the rendering of the contract illegal by a change in legislation or the outbreak of war, are two possible examples.

✳ Breach of Contract

11.68   As indicated in 4.66 above, not all breaches of contract have the effect of bringing the contract to an end, and in most cases the injured party may choose to continue with the contract if he wishes. The same is true for contracts of employment, but the special relationship which exists between employer and employee renders it more likely that the aggrieved party will wish the contract to end.

11.69   When it is the employer who is in breach of contract to any material extent (*e.g.* by failing to pay wages or by wrongly demoting the employee), then the employee may regard this as a "constructive dismissal,"[27] terminate the contract and seek damages as if he had been unfairly dismissed. Alternatively, he may remain in the job but seek compensation, as in *Rigby* v. *Ferodo Ltd.*,[28] in which an employee successfully sued for arrears of underpayment of £30 per week over a five year period.

11.70   When the employee is the one in breach, the employer has to decide whether the offending action is sufficiently material to justify his dismissing the employee with or without notice (and run the gauntlet of a possible unfair dismissal claim), or whether he should make his discontent felt by an appropriate deduction in wages. Dismissal without notice and without payment in lieu of notice is known as "summary dismissal." A reduction in wages is sometimes perfectly permissible in law, as the employer proved in *Miles* v. *Wakefield Metropolitan District Council*,[29] by successfully deducting money from the salary of a Registrar of Births, Deaths and Marriages who refused to conduct marriage ceremonies on Saturday mornings during an industrial dispute.

11.71   In most cases of breach by an employee, however, dismissal is the response by the employer. Among the more obvious grounds

---

[27] For which see 11.24 below.
[28] [1987] I.R.L.R. 516.
[29] [1987] A.C. 539.

for this are dishonesty,[30] and refusal to obey lawful, reasonable and authorised instructions.[31] Other examples are *Sinclair v. Neighbour*[32] considered in 11.35, and *Alidair v. Taylor*[33] in which a pilot landed a chartered flight with such force that it took off again. It cannot be emphasised too strongly, however, that all dismissals are theoretically subject to the unfair dismissals procedure considered below, if the employee qualifies for the right to apply.

⅍ The Giving of Notice

11.72 The most normal way for a contract of employment to terminate is by one or other of the parties giving notice to the other. An alternative, theoretically available to either party, is for the notice to be replaced by wages in lieu of notice, so that the employee leaves on the day of the notice, receiving the money which he would have received had he worked for the applicable notice period. It must again be emphasised however that the mere fact that the employer gives the employee the correct amount of notice, or wages in lieu thereof, does not render the dismissal itself automatically fair, and that most employees may challenge the dismissal if they believe it to be unfair.

11.73 Almost all the rights which a modern employee possesses in respect of notice and dismissal are the creation of statutes passed in the last thirty years or so. At common law, the employee had the right only to a "reasonable" period of notice (which was determined on a case by case basis) or payment in lieu thereof, and no right to any reason for his dismissal. He also had no right of redress at all if he was given the correct amount of notice; the reason for the dismissal, however outrageous, was unchallengeable, assuming

---

[30] As in *Dalton v. Burtons Gold Medal Biscuits Ltd* [1974] I.R.L.R. 45, in which an employee with an exemplary record was dismissed for a first offence of falsifying a time clock card; this was held to be fair.

[31] See *Pepper v. Webb* [1969] 1 W.L.R. 514, in which a private gardener was validly dismissed for informing his employer that "I couldn't care less about your bloody greenhouse and your sodding garden."

[32] [1966] 3 All E.R. 988.

[33] [1976] I.R.L.R. 420. For a more recent and well-publicised example of a legitimate "summary" dismissal, see *Tehrani v. Argyle and Clyde Health Board* (No. 2), 1990 S.L.T. 118.

that the employer condescended to give one. If he did not receive the correct amount of notice (whatever the court might decide that should have been) he had a right to damages for "wrongful dismissal," the damages being largely restricted to the unpaid wage during the notice shortfall period.

11.74   As will emerge below, all this has changed dramatically, and in several ways. To take perhaps the simplest point first, section 15 of the Employment Act 1989 gives every employee with two years' service a right to written grounds of dismissal, which he may use in evidence at any later hearing.[34] Employees with less than two years' service have limited rights of redress, as will be seen below. For this reason, if for no other, employers are unlikely to dismiss employees without very good reasons (breach of contract, redundancy, etc.) and the giving of notice is the almost exclusive preserve of the employee, at least once the employee has acquired two years' service. For employees with less than two years service, or who choose not to challenge the dismissal, it is still, however, a lawful way for the employer to terminate the contract. Such employees retain the limited protection of a wrongful dismissal action.

11.75   Another statutory intervention, which preceded the unfair dismissal provisions and has in many ways been overtaken by it, was the introduction of minimum periods of notice. These are now to be found in section 49 of EPCA, and all employees with up to two years' service are entitled to a minimum of one week's notice for each year of completed service up to a maximum of 12 weeks' notice (for twelve years' service or more). The employee, on the other hand, need only give one week's notice, regardless of his length of service. The parties remain free to negotiate longer periods of notice (either way) as part of the terms of the contract, but these are the legal minima. The length of notice required from either side is one of the basic terms of the contract which must be communicated to the employee at the start of the employment, as explained in 11.23 above.

---

[34] Thus, in *Hotson* v. *Wisbech Conservative Club* [1984] I.C.R. 859 it was held that an employer who had given the written grounds for dismissal as inefficiency could not, at the subsequent tribunal hearing, claim that the real reason was dishonesty.

11.76 But by far the most important improvement in employee rights at the end of a contract of employment came with the introduction of the "unfair dismissal" laws, which may now be considered in their proper context.

Dismissal

11.77 Although the title of this subsection is "dismissal," it deals almost exclusively with the concept of "unfair dismissal," which runs right across the various forms of termination of a contract of employment considered above. As has been pointed out frequently in the previous passages, virtually any form of dismissal chosen by the employer, including the giving of the correct period of notice, is challengeable by any digruntled employee who feels that it was "unfair."

11.78 In order to facilitate the swift and inexpensive bringing of claims for unfair dismissal by aggrieved former employees who might be intimidated by the normal court process, Parliament introduced the industrial tribunal process, which now has exclusive jurisdiction in almost all disputes arising out of alleged violations of individual employee rights.

11.79 Each tribunal consists of a legally qualified chairman, a member drawn from a panel nominated by trade union bodies and other employee representative groups. Tribunal powers vary from issue to issue (*e.g.* they are different in unfair dismissal cases from maternity pay cases)[35] but most tribunal applications are preceded by pre-hearing assessments and reviews, plus offers of conciliation by officers of ACAS, in an effort to reach a settlement without the need for a tribunal to adjudicate on the matter.

11.80 The law on unfair dismissal has grown dauntingly complex in a relatively short period of time, and is best approached by dividing the subject up as follows.

---

[35] For which see 12.46 below.

Eligibility to Claim

11.81 Not all employees are protected by the unfair dismissal provisions. The following are the most important of those left out:

11.82 (a) *Employees with less than two years' "continuous service."* This normally means with the *same* employer, unless periods of service with a previous employer are specifically counted in at the start of the employment, which fact will normally have been communicated to the employee.[36] To qualify as a "week" of service, the employee must normally be under contract to work for at least 16 hours (eight hours after five years), but service will not be broken by weeks of sickness (maximum 26 weeks), temporary cessation of work, or pregnancy leave. Weeks on strike do not break continuity, but are not counted as "service" weeks (*e.g.* a worker who has been employed for 104 weeks, of which weeks 50 and 51 were strike weeks will be deemed to have 102 weeks of service to his credit.

11.83 An employee allegedly dismissed for "trade union reasons"[37] need not, however, prove two years of continuous service before he may claim.

11.84 (b) *Employees over the normal retirement age.* This means the normal retirement age for the job in question, or if none is fixed, 65 for employees of either sex. Once again, workers dismissed for "trade union reasons" are not barred by age from applying for unfair dismissal compensation.

11.85 (c) *Certain types of employment.* Parliament has chosen to deny protection from unfair dismissal to certain classes of employee. The main categories are "share" fishermen, police officers, servicemen, certain "security" employees (*e.g.* counter-intelligence officers) and those employed abroad. Also exempted are employees on a fixed-term contract of two years or more who have agreed in writing to forgo their rights in respect of unfair dismissal.

---

[36] See 11.23 above.
[37] See 11.114 below.

11.86 (d) *Employees who have not been "dismissed."* Since the law prohibits unfair "dismissal," it follows that someone who has not been dismissed, but who has resigned, should not be protected. The fine distinction between the two in cases of employees who were in effect harrassed into resigning caused endless problems for the tribunals until the concept of "constructive dismissal" was created under section 55 of EPCA. It is dealt with separately in 11.124 below, and "dismissal" for normal purposes may be taken to mean what it says, including both the termination of an open-ended contract or the failure to renew a fixed-term one.

11.87 (e) *Applicants who are out of time.* An application in respect of alleged unfair dismissal must normally be made within three months of the "effective date of termination." In order to extend this period, the employee must show that it was not "reasonably practicable" to present it earlier. This will normally be *e.g.* for reasons of ill-health, and negligence on the part of the employee's solicitor will not normally be accepted!

Grounds for Dismissal

11.88 Once the employee has shown that he qualifies as an applicant for an unfair dismissal claim, on the basis indicated above, it is for the employer first of all to specify the grounds for dismissal, and then to show not only that the reason for the dismissal was in itself a fair one, but also that the dismissal was accomplished in circumstances of procedural fairness. The procedural rules are considered below, and this section concentrates upon the grounds for dismissal.

11.89 Section 57(2) of EPCA contains a list of those grounds for dismissal which will normally be regarded as fair, although the final one in the list somewhat begs the question so far as the remainder are concerned. These grounds are (a) the capabilities or qualifications of the employee; (b) the conduct of the employee; (c) redundancy; (d) illegality under statute, and (e) some other substantial reason.

11.90 (a) *Capability or qualifications.* "Capability" includes availability as well as ability, and no employer is expected to tolerate, for more than a "reasonable" period, the incompetence or non-attendance of an employee. Serious cases of incompetence might well justify dismissal for a first offence (as in *Alidair* v. *Taylor* referred to in 11.71 above), but in the majority of cases the tribunal will look for evidence that the employee in question was offered appropriate support in the form of supervision, training, counselling, etc.

11.91 Persistent absence for no good reason will clearly give the employer a strong ground for dismissal, but where the cause is domestic or social, once again the employer is expected to offer some sort of reasonable supportive response, and the same is true of alcoholism or drug addiction unless the employee would be a continuing source of danger to others. Ill-health has already been referred to in 11.66, and in the end such cases are normally resolved by applying the "reasonableness" test to factors such as the nature of the illness, the expected period of absence, the long-term effects on the employee and the importance of his services to the employer. Long-term absence due to a prison sentence would also normally be classed as a fair reason for dismissal.

11.92 The "qualifications" part of the ground covers not only the employee who has falsely claimed qualifications which it transpires he does not possess,[38] but also the employee who fails to acquire a qualification after a reasonable period of time allowed to him by the employer, whether as part of an in-house training scheme, by day-release or whatever. Many readers of this book may fall within this category, and they would be well advised to study *Blackman* v. *The Post Office*,[39] in which it was held that an employee had been validly and fairly dismissed for failing an aptitude test three times, despite the fact that it was a requirement of the job, and notwithstanding the fact that he had, over a five year period, proved his capability to do the job.

11.93 (b) *Misconduct.* Perhaps the clearest ground for dismissing an employee will be his misconduct, whether it consists of stealing from the till or striking the foreman. Blatant cases such as

---

[38] *e.g.* the "bogus doctor" type of case, in which instant dismissal is almost always justified.
[39] [1974] I.C.R. 151.

this are rarely judged to be anything other than a fair dismissal,[40] but tribunals are frequently called upon to adjudicate in less clear-cut situations, such as personality clashes and poor attitude situations in which the employer should be prepared to show a reasonable record of warnings, counsellings, etc., for which see 11.106 below.

11.94 Two areas of misconduct in particular have led to the need for guidance etc. at the highest judicial level, and they are (1) suspected dishonesty and (2) misconduct outside work. So far as concerns the first, it was held by the Court of Appeal in *BHS* v. *Burchell*[41] that an employer may fairly dismiss an employee for suspected (as opposed to proven) theft provided that the belief is genuinely held, that there are reasonable grounds for that belief, and that the belief only followed a reasonable investigation. That investigation may have been conducted by the police, and it will make no difference to the fairness of the dismissal if the police prefer no charges, or the accused is subsequently acquitted.

11.95 Misconduct outside work may be regarded as a fair ground for dismissal when it in some way reflects upon the suitability of the employee for the post which he occupies. Thus, in *Richardson* v. *City of Bradford Metropolitan Council*,[42] theft by a public servant from his local rugby club was regarded as sufficient for a fair dismissal, while in *Bradshaw* v. *Portland Cement*[43] incest by a quarryman with his daughter was regarded as not sufficient.

11.96 (c) *Redundancy.* If an employee is genuinely redundant, then his departure will not constitute an unfair dismissal, and he will be entitled to redundancy compensation. However, in an endeavour to prevent employers from masking what is in effect an unfair dismissal in a cloak of redundancy, section 57(3) of EPCA

---

[40] See, *e.g.* the *Dalton* case in note 30 above, and *Pepper* v. *Webb* in note 31.
[41] [1978] I.R.L.R. 379. For a more recent example of the *Burchell* test in operation, see *Linfood Cash and Carry* v. *Thompson* [1989] I.R.L.R. 235.
[42] [1975] I.R.L.R. 179.
[43] [1972] I.R.L.R. 46. N.B. however that a different type of employment may make all the difference, as in *Gardiner* v. *Newport County Borough Council* [1974] I.R.L.R. 262, in which a college lecturer was fairly dismissed following a conviction for gross indecency.

allows a claim to be made for "unfair redundancy," when the selection criteria were unfair, when the employer has failed to observe proper warning and consultation procedures (for which see 12.88 below) or when the employer failed to make reasonable efforts to find alternative employment for the redundant person within the workforce.

11.97 A redundancy based on trade union reasons will be automatically unfair, as explained in 11.115 below.

11.98 (d) *Illegality under statute.* When the employer can show that to have continued to employ the worker in question would have contravened some statute or regulation, then if he can also show that it would not have been reasonable to re-employ that person in some other capacity, the dismissal will in most cases be classed as fair. The most commonly quoted example is that of the driver who has lost his driving licence, and another example might be that of a foreign worker whose work permit has expired.

11.99 (e) *Some other substantial reason.* This category was deliberately introduced in order to accommodate that residue of worthy cases in which the dismissal was clearly fair in the circumstances, but did not quite fit into the first four categories. Hardly surprisingly, it has become one of the most frequently used, and among the employees fairly dismissed under this heading were the accounts clerk in *Foot* v. *Eastern Counties Timber*,[44] whose husband opened up a rival business in the same locality (conflict of interests) and the manager in *Farr* v. *Hoveringham Gravels Ltd.*,[45] who refused to live a reasonable distance from work and thereby be available on call for emergencies.

11.100 Clearly, one cannot generalise in this area, and each case will stand or fall on its own facts.

Procedural Fairness

11.101 As indicated in 11.88 above, it is not sufficient for the employer simply to demonstrate that he dismissed the employee

---

[44] [1972] I.R.L.R. 83.
[45] [1972] I.R.L.R. 104.

for a fair reason; he must go on and show that the manner in which he went about the dismissal was also fair in itself, regardless of how justified the dismissal itself may have been. An employee may be dismissed for a fair reason but still be eligible for compensation payment if the method of dismissal was unfair.

11.102 The industrial tribunal, when assessing the dismissal procedures adopted, will first of all require proof that the "rules of natural justice" were followed. These require that the employee be made fully aware, well in advance, of the allegations made against him, that he be given a full and fair opportunity to put his side of the case, and that he be judged impartially. In any disciplinary hearing, the employee should be allowed to bring a friend or representative, either union or legal. If these basic rules of fairness are not adhered to, the employee is almost guaranteed an award from the industrial tribunal.

11.103 Assuming that the natural justice hurdle has been successfully negotiated, the employer must then go on to demonstrate that a reasonable set of disciplinary procedures were followed. The employer may of course establish his own if he wishes, provided that they later prove acceptable to the tribunal, but if he does, then any departure from these rules in an individual case will require to be carefully justified.

11.104 Alternatively, the employer may choose to adhere as closely as practicable, on a case by case basis, with the rules laid down for general guidance in the ACAS Code of Practice, which was released in its most recent form in 1977. It does not officially have the force of law, but a copy may generally be found at the tribunal chairman's elbow! The rules of natural justice referred to above are incorporated into the Code, and among the other important principles also found within the Code are the following:

11.105 1. Every case should be thoroughly investigated before disciplinary action is even commenced. No immediate superior should have an unfettered right to dismiss a subordinate without prior reference to a more senior manager.

11.106 2. Except in cases of "gross misconduct" (not defined, but normally taken to include dishonesty and wilful disobedience), no-one should be dismissed for a first offence, but should be issued with a warning, or counselled, as appropriate. The number of warnings will depend upon the severity of the fault.

11.107 3. Reasons in writing should follow any disciplinary decision, and a right of appeal to a higher, different, authority should be built into the system.

11.108 4. Special provisions should be maintained for nightshift workers, or workers in isolated locations.

11.109 5. No action other than an oral warning should be taken against a union official without reference to a senior union official.

11.110 6. The disciplinary code to be operated within the workplace should be publicised among all staff in clear simple terms as soon as they commence work. It should in fact be part of the written information supplied at the outset (see 11.23 above).

The Reasonableness Test

11.111 Frequent reference has been made above to the fact that both the reason for a dismissal, and the method by which it was carried out, must be "reasonable." This flexible concept will make allowances for the size and nature of the employer's business, and the circumstances of every individual case. In addition, the reasonableness is judged at the time of the dismissal, and not with the benefit of hindsight, although matters which come out subsequently may well affect the size of the award. Thus, in W. *Devis and Sons* v. *Atkins*,[46] an employee dismissed unfairly for unsatisfactory work had his award reduced to nil, but the finding of unfair dismissal was upheld, in the light of evidence which came to light after his departure to the effect that he had in fact been embezzling money from his employer.

11.112 Provided that the tribunal is satisfied that the employer acted reasonably, both in terms of the ground for dismissal and

---

[46] [1977] I.R.L.R. 314.

the method thereof, it must find for that employer, even though it does not agree with his decision.

Automatically Unfair Dismissal

11.113 In three special cases, a dismissal will be automatically unfair, and will result in an award, once the grounds in question have been proved. Not even an industrial tribunal can rule that a dismissal for one of these three reasons was fair, and they are as follows:

11.114 1. *Trade union membership or activities.* Section 58 of EPCA makes it automatically unfair for an employer to dismiss an employee simply because he is a union member, or proposes to become one, or because he proposes to take part in its activities at an "appropriate time" (*i.e.* normally outside working hours). It will also be automatically unfair to dismiss an employee for not being a union member if he chooses not to be, or refuses to join. The normal two-year service requirement does not apply in such a case, but an employee with less than two years service will bear the burden of proof on the question of the real reason for his dismissal. Any union planning pressure on an employer to sack such a worker can also be dragged into the proceedings as a third party by the employer.

11.115 2. *Redundancy.* Normally, redundancy is a fair ground for dismissal, as indicated in 11.96 above. However, if the employee can show that he was selected for redundancy because of a reason specified in section 58 above, then the case will, by virtue of section 59, become automatically one of unfair dismissal. The same will be true when there is no hidden union motive behind the redundancy, but the employee can show that his selection was in contravention of a customary arrangement or agreed procedure without any justified reason. Once again, the employee does not require two years continuous service to qualify under section 59.

11.116 3. *Pregnancy.* By virtue of section 60 of the Act, an employee will be regarded as having been unfairly dismissed if the principal reason for that dismissal was pregnancy-related. The two exceptions to this rule arise when, because of her condition she will become incapable of adequately performing her work, or she will be in breach of a statutory rule (see 12.44 below) and no suitable alternative is available. An employee requires two years continuous service in order to qualify under this head.

Remedies for Unfair Dismissal

11.117 Once a tribunal is satisfied that an employee has been unfairly dismissed, it may make one of the following orders.

11.118 1. *Reinstatement.* This order requires the employer to take the employee back into precisely the same job he had before, with no loss of seniority, benefits, etc. In the words of the Act, the result for the employee will be ". . . . . as if he had not been dismissed."

11.119 2. *Re-engagement.* Following such an order, the employer must place the employee back on the payroll in a position "comparable with that from which he was dismissed, or other suitable employment," with or without arrears of pay. This would be the appropriate order, for example, when the tribunal finds that because of declining faculties, the employee cannot really perform his old job, but that it was unfair to dismiss him in the manner in which the employer did.

11.120 3. *Non-compliance award.* If the employer refuses to honour either a reinstatement or a re-engagement order (and he cannot be forced to do so directly), then the employee may return to the tribunal, and in addition to substituting a "compensation order" (see below) the tribunal will also then make an additional award of between 13 and 26 weeks pay (26–52 weeks pay when the original ground for dismissal was an act of sexual or racial discrimination).

11.121 4. *Compensation order.* When a reinstatement or re-engagement award is not appropriate (*e.g.* when the employee does not want it) or it has been ignored by the employer, the tribunal may make a compensation award. This consists initially of a basic award based on a normal week's pay (half a week's pay for every year of completed service during which the employee was aged 21 or under, one week's pay for every year of service aged 22 to 40, and one and a half weeks' pay for every year of service over 41).

Dismissal 239

Once the employee has reached 64, or entered his final year before retirement in accordance with the firm's rules, his award is reduced by one-twelfth for every month of continued service, scaling down to zero on the day of his retirement. There are limits (which are raised upwards regularly) on the maximum weekly earnings which can be used in the calculation.

11.122 Secondly, the tribunal may make an *additional* compensatory award to reflect the true loss to the employee in terms of lost opportunity and the manner of the dismissal. Once again, a statutory maximum applies at any given time, and this element of the award may be reduced by any contributory fault on the part of the employee.

11.123 A special award may be made when the dismissal falls within section 58 or section 59 of EPCA (see 11.114 and 11.115 above).

Constructive Dismissal

11.124 As indicated in 11.86 above, there are situations in which an employee can be the one who brings the employment contract to an end by resigning but still qualify for an unfair dismissal award because he has in effect been forced out by behaviour on the part of the employer which constitutes "constructive dismissal."

11.125 Before this will be justified, the employer must have committed ". . . conduct which is a significant breach going to the root of the contract of employment"[47] and obvious examples would be a failure to pay wages, sexual abuse of an employee or, as in *B.A.C.* v. *Austin*[48] a failure to provide safety goggles where to do so was reasonable and the staff had been demanding them for some considerable time.

11.126 Any behaviour by the employer which degrades the employee or effectively demotes him is potentially a constructive dismissal, but much will depend upon the circumstances. Thus,

---

[47] Lord Denning in *Western Excavating Ltd.* v. *Sharp* [1978] I.R.L.R. 27.
[48] [1978] I.R.L.R. 332.

whereas in *Isle of Wight Tourist Board* v. *Coombes*[49] it was held
to be constructive dismissal for a director of the Board to say of
his personal secretary that "she is an intolerant bitch on a Monday
morning," it is doubtful whether the same sensitivity would be held
to exist between a rigger and a roustabout on an oilrig.

11.127   Difficult questions arise when the employer is obliged to
restructure the organisation, and offers the employee continued
employment on different terms. This is frequently a technical
redundancy (for which see 12.71 below) and it may well be a
dismissal, but whether or not it is unfair, and therefore entitles
the employee to claim for constructive dismissal, is another matter
altogether. Most of the case law is in favour of the employer in
such cases, unless the new terms and conditions constitute a studied
insult.

[49] [1976] I.R.L.R. 413.

12. EMPLOYMENT STATUTES

12.1 As indicated in 11.1 above, the past 30 years has witnessed a vast improvement in the rights of employees, due almost entirely to a series of statutes designed to supply each individual employee with a basic but comprehensive "floor of rights." These form no cohesive pattern, since they are largely the result of a series of different initatives, but they may be grouped for consideration under broad headings which reflect their basic purpose.

EQUALITY AT WORK

12.2 The statutory law relating to what might loosely be described as equality at work falls into the following categories.
1. Equal pay.
2. Sex discrimination.
3. Racial discrimination.
4. Maternity provisions.
5. Rehabilitation of offenders.
6. Disability.
7. Trade Union membership.

Equal Pay

Introduction

12.3 The current state of United Kingdom law on equal pay for women is almost entirely the result of the pressure placed upon successive governments to implement Article 119 of the Treaty of Rome, which lays down a comprehensive requirement that men and women receive equal "pay" (including fringe and other benefits) for equal work. This led to the Equal Pay Act of 1970 (effective from 1975) which was partially successful, and the Equal Pay (Amendment) Regulations of 1983, which introduced the concept of "work of equal value" in an endeavour to meet the criticisms of the shortfalls in the 1970 Act.[1]

12.4 Any person (normally a female) who believes that she is being under-rewarded for her work by comparison with a male performing similar work may challenge the situation not only in the United Kingdom industrial tribunals (considered below) but also in the European Court of Justice, whose decisions are binding in United Kingdom law. Such challenges by workers have borne fruit in cases such as *McCarthy's Ltd* v. *Smith*,[2] which allowed a female applicant to seek parity of pay with her male predecessor in the job, *Garland* v. *British Rail Engineering*,[3] in which female retirees of British Rail won the right to concessionary travel for dependents, and *Barber* v. *Guardian Royal Exchange*,[4] in which an employer was forced to equalise methods of redundancy compensation among male and female former employees.

Definition of Equal Pay

12.5 The 1970 Act and the 1983 Regulations, between them, describe three situations in which employees should receive equal pay regardless of sex. Put another way, a woman should be receiving exactly the same rewards as a man who performs "like work," "work rated as equivalent," or "work of equal value." Each of these concepts may now be considered in turn, and where the applicant's case is made out, the effect as if the contract of employment contained a clause to the effect that equal pay would be given.[5]

1. Like Work

12.6 This may be defined as the same work, or work which is broadly similar. The applicant (assuming her to be female) will

---

[1] Which came to a head in *Commission of European Communities* v. *United Kingdom* [1982] I.R.L.R. 333, a direct challenge from the EC for the United Kingdom to enact the appropriate legislation.
[2] [1980] C.M.L.R. 205.
[3] [1982] E.C.R. 359.
[4] [1990] I.R.L.R. 240.
[5] *i.e.* it is one of the implied terms referred to in 11.28 above.

identify a male employee in the workforce whose work she regards as "like" hers, and will then use him as the "comparator" in her claim. This comparator must be on the staff of the same employer as the applicant, or an "associated" employer.

12.7 Using this process, 16 female canteen staff in *Capper Pass* v. *Allan*,[6] sought parity with a male colleague on a different grading, but failed because the staff on the higher grading were required to work unsupervised and undertake responsibility for cash and stock control. More successful was the female applicant from the same firm in *Capper Pass* v. *Lawton*,[7] a female cook working in the director's dining room preparing between 10 and 20 lunches per day who obtained parity with two male assistant chefs preparing many more meals in the main works canteen.

12.8 An employer will frequently seek to justify wage differentials on the grounds that the (male) comparator has additional responsibilities to carry. When further analysed, these can turn out to be spurious, as in *Shields* v. *Coomes*,[8] in which an employer sought to justify paying male betting shop staff more than females by insisting that the male employees were required to deal with difficult, and sometimes violent, customers. This defence failed when it emerged that male employees had never been called upon to carry out these functions, which was perhaps as well as they had received no appropriate training.

12.9 Similarly, in *National Coal Board* v. *Sherwin and Spruce*,[9] the tribunal disregarded claims by an employer that a higher hourly rate was justified on the grounds of shift work, pointing out that a flat shift allowance would compensate for that, and refused to entertain the argument that no man could be recruited to work for the money which the women were being paid!

[6] [1980] I.C.R. 194.
[7] [1976] I.R.L.R. 366.
[8] [1978] I.R.L.R. 263.
[9] [1978] I.R.L.R. 122.

2. Work Rated as Equivalent

12.10 This rather difficult concept proceeds on the assumption that the employer has discovered, following a job evaluation study, that the job performed by a female applicant has been "rated as equivalent" to that of a male comparator whose actual job is totally different from the female's. One may, for example, be comparing the "value" of the factory manager's secretary with that of the foreman in the dispatch warehouse, making use of factors such as the qualifications and training required, and the requirement to work unsupervised. The main failing in this system was that under this heading, no employer could be forced to conduct such a job evaluation exercise, hence the challenge to the United Kingdom by the EC in the cases referred to in 12.4 above. This in turn resulted in the 1983 Regulations, which introduced the third of the three tests currently in use.

3. Work of Equal Value

12.11 The concept of "work of equal value" is essentially the same as that of "work rated as equivalent," with the important additional factor that an industrial tribunal can order the employer to submit to the appointment of an independent expert to carry out the study, should preliminary attempts at conciliation fail. An early success under this heading was a female cook in the works canteen in *Hayward* v. *Cammell Laird Ship Builders Limited*,[10] who obtained parity with a joiner, a painter and an insulation engineer (all male) in the same firm.

Procedures and Defences

12.12 All applicants for equal pay bring their applications before an industrial tribunal, either whilst in employment or within six months of leaving. Two years' arrears of benefit may be awarded by the tribunal. Once the basic claim is made out under one of the previously considered headings, the only remaining defence open to the employer to justify the rewards differential is for him to

---

[10] [1988] 2 All E.R. 257.

show that it is justified on the grounds of some "material" factor which is other than sexual.

12.13 This may well be related to personal differences in the quality of the applicant and the comparator (for example, graduate/ non-graduate), or in the nature of the duties undertaken (*e.g.* duty in London, with its increased living expenses). Normally, "market forces" will not be accepted if this is another way of justifying the employment of men at higher rates because they will not work for less, whereas women will. However, economic realism won the day in *Rainey* v. *Greater Glasgow Health Board Eastern District*,[11] in which the Board justified a higher payment rate to male prosthetists in order to attract them from private practice than that paid to a female prosthetist who had no private practice experience, and who was recruited directly into a newly created Board prosthesis unit.

Sex Discrimination

Introduction

12.14 The Sex Discrimination Act of 1975 makes it unlawful for an employer to "discriminate against" an employee on the grounds of his or her sex. "Discrimination" is defined broadly as to consist of treating an employee in any way differently from persons of the opposite sex, and the provisions cover all aspects of employment, from advertising for staff, through recruitment, promotion, training and dismissal. Since 1986, it has also covered retirement provisions when they affect promotion, transfer, training, demotion or dismissal. Equal terms of pay and remuneration are of course covered by the 1970 Act considered above. It is, as can be seen, just as unlawful to hold a person back from promotion on the grounds of his or her sex as it is to refuse to employ that person in the first place.

12.15 It is unlawful to discriminate against someone on the ground that he or she is married, but not because the person is single. For example, an employer can still lawfully advertise for a married couple for a residential post, thereby discriminating against

---

[11] [1987] I.R.L.R. 26.

single people. What he may not do is advertise for a single person.

12.16 Discrimination, in terms of sections 1 and 4 of the 1975 Act, can take one of three forms, namely direct, indirect and victimisation. No minimum length of service is required in order to claim under any of these three heads.

Direct Discrimination (Section 1)

12.17 Direct discrimination consists of an overt and blatant act of discrimination, and motive is irrelevant, as was illustrated in *Greig v. Community Industry*,[12] in which it was held to be unlawful discrimination for an employer to refuse to allow a female employee to join an all-male team working outside, out of concern for her moral welfare. Another misconception was exploded in *Wylie v. Dee and Company (Menswear) Ltd.*,[13] in which a tribunal ruled against a Glasgow menswear store which refused a job to a female applicant because the job might involve taking customers inside leg measurements. The tribunal patiently pointed out that other (male) employees could perform this function.

12.18 Sexist assumptions were also to blame in *Hurley v. Mustoe*,[14] which also provides a good illustration of the application of the law against "marriage" discrimination. Mrs. H. had been working satisfactorily, "on trial" as a waitress in a bistro when the owner discovered that she had four children. She was paid off because of a management policy not to employ women with children because they were unreliable. This was direct discrimination against women (since the owner could not prove that he would have reacted the same way to a man with children) and, as will be seen below, indirect discrimination against a married person.

12.19 A final example was *Coleman v. Skyrail Oceanic Ltd.*,[15] in which two rival travel agencies discovered that they each had one

---

[12] [1979] I.R.L.R. 158.
[13] [1978] I.R.L.R. 103.
[14] [1981] I.R.L.R. 208. *N.B.* that recent decisions in the European court also make it unlawful to discriminate against a pregnant employee. This is binding on United Kingdom tribunals.
[15] [1981] I.R.L.R. 398.

of two married persons working for them. While theoretically such a situation might create a lawful ground for dismissal (for reasons explained in 11.99 above), the dismissal of the wife was held to be unlawfully discriminatory when it was proved that the reason for choosing her was that the husband had been presumed to be the "bread-winner" of the family.

Indirect Discrimination (Section 1)

12.20 "Indirect" discrimination consists of imposing conditions or requirements on employees or potential employees which persons of one sex would find it disproportionately difficult to comply with. A good example of the process was found in the Civil Service in the early years of the legislation, and in *Price* v. *Civil Service Commission*,[16] Mrs. Price successfully challenged, as indirectly discriminatory of women, the Civil Service requirement that applicants for executive status be aged 28 or under. The reason why it was discriminatory, of course, was because many women in that age category (*i.e.* 18–28) take time out to raise young families.

12.21 A slightly more subtle, but equally unlawful, practice was ruled against in *Clarke and Powell* v. *Eley (IMI) Kynoch Ltd.*,[17] in which an employer seeking candidates for redundancy chose to dismiss all part-timers first. All the part-time employees were female, whereas the full time employees made redundant (selected on a last-in-first-out basis) were split roughly 55 per cent women to 45 per cent men. Clearly, women had been discriminated against by virtue of the requirement that employees be full-time in order to be selected on a last-in-first-out basis.

12.22 Indirect discrimination was also encountered in *Hurley* v. *Mustoe*, referred to in 12.18 above, because a smaller proportion of married people of either sex could comply with the employer's requirement that they be childless. This clearly constituted indirect discrimination against married persons.

12.23 A fairly recent extension of the law in this area has found some employers taken to task for not allowing post-natal

---

[16] [1977] I.R.L.R. 291.
[17] [1982] I.R.L.R. 131.

employees to return to work on a part-time basis when there is no obvious justification for requiring full-time staff in the post. This is particularly crucial when "job-share" could be an alternative, but employers may escape this requirement when they can show that administrative efficiency requires a five-day week.[18]

Victimisation (Section 4)

12.24 Discrimination by victimisation arises when an employee has exercised his or her right to bring proceedings under the 1975 Act or the Equal Pay Act of 1970, or given evidence in such proceedings, or even made allegations of unlawful behaviour under either Act, and has then been treated "less favourably" by the employer. It will even arise if the employee in question has threatened such proceedings, but in all these situations, the employee will lose his or her protection from discrimination if it is shown that he or she instigated the original proceedings etc. in bad faith.

Exceptions

12.25 There are certain situations in which the provisions of the 1975 Act will not apply. The main ones involve employment in the police or prison services, as ministers of religion, or overseas. It is also not deemed discriminatory of men for women to be afforded special terms and conditions related to childbirth and pregnancy generally.

Procedures and Defences

12.26 1. *Tribunal Applications (Section 65).* Employees with a grievance under the 1975 Act may apply to an industrial tribunal (for which see 11.78 above), which may make an order declaring what the rights of the parties are, and/or order compensation equivalent to the "compensatory award" in unfair dismissal cases (for which see 11.122 above). Another possible course by the tribunal may be a recommendation that the employer take a certain

---

[18] As in the case of the health visitor in *Greater Glasgow Health Board* v. *Carey* [1987] I.R.L.R. 484.

course in order to redress the grievance (*e.g.* promote or relocate the employee); if the employer fails or refuses, an award may be made as above. Employees with two years' service whose discrimination claim is dismissal-based will normally, of course, apply directly for unfair dismissal compensation as explained in Chapter 11.

12.27 2. *Genuine Occupational Qualification Defence (Section 7).* The only defence available to an employer who is judged to have discriminated against an employee on sexual grounds is to demonstrate that being of a particular sex was a "genuine occupational qualification" of the job in question. These are described in the legislation as being related to physiology (*i.e.* appearance, not strength or stamina), decency or privacy, single-sex living accommodation when living on site is part of the job, work in single sex prisons, hospitals or other institutions, social work or guidance posts, compliance with foreign laws or customs in overseas postings and "married couple" posts. To take a few examples, one could insist on a male actor to play the role of Rambo, a female prison officer in Cornton Vale Prison and a male roustabout on an oil rig.

12.28 The fact that not all genuine occupational qualification claims are successful is amply demonstrated by *Wylie* v. *Dee and Company (Menswear) Ltd.* in 12.17 above.[19]

12.29 3. *Equal Opportunities Commission.* The Equal Opportunities Commission presides over the 1975 legislation as a whole, and concentrates on formulating general guidance policies. It is also given the exclusive power to issue non-discrimination notices to employers in regard to discriminatory practices which it wishes to see discontinued. This is particularly useful when a blatant abuse is going unchecked because no "victim" can, or will, come forward; in such cases, an employer who ignores the notice may be interdicted in the sheriff court. The Equal Opportunities Commission may also issue codes of practice.

---

[19] See also *Etam plc* v. *Rowan* [1978] I.R.L.R. 150, in which a male evened the score by successfully claiming a job in a ladies' fashion shop!

Positive Discrimination (Section 48)

12.30 This virtual contradiction in terms refers to the lawful process whereby an employer takes steps to correct a previous sexual inequality in his workforce by positively promoting the interests of the erstwhile victims. Put more simply, he may for example select only females for a particular training course in order to even up the male/female ratio of those on his staff with such training. This is lawful when, and only when, it is limited to the field of training, and relates to an imbalance such that a particular type of work has been done mainly or exclusively by persons of a particular sex during the past 12 months. The employer may not, however, push the principle beyond the field of training (*e.g.* in his appointments policy, which must remain entirely non-sexual in its basis).

Racial Discrimination

Introduction

12.31 The Race Relations Act of 1976 makes it unlawful for any employer to discriminate on "racial" grounds, which are defined as the grounds of colour, race, nationality or ethnic or national origins. The term "ethnic" was extended to a religious group, the Sikhs, in *Mandla* v. *Dowell Lee*,[20] while in *Commissioner for Racial Equality* v. *Dutton*,[21] the term "racial" was allowed to incorporate Romany gypsies.

12.32 Discrimination for racial purposes is defined in precisely the same terms as in the Sex Discrimination Act (see 12.14 above), and takes the same three forms, considered below, of direct, indirect and victimisation. The area of work covered (recruitment, training, etc.) is also precisely the same, for the very good reason that the 1976 Act was modelled on the 1975 Act.

Direct Discrimination (section 1)

12.33 As with sexual discrimination, direct racial discrimination consists of blatantly treating someone less favourably on racial

---

[20] [1983] I.R.L.R. 209.
[21] [1989] 1 All E.R. 306.

grounds. A good early example was *Race Relations Board* v. *Mecca*,[22] in which a woman telephoning to enquire about an advertised post asked the manager if it would make any difference that she was black. The manager replied in the affirmative and hung up, and a tribunal later deemed this to be discrimination.

12.34 Direct discrimination can sometimes arise in an indirect way, as in *Showboard Entertainment Centre* v. *Owens*,[23] in which the white manager of an amusement arcade was sacked for refusing to operate a colour bar. This was held by the tribunal to be discrimination.

Indirect Discrimination (section 1)

12.35 As with sexual discrimination, indirect racial discrimination consists of imposing upon a group of workers (allegedly without discrimination) a condition which a particular racial group might find impossible or difficult to comply with by comparison with the rest. An obvious example is the wearing of turbans by Sikhs in situations in which such headgear is inconvenient (*e.g.* under police hats), but in *Panesar* v. *Nestle Co. Ltd.*,[24] it was held that a rule against long hair which was disproportionately difficult for Sikhs to comply with was justified on grounds of hygiene.

Victimisation (section 2)

12.36 In just the same way that the sexual discrimination laws forbid any subsequent victimisation of anyone who has played a part in the enforcement of those laws, the 1976 Act contains provisions against victimisation on racial grounds, and for exactly the same reasons (see 12.24 above).

---

[22] [1976] I.R.L.R. 15.
[23] [1984] I.R.L.R. 7; see also *Zarczynska* v. *Levy* [1979] I.C.R. 184; [1978] I.R.L.R. 532 for a similar ruling.
[24] [1980] I.R.L.R. 64; for a similar ruling in a case involving the wearing of a beard in an Edinburgh sweet factory, see *Singh* v. *Rowntree Mackintosh Ltd.* [1979] I.C.R. 554.

Exceptions

12.37 The 1976 Act provisions do not apply at all in the case of employment in a private home[25] or in the case of employment overseas. There are also permissible nationality requirements imposed in certain areas of the Civil Service.

12.38 As with sexual discrimination, exceptions are also permitted where being of a particular race, colour, etc. is a "genuine occupational qualification" for a particular job. Section 5 of the 1976 Act specifies authenticity in the theatre or for modelling, authenticity in an ethnic restaurant and posts concerned with welfare in racial or ethnic groups (*e.g.* immigrant case workers or community liaison officers).

Procedures

1. *Tribunal Applications*

12.39 Employees with a grievance concerning alleged racial discrimination in employment may apply to an industrial tribunal just as if they had been the victims of sexual discrimination, and precisely the same procedures and remedies apply (for which see 12.26 above). Once again, an employee with two years' service would normally base his claim on an unfair dismissal on racial grounds.

2. *Commission for Racial Equality*

12.40 In the same way that the sex discrimination legislation is presided over by the Equal Opportunities Commission, the Commission for Racial Equality supervises the operation of the laws against racial discrimination, with broadly similar powers in respect of non-discrimination notices and interdict applications as the Equal Opportunities Commission (see 12.29 above).

---

[25] Thus absolving the hopeful employer who advertised for a "genuine Scotswoman" to cook his porridge!

Positive Discrimination

12.41   Section 38 of the 1976 Act contains provisions identical to those of section 48 of the 1975 Act with respect to positive discrimination to redress a particular imbalance previously evident in the racial distribution of an employer's workforce; see 12.30 above.

Maternity Provisions

Introduction

12.42   In an endeavour to prevent what might otherwise have been a particularly insidious form of indirect discrimination against women in the workforce,[26] Parliament took the opportunity of the Employment Protection (Consolidation) Act 1978 to establish basic rights for female workers who wish to preserve their careers while pausing (briefly) in order to have children. Some had been in existence prior to 1975 and some were amended in 1980 and 1986. The four basic rights thus implemented are as follows:

1. The right to time off for ante-natal care.
2. The right not to be unfairly dismissed for pregnancy.
3. The right to maternity pay.
4. The right to return to work after pregnancy leave.

Time Off for Ante-natal Care

12.43   A pregnant woman is entitled to "reasonable" time off work, *with* pay, in order to seek the normal ante-natal care to which she is entitled. The employer may insist on a medical certificate and an appointment card, but if such time off with the usual rate of pay is unreasonably refused, the employee has three months in which to complain to an industrial tribunal, regardless of her length of service.

---

[26] Since employers could always claim that they would be prepared to treat pregnant men in exactly the same way!

Protection from Pregnancy-related Unfair Dismissal

12.44 As indicated in 11.116, it is automatically an unfair dismissal if an employee is sacked simply because she is pregnant, unless the employer can show that she has become incapable of performing the work she was employed to perform,[27] or that her continued employment in that condition would be unlawful. Even then, other "suitable" work must be offered to her if it is available. However the employee must have two years' continuous employment before she may claim under this head.

12.45 An interesting interpretation of the phrase "reason connected with pregnancy" arose in *George* v. *Beecham Group*,[28] in which an employee with a poor attendance record on medical grounds was placed on what amounted to six months' probation for attendance. During that period she was off work with a miscarriage, and her resulting dismissal was deemed to be unfair.

Right to Maternity Pay

12.46 Since 1975 (and now under Regulations issued in 1986), a woman who becomes pregnant while working for an employer by whom she has been employed for at least six months is entitled to what is called "statutory maternity pay" which is in effect paid time off to have her child. She may claim this right at any time from the fifteenth week prior to the expected date of the birth (referred to as the "qualifying week") and payment is for a period of 18 weeks, starting no later than six weeks before the expected birth (*N.B.* it can, of course, start earlier). In order to qualify, the employee must of course actually take the time off, and the employer may lawfully demand a certificate of the expected date of birth. The employee is also required to give three weeks' notice of her intending departure, when possible.

12.47 The rate of pay depends upon length of service. For employees with at least two years' "continuous service" by the end of the qualifying week (*i.e.* a minimum of two years' service on a

---

[27] As in *Brear* v. *Wright Hudson* [1977] I.R.L.R. 287, the lifting of heavy boxes.
[28] [1977] I.R.L.R. 43. But see *Grimsby Carpet Co.* v. *Bedford* [1987] I.R.L.R. 438.

minimum of 16 hours per week, or eight–16 hours per week after five years), the payment is 90 per cent of normal weekly earnings for six weeks, followed by 12 weeks at the "lower rate," which is a fixed rate according to Regulations issued from time to time.[29] Employees with between six months and two years' service receive the lower rate for the entire 18 weeks.

12.48 Although the employer makes the payment initially, he may reimburse himself via the normal social security mechanism (*i.e.* by deductions from national insurance contributions payable in respect of other staff).

Return to Work after Confinement

12.49 An employee who has two years' continuous service by the eleventh week prior to confinement, and who remains until that date (unless dismissed for reasons of pregnancy) is entitled to her original job back, without loss of seniority, accrued rights, etc., when she has had her child. In order to stake her claim, she must give the employer written notice at least three weeks in advance of her intention to take time off to have her child, of the date of the expected confinement and of her intention to return afterwards.

12.50 She may then exercise this right within 29 weeks of having her child, after giving her employer 21 days' notice of her intended return date. The employer may postpone this return by a further four weeks in order to make the necessary arrangements, and the employee herself may extend the period to 33 weeks with a suitable medical certificate.

12.51 The employer himself may, no earlier than 49 days after the expected date of confinement, send a written request for the employee to confirm that she will still be returning. She is entitled in that request to be advised by the employer that she must confirm in writing that she is returning, or may forfeit her right to do so.

12.52 Failure to honour a woman's right to reinstatement after confinement is classed as an unfair dismissal. However, under the

---

[29] It is in fact the rate applicable to statutory sick pay.

Employment Act of 1980, an employer with five or fewer
employees may escape the need to reinstate if he can show that it is
not "reasonably practicable" for him to do so. Also, any employer,
regardless of the size of the workforce, may avoid giving the
employee precisely her original job back if he can show that it is
not "reasonably practicable" to do so, and he has offered her an
alternative job whose terms and conditions are "not substantially
less favourable" than her old job.

Rehabilitation of Offenders

12.53 The Rehabilitation of Offenders Act of 1974 was passed
in order, where appropriate, to allow someone who has been con-
victed of criminal behaviour in the past to "wipe the slate clean"
after so many years without re-offending. After such period as is
laid down under the Act,[30] the conviction is "spent" and may never
be used against the former offender for most purposes, and the
offender need not disclose it in most job applications.[31] It will be
automatically an unfair dismissal to dismiss someone already in
employment because the spent conviction becomes known, but
curiously there is no remedy under the Act for anyone whose conviction becomes known prior to interview, and who is not
employed as a result.

Employment of Disabled Persons

12.54 The Disabled Persons (Employment) Acts of 1944 and
1958, designed to enhance the employment prospects of registered
disabled persons, require all employers with a workforce of more
than 20 employees to give priority in certain designated jobs (*e.g.*
lift attendants) to such persons, and to honour a "quota" of 3 per
cent disabled employees. The only sanction is prosecution; there is
no remedy for an applicant discriminated against because of his
disability, and the legislation is long overdue for replacement by
something more effective.

---

[30] Which varies according to the sentence imposed, being seven years for all offences
resulting in not more than six months' imprisonment. No sentence of more than
30 months ever becomes "spent."
[31] *N.B.* however that it must be disclosed by intending solicitors, doctors, dentists,
accountants, nurses, opticians, pharmacists and teachers.

Trade Union Membership

12.55   The main purpose of the Employment Act of 1990, which
is the latest of a series of Acts relating to trade union membership
rights and which began in 1971, is to ensure that an employee is
not penalised if he wishes to be a trade union member or partake
in union activities; but at the same time the employee is not forced
to do either simply in order to acquire or retain his job in a "closed
shop" situation. Section 1 of the 1990 Act allows an individual to
complain to an industrial tribunal if he is refused employment on
either ground (*i.e.* that he is or is not a trade union member). The
question of unfair dismissal on the same grounds was considered
in 11.114 above.

TIME OFF WORK

12.56   The right of a pregnant employee to take time off work
for ante-natal care was considered in 12.43 above. In addition,
most employees have a right to time off work in respect of trade
union duties or activities, public duties, impending redundancy and
safety representative duties.

Time off Work for Union-related Matters

12.57   This right falls into two separate categories.

Time off for Trade Union Duties

12.58   Under section 27 of EPCA, an official of an independent
trade union which is recognised [32] by the employer is entitled to
"reasonable" time off, *with* pay, in order to carry out his union
duties insofar as they concern relations between the employer and
his employees, or involve training of the official in aspects of industrial relations which relate to his duties, or which are approved by
the TUC or his particular union.

---

[32] *i.e.* one which the employer has agreed shall represent the interests of all or some
of his employees.

Time off for Trade Union Activities

12.59 Section 28 of EPCA allows ordinary union members the right to "reasonable" time off *without* pay, in order to engage in union activities which fall short of industrial action. Once again the union must be recognised by the employer.

12.60 What is "reasonable," in either case, is a matter for an industrial tribunal to determine should the matter become disputed, and ACAS Codes of Practice give practical guidance.

Time off Work for Public Duties

12.61 Section 29 of EPCA allows employees who are J.P.s, local councillors, tribunal members or holders of other public offices "reasonable" time off, without pay, in order to perform the duties associated with such offices. Once again, the concept of "reasonable" is a flexible one which will be applied case by case, and may ultimately be decided by an industrial tribunal.[33]

Time off for Safety Representative Duties

12.62 As is explained in 12.107 below, employees are entitled to be represented in health and safety matters by safety representatives appointed by their unions in terms of the Health and Safety at Work Act 1974. Such safety representatives are entitled to "reasonable" time off work, with pay, in order to carry out their duties or to attend appropriate training.

WAGE PROTECTION

12.63 Various statutes passed in recent years have been aimed at protecting the wage position of the individual employee, and ensuring that his vulnerabililty in this area is not exploited by the

---

[33] As in *Ratcliffe* v. *Dorset County Council* [1978] I.R.L.R. 191, in which it was held that it was not "reasonable" for the employers of a college lecturer who was also a local councillor simply to re-allocate his teaching hours. "Time off" was to be precisely that, and not "time re-allocated."

employer. The main manifestations of this process have been as follows.

1. Wages Act 1986—fully considered in 11.43 and 11.44 above.
2. Statutory Sick Pay.
3. Insolvency Rights.
4. Guarantee payments.
5. Itemised pay statements.

Statutory Sick Pay

12.64 Under Regulations issued in 1982, most employees are entitled to payment of Statutory Sick Pay (SSP) if they are absent from work due to illness, howsoever caused. This right exists for 28 weeks, and consists of a weekly payment based on the employee's normal average earnings divided by the number of days of sickness which are being claimed for. In practice, the actual payment rates per week are fixed by Regulations which vary from time to time, so that all employees within a certain earnings' "band" are paid the same amount. The amount is paid initially by the employer, who then deducts this amount from his overall national insurance contributions.

12.65 There are various exceptions to the entitlement, including those who earn below the national insurance "threshold," staff who already qualify for Statutory Maternity Payment (for which see 12.46 above) and staff over the state retirement age. In addition, the first three days of sickness do not count, with the result that payment only begins on the fourth day.

Insolvency Rights

12.66 Under EPCA, as amended in 1989, an employee whose employer becomes insolvent or bankrupt, is entitled to be paid arrears of wages by the State as a form of statutory preferential payment, whether the Government is able to recover that amount or not. In practice, there is a maximum amount, based on a maximum weekly wage and a maximum number of weeks, plus payment of amounts due in respect of notice, sickness, paid time off, etc. The maximum amount is currently £800.

Guarantee Payment

12.67 By virtue of sections 12–18 of EPCA, workers are granted the right to a "guarantee payment" (which in practice is restricted to a maximum amount fixed by Regulations) in respect of each "workless day" which they suffer as the result of a reduction in work which arises as the result of some disruption in the employer's business and which is not caused by industrial action. In order to qualify, the employee must have been employed for at least 16 hours per week for at least four weeks before the lay-off, and the employee will disqualify himself from the right to guarantee payment if he unreasonably refuses "suitable" alternative work or does not comply with reasonable requirements imposed by the employer to ensure that he is available if and when work becomes available.[34]

12.68 Among the limitations on the right to guarantee payment are the fact that it is only payable in respect of five workless days in any three month period. Complaints in relation to non-payment of guarantee payments are heard by an industrial tribunal, which has the power to award payment of arrears.

Itemised Pay Statements

12.69 Under EPCA, section 8, every employee has the right to demand from his employer, at the time of the payment of his wages, an "itemised pay statement" which specifies in writing the amount of the gross wage, the amount(s) of any fixed or variable deductions from that wage, and the reason(s) therefore, the net wage, and, where different parts of the net amount are paid in different ways, the amount and method of payment of each part-payment. A "standing statement" every 12 months is sufficient for fixed item deductions.

---

[34] As in *Meadows v. Faithfull Overalls* [1977] I.R.L.R. 330, in which employees whose premises were rendered too cold by a lack of central heating oil lost the right to guarantee payment when they failed to remain in the canteen (supplied with free hot tea) for a further hour as requested, in order to await the arrival of more oil.

REDUNDANCY

12.70 A genuine redundancy will not be regarded as an unfair dismissal,[35] but it will bring the contract of employment to an end, and it is hedged around with a variety of statutory restrictions. It also gives the employee concerned the right to financial compensation, as explained in 12.87 below.

Definition of Redundancy

12.71 In order for there to be in law a redundancy, the employee must suffer a particular type of work loss, and that loss must occur for certain reasons.

Type of Work Loss

12.72 Before an employee may claim that he has been made redundant, he must show that he has been dismissed, or has suffered a "lay-off" or "short time." The case of dismissal raises no difficulty,[36] but a "lay-off" is defined as being a situation in which the employee is laid off completely for either four consecutive weeks or six weeks out of any 13, during which he receives no payment of any kind from the employer. "Short time" is defined as the inability of the employee to earn at least half his normal weeks pay for either of the above periods of time.

12.73 In the "lay-off" or "short time" situations, the employee may serve upon the employer an official notice announcing his intention to claim redundancy compensation. The employer may then, if believes the lean spell to be temporary, issue a counter-notice within seven days promising a period of 13 weeks' full time employment commencing within the next four weeks. Alternatively, of course, he may simply accept the notice.

---

[35] But see 11.96 above.
[36] Apart from those cases in which it is a "constructive dismissal," for which see 11.124 above.

Reason for Work Loss

12.74   There may be a variety of reasons why the employee has suddenly experienced dismissal or a reduced working week, and not all of them entitle him to redundancy payment. For example, if the employee is simply advised that the job is being transferred to another location, and he is required to move with it, his refusal, and subsequent work loss may not be classed as a redundancy at all if his terms of employment contain a "mobility clause." Even if there is not, his refusal to move may still disqualify him from a redundancy payment if in all the circumstances it is "unreasonable."

12.75   Thus, whereas the court in *O'Brien* v. *Associated Fire Alarms*,[37] regarded it as totally unreasonable for an employer to expect an employee to move 120 miles with his family in order to keep a job which carried no mobility clause, in *Jones* v. *Associated Tunnelling*,[38] the tribunal held that an employee was unreasonable in refusing to move from one colliery to another within reasonable commuting distance from his home, particularly since he had already made such a move (from the same home base) some 10 years previously.

12.76   Sometimes an employee is caught in a "management efficiency" situation in which his or her job is preserved provided that they agree to a change in work practices. If this does not amount to the sort of reduced status which can constitute a constructive dismissal (for which see 11.124 above), it will not normally be a redundancy either. Thus, in *Johnson* v. *Nottinghamshire Combined Police Authority*,[39] it was held that two police typists were not being made redundant simply because they were asked to change from day shifts to alternating shifts, in order to cover more working hours between them without working more hours individually.

Persons Excluded from Redundancy Rights

12.77   The right to claim redundancy compensation is denied to employees with less than 104 weeks "continuous service" (see

---

[37] [1969] 1 All E.R. 93.
[38] [1981] I.R.L.R. 477.
[39] [1974] I.C.R. 170.

below), those who normally work for less than 16 hours per week (eight hours per week after 5 years' service), those who are under 18 or over 65 (or "the normal" retirement age where this is lower), employees in certain posts (*e.g.* Crown employees and office holders such as police and prison officers) and employees who are covered by approved private schemes. Also, no claim may be made by an employee on a fixed term contract of two years or more who has signed away his right to claim redundancy compensation.

12.78 "Continuous service" in this, as in all other employment law contexts governed by statute, means a period of weeks which is not broken by any gap *other than* one involving sickness (maximum 26 weeks), temporary cessation of work, pregnancy leave, and any temporary break which by custom or arrangement is regarded as not breaking continuity of employment. For the effect of strike action, see 11.82 above.

Reasonable Alternative Employment

12.79 An employee may disqualify himself from the right to claim redundancy payment if he refuses an alternative job offered to him by the employer which it would have been "reasonable" for him to take (or, more accurately, it was "unreasonable" of him to refuse). In order to qualify, such a job must be offered so as to take effect no more than four weeks after the termination of the previous job.

12.80 The new job must be a "reasonably suitable" alternative to the former one, and it is for the employer to prove both the suitability of the new job and the unreasonableness of the employee in refusing it. It is always a question of fact in each case, and previous case precedents are not always helpful. However, one can appreciate why the tribunal in *Taylor* v. *Kent County Council*,[40] held that a headmaster was reasonable in refusing reduction to the status of supply teacher, even though his salary was preserved. Less explicable perhaps was the ruling in *Fuller* v. *Stephanie Bowman*

---

[40] [1969] 2 Q.B. 560.

(Sales) Ltd.,[41] that a respectable middle-aged lady had been unreasonable to refuse a transfer to new working premises in the heart of Soho, upstairs from a sex shop.

12.81 Factors normally taken into account will be salary, fringe benefits, status, working hours and skills required.[42] To enable the employee to sample the new job, EPCA allows the employee a four week "no obligation" trial period (which may be extended by agreement) in the new job. The same tests as above are then applied after the trial period.

Transfer of Undertakings

12.82 The Transfer of Undertakings (Protection of Employment) Regulations of 1981 were passed with a view to protecting the position of employees whose employers sold their businesses. The effect of these Regulations, coupled with the unfair dismissal and redundancy provisions of EPCA, is that where the business is not sold as a "going concern" (*e.g.* if all that is being sold are the physical assets), then the outgoing proprietor will be liable to the employees either in respect of unfair dismissal or redundancy compensation. Where, on the other hand, the business transfers (whether by sale or some other lawful process such as inheritance) as a going concern, the accumulated continuous service of the employees is transferred with them, to become the liability of the purchaser, etc. should any of those employees subsequently become unfairly dismissed or redundant. A glaring loophole in the Regulations is that they do not apply in respect of corporate merges or takeovers.

12.83 It was not entirely certain what was the position of employees dismissed by the outgoing employer only hours or days before the transfer, since the Regulations only apply to those employed by the outgoing employer "immediately before" the

---

[41] [1977] I.R.L.R. 87.

[42] In *Thomas Wragg and Sons* v. *Wood* [1976] I.R.L.R. 145, the tribunal held that the employee could reasonably refuse on the ground that he had found another job to start the day after the redundancy notice took effect. He still received his redundancy pay, since the offer of a new job by the old employer had been delayed until after the employee had found the new job.

transfer. The question of whether they were the legal responsibility of the outgoing or incoming employer was settled in *Litster* v. *Forth Dry Dock and Engineering Company Limited*,[43] in which in just such a case the House of Lords ruled that staff dismissed one hour before the transfer, in a clear attempt to avoid the Regulations, were still to be regarded as the responsibility of the incoming employer if they would have been employed by the former employer "immediately before" the transfer of the undertaking but for the unfair dismissal by the former employer.

12.84 Regulation 8 makes it automatically an unfair dismissal to dismiss an employee before or after a transfer of a business if the principal reason for it is the transfer itself. In practice there is an exception (which means that in such cases the normal reasonableness test applies) where the reason is an "economic, technical or organisational" one. This serves to render Regulation 8 impotent in most cases, for fairly obvious reasons.

The Effect of Industrial Action

12.85 By virtue of the provisions of EPCA, if an employee who is aware of an impending, or probably impending, redundancy engages in industrial action justifying dismissal (*e.g.* a strike) *before* formal redundancy notices are issued, he loses his right to redundancy compensation. If, on the other hand, he goes on strike[44] *after* the issue of such notices, then he retains the right to redundancy payment.

12.86 For the effect of strikes on the calculation of continuity of service, see 11.82 above.

Calculation of Redundancy Payment

12.87 The method of calculation of redundancy payment is the same as that for the "basic award" for unfair dismissal,[45] although

---

[43] [1989] I.R.L.R. 161.
[44] But not if he engaged in any other form of industrial action for which he could be dismissed (*e.g.* work to rule); in such a case it is for the tribunal to decide whether or not redundancy compensation is lost.
[45] For which see 11.121 above.

entitlement does not begin until the employee's 18th birthday, with the result that no period of service before then will count in the calculation. Payment is made initially by the employer, and only if the employer cannot or will not pay will the Secretary of State for Employment make payment out of a contingent redundancy fund for that purpose. He may then pursue the employer for reimbursement, should this be financially worthwhile.

Statutory Consultation Procedures

12.88 By virtue of the Employment Protection Act of 1975, an employer who is contemplating redundancies amongst his workforce is statutorily obliged to consult any union recognised by him before carrying out such a policy, at least if he intends to make at least 10 or more employees redundant.

12.89 To be more specific, he must consult where 10 or more employees covered by such a union are to be made redundant within 30 days or less, or if 100 or more such employees are to be made redundant within 90 days or less. At the same time, he must advise the Secretary of State for Employment, and in the latter case, failure to do so is a criminal offence.

12.90 Although the employer's duty is only to "consult," he must in practice give reasons, numbers and descriptions of employees involved, and the method of selection proposed, together with the proposed method of dismissal. He must receive and consider proposals by the union and give reasons in writing for rejecting any such proposals.

12.91 If the employer fails to consult, the union itself[46] may apply to the tribunal for a "protective award" to cover the employees thus threatened, which may amount to an award of full pay to each of those employees for the entire protected period (*i.e.* 30 days or 90 days) or such of it as elapsed before the consultation began. Even where less than 10 redundancies are proposed, an employer who does not consult may be ordered to pay a protective award for a period not exceeding 28 days.

---

[46] Not the individuals most affected.

HEALTH AND SAFETY AT WORK

12.92 Reference was made in 11.53 above to the employer's common law duty to ensure the safety of employees at work by taking "reasonable care" for them. The main failing of this obligation is that it only establishes rules for compensation once someone has actually been injured, and makes no attempt to prevent the injury occurring in the first place. For this reason, successive governments have passed statutes designed to force the employer, on pain of criminal prosecution, to promote positive safety policies. By far the most important and comprehensive of these was the Health and Safety at Work Act 1974, which is considered in the remaining sections of this chapter.

Introduction

12.93 The 1974 Act was passed with the aim of imposing on all employers minimum standards of safety policy, regardless of the nature or type of workplace involved. It futher promotes industrial safety by making employees themselves and other stakeholders in industry (*e.g.* manufacturers and designers of plant and machinery) responsible for the observance of proper standards. A breach of the broad provisions of the Act may result in criminal prosecution whether anyone is thereby injured or not. It does not of itself, however, give rise to any civil claim, which will still normally only arise delictually once someone *is* injured.

12.94 The provisions of the Act are best considered in terms of the person upon whom duties are imposed by it.

Section 2: Duties of Employers to Employees

12.95 Section 2 is an intentionally broad section which imposes upon virtually all employers the duty to ensure the health, safety and welfare at work of all employees "so far as is reasonably practicable." Failure to do so—regardless of whether or not anyone is injured—is a criminal offence. Rather unnecessarily, in view of the broad generality of the first part of section 2, the second part thereof lists areas of safety which are particularly covered, including safe plant, machinery and equipment (in terms of both installation and subsequent maintenance), the use, storage and transport of articles and substances, proper training and supervision, provision of adequate safety information, means of entry and exit to work places and general environmental wellbeing (light, heat, ventilation, etc.).

12.96 Every employer with five or more employees must publish to his employees a written statement of his general policy on health and safety, and his health and safety procedures. He must also consult any safety representatives appointed by trade unions recognised by him, and establish a safety committee if so requested by those representatives.

Section 3: Duties of Employers to Non-employees

12.97 In addition to those duties which they owe to their own employees, all employers (and all self-employed persons) are subject to a general duty imposed under section 3 of the Act to take such steps as are reasonably practicable to ensure that no-one else is exposed to safety risks by their activities. By this means, patrons and general public members are protected from the activities of local businesses, users of public facilities such as schools and libraries are entitled to safety considerations from operators, and neighbours are protected from the activities of local industry.[47]

12.98 Equally covered are other people's employees while they are on an employer's premises (*e.g.* sub-contractors) and this point was amply demonstrated in *R. v. Swan Hunter Shipbuilders*,[48] in which a shipbuilding firm was held responsible for the deaths of 8 employees of a sub-contractor to whom they had not given the same warning regarding the dangers of oxygen in confined spaces as they had given to their own employees.

Section 7: Safety Duties of Employees

12.99 It is not just employers who are bound by safety duties in the workplace as the result of the 1974 Act; section 7 of the Act

---

[47] In fact, this section was hurriedly added at the Bill stage of the legislation in the aftermath of the Flixborough disaster in Lincolnshire.
[48] [1981] I.R.L.R. 403.

imposes a duty upon employees (with the same sanction of criminal liability in default) to ensure that, in the performance of their duties at work, they take reasonable care not only for themselves but also anyone else who may be affected by their actions (*N.B.* not just fellow workers). The Act also imposes a duty of co-operation with the employer in assisting him to perform his duties.

12.100 Prosecutions under section 7 are not numerous, but neither are they unheard of.[49]

Sections 4 and 5: Duties of Controllers of Premises

12.101 To cover certain obvious gaps in the network of duties otherwise created by the Act, section 4 imposes a duty on those who control non-domestic premises used by non-employees who work there or make use of plant or substances provided there (*e.g.* motorists using filling stations). This duty, as in other sections, is to render such plant or substances safe "so far as is reasonably practicable." Section 5 concerns control over the emission of noxious or offensive substances (*e.g.* ether fumes in a self-operated dry cleaners).

Section 6: Duties of Designers, Manufacturers, Importers, and Suppliers

12.102 To complete the network of industrial safety controls, section 6 of the Act requires designers, manufacturers, importers and suppliers of plant, equipment, tools and other items used at work to ensure that such objects are designed, installed, tested and supplied with adequate instruction to ensure "so far as is reasonably practicable" the health and safety of those using them.

Liability under the Act

12.103 As a general rule, in line with all criminal liability, responsibility for breaches of the duties imposed by the Act will normally fall upon those who bear those duties, who will normally be the persons actually at fault. However, in the case of corporate

---

[49] And they remain as a warning to potential practical jokers in the workforce.

bodies[50] this responsibility may devolve upon directors, office bearers or managers, as in the case of *Armour* v. *Skeen*,[51] in which both Strathclyde Regional Council and its Director of Highways were successfully prosecuted for a breach of statutory procedures which led to the death of a workman painting the Albert Bridge. The Director's personal liability was held to arise from his failure to implement a safety policy within his department which would result in adequate safety training and procedures.

Enforcement of the Act

12.104 At the apex of health and safety enforcement is the Health and Safety Commission, which exercises a broad control over the entire operation of the Act. The Commission is largely a public relations body charged with the duty of promoting health and safety at work via research, publications, reports, etc., and the preparation of codes of practice for use in conjunction with the Act. Appointments are by the Secretary of State, with representatives from employers, employees and professional and local government bodies.

12.105 The Health and Safety Executive is the senior enforcement body, with a network of inspectors whose function it is to police the Act via regular inspections of workplaces, investigation of accidents, etc. Eventual prosecution, in Scotland, is in the hands of the procurator fiscal service, but in collecting the evidence necessary for prosecution, local inspectors have wide powers of search and seizure, including the power to interview witnesses, take photographs and carry out tests. Since 1977, some of the powers of the Health and Safety Executive have been shared with local authorities via their environmental health officers,[52] who have the same investigative powers as health and safety inspectors.

12.106 Among the powers given to inspectors who have reason to believe that the Act is being infringed are the issue of "improve-

---

[50] *i.e.* companies, local authorities, etc.
[51] [1977] I.R.L.R. 310.
[52] The latter normally having responsibility for hotels, restaurants, shops and offices.

ment notices" which require certain processes, procedures, etc. to be improved as recommended by the inspector within a stated period of not less than 21 days, and "prohibition notices," which in effect close down a process completely when it is believed by the inspector that it is too dangerous to allow to continue pending improvement. The implementation of such a notice may be deferred pending improvement (making it in effect an improvement notice with teeth). In either case, an appeal may be lodged with an industrial tribunal.

12.107 In an effort to encourage employers and workers to police health and safety themselves, the Act contains provision for the appointment of safety representatives from the workforce. They need only be appointed when required by members of a union recognised by the employer, but even non-unionised employers have found it advantageous to appoint them. Their functions are to liaise with the employer on all matters of safety, investigate complaints, make representations to the employer, etc. As indicated in 12.62 above, such representatives are entitled to time off with pay in order to perform their duties.

12.108 If 2 or more safety representatives so request it, the employer must establish a safety committee to which safety matters are referred. The employer must then consult with the committee, but is not bound to implement its recommendations, since ultimate responsibility for implementation of the Act rests with the employer. By the same token, the mere fact that an employer has appointed safety representatives and established a safety committee will not absolve him from liability for any breaches of the Act.

Health and Safety Regulations

12.109 It will have been noted that the 1974 Act is very broad in its terms, and contains no detailed safety provisions. It is what is known as an "enabling" Act, *i.e.* it enables other persons and bodies (in practice the Secretary of State through Parliament) to enact detailed safety provisions via "statutory instruments," and other delegated legislation.[53] These are already numerous, and deal

---

[53] For which see 1.12 et seq. above.

with specific areas of specific industries, in many instances making use of regulations which existed under previous Acts of Parliament such as the Factories Acts and the Office Shops and Railway Premises Act. Such regulations are outside the scope of a book such as Premises Act. Such regulations are outside the scope of a book such as this.

12.110   Codes of practice have also been introduced, which point employers towards the correct health and safety procedures, but which themselves do not have the force of law.

13. PROPERTY

13.1 The word property is used in Scots law in two separate, but related, ways. The first is to describe the right which the "owner" has over the thing itself,[1] and the second is to describe the thing (e.g. "moveable property" or "heritable property" as defined below). A person has "a right of property" in something when he possesses a higher right to it than anyone else, but not necessarily a totally unrestricted right. Thus, for example, the "owner" of a house may have "property" in it subject to a mortgage, while most land owners are restricted in the use to which they may put their land by modern planning laws, the law of nuisance, etc.[2]

13.2 "Property" is used in this chapter to mean the thing itself.

CLASSIFICATION OF PROPERTY

13.3 There are several ways in which property may be classified in order to consider the law relating to it, but the two most common are:

1. Corporeal property and incorporeal property
2. Heritable property and moveable property.

Corporeal and Incorporeal Property

13.4 Corporeal property is property which is tangible, *i.e.* it has a physical existence. Two obvious examples are a house and a car. Incorporeal property, on the other hand, is intangible, and consists of a "right" to something (*e.g.* to the possession of a house under the repossession clause of a standard security, or to the payment of the declared dividend on a share).

---

[1] And hence the frequent reference to the "passing of property" in goods in the Sale of Goods Act of 1979 to mean the passing of ownership; see, *e.g.* 5.22 above.
[2] For which see 10.50 above.

Heritable and Moveable Property

13.5 "Heritable" property[3] consists of land and buildings, while "moveable" property is everything else. Both types of property can be either corporeal or incorporeal (*e.g.* a car is corporeal moveable property, the right to payment of money is incorporeal moveable property, a house is corporeal heritable property, and a "servitude"[4] is incorporeal heritable property because it is a right to something connected to land).

13.6 Sometimes, property can move from one classification to another according to a change in circumstances; for example, the goodwill of a business can be heritable if it depends largely on the premises,[5] but moveable if it depends upon the skill of the proprietor,[6] while crops in the ground (heritable) become moveable once harvested.

13.7 But by far the greatest difficulty with the distinction between heritable and moveable property arises in the case of "fixtures."

Fixtures

13.8 A fixture is something which has become so permanently annexed to heritable property (either the soil or a building) as in law to become part of it. Once it has, then only the owner of the heritable property may remove it, subject to certain special rules described below. It is first, however, important to grasp the rules which determine whether or not a particular item *is* a fixture.

Fixture or Non-fixture

13.9 In determining whether or not a particular item has become a fixture (assuming of course that it was not built in originally, as in the case of windows), two principle tests have emerged.

---

[3] For historical reasons concerning the old succession laws.
[4] For which see 13.38 below.
[5] *e.g.* a famous Edinburgh hostelry.
[6] *e.g.* a hairdresser's business.

13.10 1. *The purpose of annexation.* If the primary purpose for annexing the item to the heritage was to improve the heritage, rather than simply to enjoy the item, then the item is likely to be regarded in law as a fixture, regardless of how loosely it is connected to the heritage. Thus, in *Christie* v. *Smith's Exr.*,[7] it was held that a summerhouse fixed in position on the ground solely by its own weight was a fixture.

13.11 2. *The degree of annexation.* If the item in question is so firmly annexed to the heritage that it cannot be removed without damage either to itself or to the heritage, then it is likely to be regarded as a fixture. Obvious examples are fireplaces and built-in wardrobes, but the mere fact that the degree of annexation is slight will not necessarily prevent an item being a fixture, particularly not in the case of "constructive fixtures" which are "accessories" to the heritage, such as the keys to a house. However, in most cases, a light degree of annexation will not create a fixture out of something which is clearly being enjoyed for itself (*e.g.* a painting on a wall).

The Right to Remove Fixtures

13.12 As indicated above, only the "heritable proprietor" (*i.e.* the owner of the heritable property) normally has the right to remove something which has become a "fixture" of that heritage. However, the following problem cases have arisen in the past.

13.13 1. *Heir and executor.* As explained in 15.18 below, the calculation of the "legal rights" of the surviving spouse and children of a deceased requires a distinction to be made between heritable and moveable property. If the precise nature of a fixture is in dispute, hopefully the wording of any will can be relied upon to convey the deceased's intention. If not, the normal "fixture" tests apply.

13.14 2. *Seller and purchaser of heritage.* The same problems can apply when heritage is being bought and sold, and hopefully in

---

[7] 1949 S.C. 572.

such cases the contract of sale will indicate the parties' intentions. If not, the courts tend to favour the purchaser.

13.15   3. *Heritable and general creditor.* In a bankruptcy, one creditor may have security over heritable property (*e.g.* the mortgagee in a standard security) while others may have security over moveable property (*e.g.* a shopkeeper's fittings). Any dispute as to what has, or has not, become a fixture (*e.g.* shelving), and therefore belongs to the heritable creditor, will require to be solved using such guidelines as the court can find.

13.16   4. *Liferenter and fiar.* The law of liferent and fee is explained in 13.120 below. When a liferenter attaches items to the property during his liferent, a dispute may arise later as to whether or not it may be removed before the fiar takes possession. In order to encourage the liferenter to improve property, the courts tend to lean against regarding their annexations as fixtures, rather in the manner of the freedom given to tenants (see below).

13.17   5. *Landlord and tenant.* As indicated above, the law has promoted the improvement of property by allowing tenants, at the end of the lease, to remove either "trade fixtures" (*e.g.* permanent shelving) or "ornamental fixtures" (*e.g.* antique fireplaces) by way of exception to the general rule, unless such removal would substantially injure the heritage or the fixtures themselves would be destroyed or lose their essential character. Under the Agricultural Holdings (Scotland) Act 1949, this even extends to buildings put up by the tenant and removed by him within six months of the expiry of the lease.

13.18   6. *Special agreement.* The parties may always amend the normal rules by special agreement, so that for example a landlord may allow a tenant to remove a fixture when it might not otherwise be removable in law, while a tenant may agree to leave an item which he might otherwise have been entitled to remove. Such an agreement will of course bind only the parties to it, and not some innocent third party such as a heritable creditor.

LANDOWNERSHIP

13.19   This section concentrates solely on the rights attaching to the ownership of "heritage" (*i.e.* heritable property) in its corporeal form, and the various legal rules attendant upon such ownership.

Restrictions on Landownership

13.20 As indicated in 13.1 above, the mere fact that a person owns a parcel of heritable property does not mean that he can do with it what he wishes. There are restrictions imposed by statute (*e.g.* planning laws), by common law (*e.g.* the law of nuisance considered more fully in 10.50 above), and by agreements which the owner may have reached with other parties (*e.g.* a tenant if he has leased the property out, and "servitudes" considered in 13.38 below).

Exclusive Possession

13.21 Apart, however, from those restrictions considered in 13.20, the owner of the heritable property has "exclusive possession" of it "*a caelo usque ad centrum*" (*i.e.* from the sky to the centre of the earth). In law, the owner of land owns a slice from the earth's core, through the surface and into the air, and he has the right to protect all of this by means of actions for trespass, and interdict to prevent continued challenge.[8]

13.22 However, even this right is subject to limitations (*e.g.* to allow military and civilian aircraft to pass overhead, to allow minerals to be extracted, to allow police and other officials to enter one's property, etc.) which are found in various statutes designed to ensure that the interests of the community come before the interests of individual proprietors.

Natural Rights of Property

13.23 A person who owns land also owns certain "natural rights" which go with it, and are designed to ensure comfortable enjoyment of that property. They may be "alienated" (*i.e.* signed away) by the owner for the period of his ownership, but then they revert to the land at the termination of that ownership because they arise

---

[8] Thus in *Brown* v. *Lee Constructions*, 1977 S.L.T. (Notes) 61, a pursuer successfully interdicted against a crane jib passing over his property (trespass to airspace), while in *Davey* v. *Harrow Corporation* [1958] 1 Q.B. 60, the right protected was against burrowing under land.

"*ex lege*,"[9] unlike for example servitudes, which arise by agreement between the parties to them.

There are 3 main groups of natural rights of property:

1. Right of support for land.
2. Rights in water.
3. Rights protected by the law of nuisance.

13.24 The law of nuisance was considered in 10.50 above, and therefore only the first two above require further elaboration.

Right of Support for Land

13.25 For obvious physical reasons, land requires support from either side and from below, and the owner of land has a legal right to ensure that it receives it. The position may be complicated by the existence of a mineral lease (whether voluntary or imposed upon the land owner by statute), but leaving that possibility aside, the law distinguishes between land in its natural state and land which carries buildings.

13.26 1. *Land in its natural state.* The owner of land in its natural state is legally entitled to the support necessary to preserve it in that state, *i.e.* to prevent it from subsiding. Any infringement of that right gives rise to a right to damages, and interdict to prevent recurrences. It does not matter whether the subsidence comes from below or from either side, and any land owner working even his own land must cease digging sufficiently far from his neighbour's boundary to ensure that adjoining land is not affected.

13.27 2. *Land carrying buildings.* There is no natural right of support for buildings, but it may be acquired by grant, express or implied, as when a mineral lease is granted under land which already contains buildings. There is an implied term in the mineral lease to the effect that the existing buildings will remain adequately supported. The same is true even when the lessee is aware that buildings are contemplated, and the effect in both cases is that of an implied grant of the right of support to the landowner.

---

[9] *i.e.* by the automatic operation of law.

Rights in Water

13.28   A distinction must be drawn between water which is not in a definite channel, and water which exists in streams and lochs.

13.29   1. *Water not in a definite channel.* "Surface water" may be used to its full extent by the owner of the land, who may even form a pond to catch it, or sink a well to extract it. No adjoining landowner may object, even if it means that he gets none. Should the landowner wish to rid himself of excess water, then although he has the right to let it drain naturally onto lower land belonging to a neighbour (against which the neighbour has no legal redress), he may not artificially increase the run-off by pumping or channelling, except where it constitutes agricultural drainage, which is subject to special statutory rules.

13.30   2. *Streams.* A stream for legal purposes is any natural channel of water, however small or large, other than the tidal reaches of a river,[10] and all the landowners through whose land even one bank of it may be located (the "riparian owners") from the original source of that stream to its mouth have a common interest in it which creates mutual legal rights and duties.

13.31   The "alveus," or bed, of the stream belongs to the owner of the land on either side of it *ad medium filum* (*i.e.* to the centre line of it), which means of course that it is owned entirely by a landowner through whose land it flows completely, but only for that length of the stream which passes across his land.

13.32   Each riparian proprietor may take as much water as he wishes for "primary" purposes (*i.e.* drink for himself and his animals and ordinary domestic requirements), even if by so doing he exhausts the stream, leaving nothing for any lower riparian owner. However, he may not remove water for any other purpose (*e.g.* irrigation or cooling) if by so doing he infringes the rights of a lower riparian owner in respect of the quantity and quality of water he would otherwise have received.

---

[10] See 13.69 below.

13.33 A riparian proprietor may even divert a stream as it flows through his own land, provided that the water is returned to the stream before it leaves his land, so that the lower riparian owner suffers no change. However, if the upper proprietor in such a case has only one bank of the stream on his land, the proprietor of the other bank may object to such a diversion, since it diminishes the flow of water past him.

13.34 The Control of Pollution Act of 1974 imposes statutory control over the discharge of harmful substances into streams.

13.35 3. *Lochs.* Sea lochs are, for legal purposes, an extension of the sea, and as such are regarded as *regalia majora.*[11]

13.36 Inland lochs which are entirely surrounded by the land of the proprietor are his to do what he wishes with, unless they flow by stream into the land of a neighbouring proprietor, in which case the normal "riparian" rules apply as explained above.

13.37 Inland lochs which are surrounded by the lands of various proprietors give rise to a presumption[12] of joint right to the water itself (for sailing, fishing, etc.), with each proprietor owning the "solum" (bed) of the loch from his own boundary to the centre.

Servitudes

Definition

13.38 A "servitude" is a form of express or implied burden on heritable property whereby the owner of the "servient tenement" (ST) must do, or refrain from doing, something on his own property so as to benefit, or refrain from detrimenting, the land of the owner of the "dominant tenement" (DT). The word "tenement" should not be taken, in this context, as being limited to flatted dwellings, but in fact extends to all land, whether built on or not.

---

[11] For which see 13.66 below.
[12] Which may be rebutted by terms to the contrary in title deeds, or evidence of possession arrangements in the past.

13.39 Servitudes may be classified in two broad ways:

1. Positive and negative servitudes.
2. Urban and rural servitudes.

Positive and Negative Servitudes

13.40 A positive servitude arises when DT may exercise a physical right over the land of ST, an obvious example being a right of way; a negative servitude is in effect a restraint imposed on the way in which ST uses his land (*e.g.* the right of light).

Urban and Rural Servitudes

13.41 An urban servitude is one which relates to buildings, wherever they are situated, whereas a rural servitude is one which relates simply to land.

Urban Servitudes

13.42 The main urban servitudes are as follows.

13.43 1. *Support*. This has already been partly encountered in 13.25 above, but in the case of tenemental or adjoining buildings it also includes *tigni imitendi* (which allows a DT to insert a beam or other support structure into ST and keep it there), and *onus ferendi*, which entitles DT to insist that his building be supported by ST.

13.44 2. *Stillicide*. Sometimes called "eavesdrop," this allows DT to shed his rainwater on ST.

13.45 3. *Light*. Sometimes called "prospect," the right of light allows DT to insist that ST not build at all (*non aedificandi*), not build any higher (*altius non tollendi*) and not build in such a way as to cut off DT's light or view (*non officiendi luminibus*). It will have been noted that "light" is the only negative servitude of any significance.

Rural Servitudes

13.46 The main rural servitudes are as follows:

13.47 1. *Way.* A right of way in law is right possessed by DT to cross the land of ST by foot, horse or vehicle, depending on the nature of the right in question. ST is not required to keep the "way" repaired, and he may erect gates (*e.g.* to preserve stock) provided that this does not actually interfere with the exercise of the servitude. A servitude right of way (possessed only by DT) is not the same as a public right of way, which must follow a definite route.

13.48 2. *Aquaehaustus.* The right to take water from, or water cattle at, some source of water on ST.

13.49 3. *Aqueduct.* The right to convey water (by pipes or by channel) through ST. The duty of maintenance is on DT, but ST must allow him reasonable access for this purpose.

13.50 4. *Pasturage.* The right to pasture sheep and cattle on ST.

13.51 5. *Fuel, feal and divot.* The right to take, from ST, peat for fuel and turf for fencing and/or roofing.

Characteristics of Servitudes

13.52 As indicated above, a servitude exists for the benefit of the dominant tenement, and cannot be separated from ownership of that tenement. It is also a feature of all true servitudes that they only require the owner of the servient tenement to submit to action by the owner of the dominant tenement, and not to take any action himself.

13.53 All servitudes must be exercised by the dominant tenement owner *civiliter, i.e.* in the way least burdensome for the servient tenement, whose owner may otherwise enjoy his land as he pleases.

Constitution of Servitudes

13.54 Servitudes (which will not necessarily appear in any title deeds) may be created by express grant, by implied grant or implied reservation, or by prescription.

Express Grant

13.55 Such a grant will of course be made by the owner of the servient tenement, and since it relates to heritage it must be probative form,[13] normally of course a title deed, but not necessarily so.

Implied Grant or Implied Reservation

13.56 A servitude may arise by implication when it is necessary for the use of the property, for example where the DT is split into two parts, and a right of way is necessary over ST in order to join the two. An implied grant will occur when ST sells to DT that part of the property which requires the right of way, and an implied reservation will occur when DT sells the land which lies between, keeping the two sections requiring joinder to himself. The courts are less willing, however, to uphold the latter.

Prescription

13.57 Under the Prescription and Limitation (Scotland) Act 1973, a positive servitude may be created when it is possessed openly, peaceably and without "judicial interruption"[14] for a period of 20 years.

Extinction of Servitudes

13.58 Servitudes may be extinguished in the following ways.

13.59 1. *By a change in circumstances.* Compulsory purchase and destruction of either tenement are two obvious examples.

13.60 2. *Confusione.* This arises when the two tenements pass into the ownership of one single party; even if they are later separated, the servitude does not automatically revive.

---

[13] See 2.59 above. *N.B.* that an express grant is the only way of creating a negative servitude.

[14] *i.e.* by court proceedings or by arbitration.

13.61 3. *Renunciation.* This occurs when the owner of the dominant tenement expressly renounces the servitude in a probative document.

13.62 4. *By prescription.*[15] A positive servitude, if unexercised and unclaimed in court proceedings or arbitration for 20 years, is thereby lost due to the operation of the negative prescription. A negative prescription can only be extinguished by virtue of the owner of the servient tenement doing something inconsistent with the servitude for 20 years without legal challenge; an example would be building so as to reduce or obscure DT's light.

13.63 5. *By personal bar.* A court may rule that the actions or words of DT have in some way debarred him from insisting on continued enjoyment of the servitude.

13.64 6. *By court order.* Under section 1 of the Conveyancing and Feudal Reform (Scotland) Act 1970, the ST may apply to the Lands Tribunal for Scotland for a discharge of the servitude when he can satisfy it that changes in the neighbourhood have rendered the servitude unreasonable, inappropriate or unduly burdensome.

Regalia

13.65 "Regalia" are heritable property rights vested in the Crown. They are subdivided into *regalia majora* (the greater royal rights) which the Crown holds in trust for the public, and which cannot be alienated, and *regalia minora* (the lesser royal rights) which the Crown may deal with as it pleases.

Regalia Majora

13.66 The following are among the more important of the *regalia majora*:

1. *The Sea*

13.67 Within the limit of territorial waters (normally 12 miles), the sea is vested in the Crown for public fishing and navigation.

---

[15] For prescription generally, see 4.44 above.

2. The Foreshore

13.68 The "foreshore" is defined as the land lying between the high and low water marks of ordinary spring tides, and once again it is vested in the Crown for public navigation and fishing, and possibly recreation.

3. Tidal Rivers

13.69 These, insofar as they are navigable, are subject to the same rules as the sea, with the solum (bed) belonging to the Crown in trust for public navigation and fishing. The public may also navigate (but not fish) non-tidal rivers, but the solum in such cases belongs to the riparian proprietors (see 13.30 above).

Regalia Minora

13.70 Among the *regalia minora* are the following:

1. Precious Metals

13.71 Mines of gold, silver and high quality lead belong to the Crown, which must however make a grant of them to the owner of the land containing them in return for a "royalty" to the Crown for the minerals extracted. Coal belongs to the British Coal Corporation, and other minerals belong to the heritable proprietor.

2. Salmon Fishings

13.72 Regardless of the ownership of the heritage, salmon fishing rights belong initially to the Crown, which may then alienate them. Where the person with the fishing right is not the "riparian" proprietor (see 13.30 above) he has a right of access over the land to the fishings, and a corresponding right to moor boats and dry nets, but must exercise those rights *civiliter* (13.53 above).

3. The Foreshore

13.73 Subject to the *majora* rights considered above in 13.68, the Crown may alienate *minora* rights to the foreshore (*e.g.* the right to hire out deck chairs). The *minora* proprietor must not obstruct the public enjoying *majora* rights (*e.g.* of sailing).[16]

Land Tenure

13.74 The law relating to "land tenure"[17] is best understood by considering each of the following factors in turn:

1. Feudal tenure.
2. Register of Sasines.
3. Registration of title.

1. Feudal Tenure

13.75 Landholding by feudal tenure proceeds on the basic premise that all land is held initially by the Crown, and is then "feued" by the Crown to a leading nobleman, who in turn feus it out in parcels to landowners, and so on down to the level of the person actually working the land. This creates a feudal pyramid of feus, with each of the link proprietors in the chain being both the "vassal" or "feuar" of his "superior" title holder, and the "feudal superior" of the person holding from him. Each passing down of title is known as a subfeu, and the process as a whole is known as subinfeudation.

13.76 The system was originally based on the requirement of each vassal to provide military service when required; for obvious reasons this system of "ward holding" was abolished after Culloden in 1746, and was replaced by the payment of "feu duty" and the observation of any condition imposed by the superior in the feu charter. These enforceable rights vested in the superior were (and are still) referred to as the *dominium directum* (direct ownership) of the land, while the vassal in return receives the *dominium utile* (useful ownership).

13.77 In an effort to make land tenure more relevant to the modern world (*i.e.* in effect abolish feudalism), Parliament passed

---

[16] For local authority rights over the seashore, see the Civic Government (Scotland) Act 1982, ss. 120–123.
[17] *i.e.* the method of holding land.

two Acts. The first was the Conveyancing and Feudal Reform (Scotland) Act 1970, which allowed the proprietor of land to apply to the Lands Tribunal for Scotland for the variation or discharge of unreasonable, inappropriate or unduly burdensome conditions in existing feus, and the Land Tenure Reform (Scotland) Act of 1974, which set out to abolish feu duty, and thus one of the remaining links in the practical feudal chain.

13.78 Under the 1974 Act, no new feu duties may be created in any sale of land, and the feu duty *must* be "redeemed" on any sale of land which is burdened by it. It may also be redeemed by the vassal at either of the payment terms of Whitsunday (May 28) and Martinmas (November 28). "Redemption" is the buying out of the feu duty by a capital sum based on the amount required to generate the same income to the superior as if the money were invested in two and a half per cent Consolidated Stock.

13.79 It should be noted that notwithstanding these statutory changes, new feus (containing "feu burdens"[18]) may still be created if they do not involve the payment of feu duty.

2. Register of Sasines

13.80 Since 1617, title deeds to property have been kept in the Register of Sasines in Edinburgh, organised on a county basis. From the early days of handing over a symbolic clod of earth, fishing net or whatever else was appropriate, and recording details of the ceremony in an "instrument of sasine" which was then registered for posterity, modern conveyancing reached the stage at which land was exchanged by means of a deed of "conveyance" which was itself registered in the name of the new proprietor, who then, and only then, became "infeft" in the land. Also recorded in the Register were mortgages of the land in security for a loan ("standard securities").

---

[18] *e.g.* restrictions on building. For examples of the discharge of feu burdens which were no longer reasonable, in terms of the 1970 Act, see *United Auctions (Scotland)* v. *British Railways Board,* 1991 S.L.T. (Lands Tr.) 71 and *Ramsay* v. *Holmes,* 1992 S.L.T. (Lands Tr.) 53.

13.81 The majority of modern land titles are still recorded by this method, but by virtue of the Land Registration (Scotland) Act of 1979, even the register of sasines will become a thing of the past as "registration of title" takes over.

3. Registration of Title

13.82 Under this system, each portion of land in Scotland is registered on a "title sheet" which simply records the name of the heritable proprietor and any heritable creditor (*e.g.* a building society). This will replace the old system of recording bulky title deeds, since any future conveyance will simply be recorded by means of a change to the title sheet, with the new proprietor being given a "land certificate" (and a "charge certificate" for a mortgagee) by the Keeper of the Registers of Scotland.

13.83 The system began in 1981, and the theory was that it would spread, area by area, on an annual basis, until the whole of Scotland was covered. It began in Renfrew, and has become operational in Dumbarton, Lanark and Glasgow, with Midlothian to follow. It may well be the millenium before it is complete.

MOVEABLE PROPERTY

13.84 This section concentrates on "moveable" property, which it will be recalled from 13.5 above is any property other than heritable (including fixtures which may once have been moveable but which have become part of the heritable property). It will also be recalled from 13.4 that moveable property may be either corporeal or incorporeal, and this section may be conveniently subdivided along those lines.

Corporeal Moveable Property (CMP)

13.85 This consists of all property which is not only non-heritable but also has tangible form (*e.g.* a car or an item of furniture). Because it is both visible and on the whole portable, physical possession of CMP assumes some importance in the question of ownership rights. It is also relatively easily transferred in legal terms.

Ownership and Possession of CMP

13.86 There is a rebuttable presumption that the person who is in possession of an item of CMP is the owner of it, which no doubt gave rise to the generally held, but inaccurate, belief that "possession is nine tenths of the law." It does not take much evidence to rebut the presumption, particularly in the modern world of consumer credit agreements (Chapter 6) and Romalpa clauses (see 5.40 above). For this reason, anyone dealing with a person who claims to own goods which he is pledging in security (*e.g.* a pawnbroker) does so at his own peril, if the true owner is able to show the real reason for the ostensible possession (*e.g.* theft or fraud).[19]

13.87 There are two essential elements in the true possession of CMP. First of all there must be a physical holding of the item, insofar as this is practically possible.[20] The possession may also take the form of "civil" as opposed to natural, or physical, possession. Civil possession is possession through a third party such as a carrier or a tenant; in either case another party has the temporary possession, but under the control of the true owner.

13.88 The second element of possession in law is known as *animus possidendi* ("intention to possess"), and is what distinguishes true possession from mere custody. A mere intention to possess does not, of course, create a lawful title, as any thief will be quickly advised by a sentencing court.

13.89 Possession is said to be "exclusive" in the sense that no two persons can have full possession of the same item. However, possession may be shared or divided, as in common ownership (see 13.107 below), provided that between them the two possessors possess the full right to the item.

---

[19] And hence the need for special rules in certain cases involving sale of goods considered in 5.56 above, which are necessary in order to protect the innocent buyer.
[20] *e.g.* in the case of a yacht, the keys to the vessel and the payment of mooring fees would be sufficient.

13.90 Normally, a person acquires possession of CMP by acquiring it from someone else (*e.g.* buying a car or inheriting a gold watch), but in special cases the new owner may have acquired valid title by more unusual means. "Occupation" is the name given to acquisition of lawful title by the simple process of taking the property with the intention of owning it. This is distinguished from theft by the fact that the object thus "occupied" had no lawful owner previously (*e.g.* wild animals which have not been "poached").

13.91 "Treasure trove" found in the ground and whose owner cannot be identified belongs to the Crown and not the finder, and the Civic Government (Scotland) Act 1982 makes a criminal offence out of the old tradition of "finders keepers."

13.92 Another form of acquired ownership is "accession," whereby a person becomes the owner of an item of CMP by reason of his ownership of something else. The clearest example is that of a calf born to a cow, and of course the same process is observed once something once moveable becomes a fixture to heritage (see 13.8 above).

Transfer of CMP

13.93 As indicated above, the transfer of title to CMP is relatively simple, given the physical nature of it, and the symbolic nature of possession.[21] The mere physical transfer of the item from A to B is not, for the reasons explained in 13.86 above, sufficient in law, and there must additionally be evidence of *animus donandi*[22] on the part of the former owner. There is a presumption against simple gift, and the courts would normally seek evidence of some sort of commercial arrangement (*e.g.* exchange for money), in the absence of clear evidence of *animus donandi*.[23]

13.94 The delivery of the item itself may be actual (*e.g.* when goods are placed in a shop bag by the sales assistant and handed

---

[21] Detailed rules concerning transfer of title in sale of goods situations are laid down under the Sale of Goods Act of 1979, considered in 5.22 et seq.

[22] "Intention to give."

[23] *e.g.* by an aunt to a favourite nephew.

to the buyer), symbolic (*e.g.* when a "bill of lading" for goods loaded on to a ship is handed to the deliveree, who may use that bill to acquire the goods when they are unloaded at the other end) or constructive, as when a delivery order addressed to the storer of goods (*e.g.* in a warehouse) is handed to the storer in respect of "ascertained" goods.[24]

Incorporeal Moveable Property (IMP)

13.95   As indicated in 13.4 and 13.5 above, IMP consists of legal rights to items which are in themselves not heritable. Rights to shares in a company, copyright in music and patent and trade mark rights are good examples. The main legal difficulty with IMP is of course the fact that the property cannot be physically transferred, as in the case of corporeal moveable property such as a car, and far more emphasis is therefore laid on the legal transfer, which in many cases is regulated by specific statute anyway, much of which is outside the scope of this book.

Transfer of IMP: General Rule

13.96   Whereas corporeal moveable property is transferred by physical delivery in most cases, IMP is transferred by a process known as "assignation," which normally takes the form of a deed or a document prescribed by statute. The person making the transfer is known as the "cedent," and the person to whom the transfer is being made is called the "assignee." As a general rule, any IMP may be transferred by assignation, but there are exceptions (*e.g.* alimentary liferents considered in 13.133 below).

13.97   There is no generally prescribed form of assignation, and as between the cedent and the assignee, mere delivery of an "executed"[25] assignation is sufficient. But when third parties are involved,[26] then the transfer will not be effective between the assignee and the third party until the assignation is intimated to

---

[24] For the meaning of which see 5.22 above.
[25] *i.e.* signed and witnessed—see 2.65 above.
[26] *e.g.* a debtor or a life insurer. For a case involving inadequate intimation to a third party, see *Gallemos (In Receivership)* v. *Barratt Falkirk*, 1990 S.L.T. 98.

that third party. This process is controlled by the Transmission of Moveable Property (Scotland) Act 1862,[27] and normally requires the services of a notary public. The courts will also often recognise less formal types of intimation when it is proved that the third party was already aware of the assignation having taken place.

13.98 The effect of assignation of IMP is to place the assignee in the position of the cedent, warts and all. By means of the principle *assignatus utitor jure auctoris*,[28] the assignee will be subject to any claims by a third party which were maintainable against the cedent, unless the third party, clearly and expressly, waives any such claims as part of the assignation process.

Transfer of IMP: Special Rules

13.99 Many of the more common modern examples of IMP are governed by special statutory rules insofar as concerns transfer. Consideration of these rules is largely outside the scope of this book, but the following outline summary will serve to illustrate the statutory process in the case of negotiable instruments, trade marks, patents and company shares.

13.100 A "negotiable instrument" (of which the best modern example is a cheque) is a document drawn by A requesting that B make payment to C. Under the Bills of Exchange Act of 1882, the effect of simply delivering a negotiable instrument is to transfer to the assignee the right to the payment specified in it without prior intimation to B, and a person who qualifies as the "bona fide holder for value" of it[29] will take the right to the money free of any defects in title suffered by previous holders of it, including the cedent.

13.101 A trade mark is a name or a symbol by means of which a manufacturer or trader seeks to make his goods instantly distinguishable from others. In order to protect this uniqueness, the owner of the trade mark must register it with the Patent Office for

---

[27] Where no special alternative rules have been laid down by statute.

[28] See 4.33 et seq., and particularly *Scottish Widows* v. *Buist*.

[29] *i.e.* someone who has taken it in good faith and given something (*e.g.* goods) in return for it.

a renewable seven year period. Should he decide to assign it (*e.g.*
upon the sale of the business) he may only do so in accordance
with the specific rules laid down under the Trade Marks Acts of
1875 to 1986.

13.102   A patent is the exclusive right to exploit an invention
commercially, and to prevent others from doing so. The Patents
Act of 1977 requires the inventor to apply for a patent for a period
of 20 years, and that patent may be assigned by the original, and
any subsequent, grantee of it. The patent is registered, and the
assignation and re-registration procedures are prescribed under the
Act.

13.103   Shares in a company normally give the shareholder a right
to take part in the management of the company in general meeting,
and to enjoy any dividends declared for the benefit of shareholders
out of profits made by the company. A shareholder will be registered as such in the register of shareholders maintained by the
company secretary, and the method required for the effective transfer of shareholding rights will be laid down in the company's Articles of Association.[30] The document evidencing ownership of
shares is known as a share certificate, and assuming that a particular share is assignable, it is incumbent upon the assignee to ensure
that following normal assignation procedures (either prescribed in
the Articles or as described in 13.96 above) the change is intimated
to the company secretary, so that the share register may be
amended, and a new share certificate issued in the name of the
assignee.

JOINT PROPERTY

13.104   Property, whether heritable or moveable, may be owned
jointly by A and B. What this means is that neither of them may
be said to have a separate right in the property (not even 50 per
cent), but each has the property vested in them in *pro indiviso*[31]
shares. There may be more than two joint owners.

---

[30] For which see 9.55 above.
[31] *i.e.* indivisibly.

13.105 No joint owner may dispose of his property during his lifetime (*inter vivos*) or even on his death (*mortis causa*). When one joint owner dies, his share is added to the share(s) of the other joint owners.[32]

13.106 The clearest examples of joint property in practice are the shares of a partner in partnership assets and the rights of members of an unincorporated club to club property. Joint liferents[33] are another example.

COMMON PROPERTY

13.107 By contrast with joint property, property held "in common" is held by A and B (or any number of common proprietors) in such a way that each enjoys unrestricted title to his own share, which he may dispose of as he wishes. On his death, his share in the common property passes under the normal laws of succession.

13.108 Each common owner has the right to participate in the management of the common property, and each of them may veto any attempted "extraordinary use" of that property (*e.g.* the creation of a servitude over it). It appears that ordinary repairs and maintenance do not fall into this category. It would also seem that if any legal action (other than against trespass) is to be taken in defence of the property, the concurrence of all proprietors must be acquired.

13.109 If any one of the common owners wishes, he may call upon the others to have the property divided or, if this is not reasonable or practicable, on a sale of the whole and a division of the proceeds. The most common example of this process in action is now the sale of matrimonial homes, for which see 14.35 below.

13.110 Common property is most commonly found in tenemental, or flatted, houses, and these are considered below. First of

---

[32] It is said to "accresce" to them.
[33] For which see 13.120 below.

all, however, it is necessary to contrast common property with common interest.

COMMON INTEREST

13.111 Even though two or more proprietors have a completely separate and distinct piece of property, it may well also be that each of them must act with due regard for the interests of the other in the way in which his property is managed.

13.112 One good example is the duty of each "riparian" owner to the other concerning the use to which he puts the river which they have a common interest in (for which see 13.30 above). Another is the common interest which each "town square" proprietor has in the gardens which frequently form the centre of the square.

13.113 But by far the most important example of common interest in property arises under what is usually called "the law of the tenement."

THE LAW OF THE TENEMENT

13.114 A "tenement" is basically any property divided up in such a way that different floors (and often different areas of different floors) are owned by different proprietors. If the respective title deeds to each of the properties contain no provisions relating to management of common areas,[34] then the common law of the tenement prevails as follows.

13.115 The owner(s) of the ground floor (solum) of the tenement own it, and any surrounding garden, yard, drying green, etc., but they must maintain that ground so as to ensure continuing support for the upper proprietors. They must also not build so as to exclude or restrict light to those proprietors. Equally, the owners of each of the lower storeys must maintain them so as to maintain support

[34] As modern tenemental titles normally do. For an example of such a "deed of conditions," see *Arnold* v. *Davidson Trust*, 1987 S.C.L.R. (Sh.Ct.) 213.

for those above them, but only to the extent that to fail to do so would be actionable in negligence.

13.116 The external walls which comprise the tenement are the property of each of the proprietors as it forms the outer wall of his property, but there is a "common interest" between all proprietors which entitles them to object if any of the proprietors takes, or proposes to take, any action to endanger the physical security of the tenement as a whole.

13.117 The upper storey proprietor(s) also own(s) the roof, but since each of the proprietors has a common interest in the cover which it supplies to his own property, the upper proprietor(s) may be compelled to carry out such repair and maintenance as is necessary to ensure that the roof is an effective cover for the tenement as a whole.

13.118 Gables, floors and ceilings are common property as between the proprietors whose property they enclose. Thus, a party wall between two flats is divided down the inside by an imaginary centre line, as are horizontal surfaces which form the floor of one flat and the ceiling of another. There is also a common interest in all the proprietors to ensure that such items are not treated so as to prejudice the stability of the building.

13.119 Entrances, passages and stairs are common property among all to whose property they give access, and the stairway walls are common property between all the remaining proprietors and the persons whose property is on the inside of them.

LIFERENT AND FEE

Introduction

13.120 A liferent, as its name implies, is a right to enjoy and use property during one's lifetime, without destroying or depleting the *corpus*, or body, of the property, which will upon the death of the liferenter revert to the "fiar," who is the person in whom the "fee," or final ownership, of the property is vested. A liferent may exist in either heritable or moveable property, and it is in effect the right to enjoy the fruits or profits of something without depleting the capital. In this regard it may be contrasted with an annuity, which is the right to an annual fixed amount, even if it is necessary to eat into capital to achieve this. At the same time, a liferent is more than a mere right of occupancy, even if the latter is measured in terms of a human life.[35]

13.121 There are various ways of classifying liferents, each of which gives a fuller idea of the precise nature of the right.

Liferents by Constitution or by Reservation

13.122 A liferent by constitution[36] is one created by the proprietor in favour of another person; he may either retain the fee for himself or convey that to someone else at the same time (*e.g.* a father disponing his estate to his wife for her lifetime and thereafter to his son in fee, which is a common arrangement under a will).

13.123 A liferent by reservation, on the other hand, is one reserved by the grantor to himself while conveying the fee to someone else.

Legal and Conventional Liferents

13.124 A legal liferent is simply one created by law, whereas a conventional one arises out of an agreement between parties, or the expressed intention of the donor (e.g. by will). Since 1964, when the last legal liferents were abolished, all new liferents have been conventional.

Proper Liferents and Beneficiary Liferents

13.125 A proper liferent is one which directly arises from a straight grant creating liferent and fee, without the need for any intervening trust. A beneficiary liferent, on the other hand, arises through the medium of a trust, in which the property is vested in trustees who administer it for the ultimate benefit of the liferenter. At the end of the liferent, the property becomes vested in the fiar.

---

[35] *e.g.* a widow's right to remain in the matrimonial home for the rest of her life.
[36] Popularly called a "simple liferent".

Rights of a Liferenter

13.126 As indicated above, the basic right of a liferenter is to enjoy the fruits or income of the property, but not to encroach upon the capital of it. This is sometimes expressed in the Latin phrase *salva rei substantia* (which translates as "without destruction of the substance") and this reflects accurately the position of the liferenter.

13.127 It is sometimes necessary to make fine distinctions between income and capital, not only in terms of which of the parties (liferenter or fiar) is entitled to a particular receipt, but also on the question of whether a particular item of expenditure is chargeable against income or capital. To complicate matters further, some items of property subject to a liferent may be such as will deteriorate over time anyway (*e.g.* a yacht or furniture), while types of income will vary from property to property (*e.g.* rents from land or profits from company shares).

13.128 In the case of an estate of timber, the rule appears to be that the liferenter is entitled to ordinary windfalls, to copse-wood cut in the normal course of maturity and to wood cut for estate purposes such as fencing, while the fiar is entitled to the final mature trees and trees blown down by "extraordinary storm."

13.129 So far as minerals are concerned, the liferenter is entitled to royalties from mineral workings (which of course deplete the capital) which were let or worked during the lifetime of a donor who left a testamentary liferent knowing the extent of the workings, but not in respsect of minerals let or worked since the donor's death.

13.130 When the liferent property takes the form of shares, the liferenter is entitled to the dividends from those shares and to any other cash payments made by the company out of profits. Bonus shares will be classed as capital (and hence the property of the fiar) if the company issues them as such, but will be claimable by the liferenter if the company declares them to be in lieu of a cash payment.

Liabilities of a Liferenter

13.131   A liferenter must bear the annual and other periodic costs of the property such as insurance premiums and rates, but will not be liable for normal wear and tear on the property, or even accidental destruction.

13.132   While the liferenter must pay for ordinary repairs, the cost of extraordinary repairs and rebuilding will fall on the fiar.

Alimentary Liferents

13.133   An alimentary liferent is one which is declared in a trust deed to be for the personal maintenance of the liferenter; the effect is that the liferenter who accepts cannot thereafter assign it to anyone else, nor can it be "attached" by the liferenter's creditors. An alimentary liferent cannot be created other than as a beneficiary liferent (for which see 13.125 above).

13.134   Two other conditions which must be satisfied for the creation of a valid alimentary liferent are that the person who is to benefit must not be the grantor himself, and that the amount involved must not reasonably exceed what the liferenter is likely to require for his or her maintenance; to the extent that it does, it may be attached by his or her creditors.

Assignation of Liferents

13.135   Although a proper liferent may not be assigned as such, the liferenter may assign the income from it, even though the assignee will thereby acquire only a "personal" right of action against the liferenter, and no right to the liferent itself. A beneficiary liferent, on the other hand, may be assigned if it is not alimentary in nature. The assignation must be intimated to the trustees before they need pay the income to the assignee. Since the *assignatus* principle applies (see 13.98 above), the liferent will still come to an end at the death of the original liferenter.

Extinction of Liferents

13.136   A liferent clearly terminates upon the death of the liferenter, or upon the occurrence of some other event which has been fixed as terminating the liferent. The liferenter himself may terminate the liferent in the case of all but alimentary liferents, and the liferent may become extinguished by consolidation (*i.e.* the merger of liferent and fee when the liferenter becomes the fiar).

HERITABLE POSSESSION

13.137 The importance of physical possession in the context of moveable property was considered in 13.86 above. So far as possession of heritage is concerned, there are at least three ways in which being in physical possession of it can be important from a legal point of view, and they are as follows.

Possessory Remedies

13.138 A person who has been in open and peaceful possession of heritable property for a minimum of seven years, in circumstances in which such possession has been exercised as a matter of right under some form of title which falls short of a registered title (*e.g.* under a lease), may make use of interdict to defend himself from threatened eviction pending a fuller investigation into the precise legal position, and an action of removing in order to regain lost possession.

Bona Fide Possession

13.139 A person who has honestly but mistakenly believed himself to be the owner of heritage, with "probable" grounds for that belief, may claim the fruits of the property severed by him during his period of possession (including rents), the money expended by him on improvements to the property, and immunity from action for "violent profits" (*i.e.* in effect damages which would otherwise have been payable to the rightful owner).

Positive Prescription

13.140 Possession of heritage under an *ex facie* ("on the face of it") valid title registered in either the Register of Sasines (see 13.80 above) or the Land Register (see 13.82 above) for a period of 10 years acquires an inviolable title to it, even if it transpires that the title was invalid or forged. The period is 20 years in some cases (*e.g.* positive servitudes). The 10 years must, however, have been of possession openly, peaceably and without any legal claim.

RIGHTS IN SECURITY OVER PROPERTY

Introduction

13.141 A right in security is a power which a creditor requests over the property of a debtor as an additional safeguard to him should the debtor default in payment. It may apply to either heritable or moveable property, and the effect is to allow the creditor to seize and perhaps sell the property in question in certain predefined circumstances. The right which the debtor thus acquires over the property is said in law to be a "real" right.

13.142 It is convenient for the purposes of the rest of this section to distinguish between those rights in security which require some form of delivery, and those which do not.

Rights in Security Requiring Delivery

13.143 A distinction must be drawn between heritable and moveable property.

Heritable Property

13.144 Clearly there can be no actual delivery of land or buildings, and the closest that one can come is for the title to the property to be in some way secured in priority to the heritable creditor. This is achieved by means of what is popularly called a mortgage, but which is known in law as a "standard security."[37] The effect of such a security, which is registered as a title for the benefit of the creditor, is that pending the repayment of the loan the creditor has the option of taking over the property and selling it should the debtor default in payment in circumstances closely defined in the 1970 Act. Alternatively, the debtor will repay the loan as agreed,

---

[37] The only permissible form of mortgage since 1970; see the Conveyancing and Feudal Reform (Scotland) Act 1970.

whereupon the creditor is obliged to "discharge" the standard security.

Moveable Property

13.145 Securities over moveable property may be created either by express contract or by the operation of the law of lien.

Express Contract

13.146 An express contract in security of corporeal moveable property (*e.g.* goods) which incorporates delivery of the goods by the debtor to the creditor is normally known as "pledge" but is more popularly referred to as "pawning." Pawnbroking transactions are closely controlled under the Consumer Credit Act of 1974, and delivery may be actual, symbolic or constructive.[38]

13.147 A right in security over incorporeal moveable property is created by a formal assignation of it, using the procedure explained in 13.96. The security agreement will of course contain a clause binding the creditor to assign the property back again following the payment of the debt.

Lien

13.148 A lien is a right created by law whereby a creditor may retain property belonging to a debtor which he has already in his possession. In the case of a "special lien," that property will have come into the possession of the creditor as the result of the contract which gave rise to the debt. For example, a hotel proprietor may exercise a right of lien over guests' luggage until the accommodation account is paid, while a garage proprietor may retain the vehicle he has repaired until the repair bill is met in full.

13.149 A "general lien" is possessed by certain professionals in respect of any property belonging to the client/debtor which they happen to have in their possession in respect of any general indebtedness to them by the debtor. For example, a solicitor could

---

[38] See 13.94.

retain a client's property deeds until a bill is paid relating to court work.

13.150 Whether or not the lien also carries with it a right of sale depends upon the individual case.[39]

Rights in Security not Requiring Delivery

13.151 The two main securities over moveable property which do not require delivery are floating charges and hypothecs.

Floating charges

13.152 These may be granted only by companies or industrial and provident societies. They do not attach to any particular property, but float over the moveable property of the debtor generally until some event occurs to crystallise the charge. Until that time, the debtor may deal normally with the property. The process is heavily regulated by statute.

Hypothecs

13.153 These are common law rights over property for which the creditor does not require delivery. They may be either conventional (*i.e.* created by agreement) or legal (*i.e.* implied by law).

13.154 The only conventional hypothecs recognised by Scots law are the somewhat obscure "bonds of bottomry" and "bonds of respondentia," which the master of a ship may grant in order to raise money to allow the vessel to continue its voyage. A bond of bottomry covers the ship itself, and a bond of respondentia the cargo.

13.155 Legal hypothecs are granted to feu superiors[40] over moveable items[41] belonging to the vassal in security for unpaid feu-duty,

---

[39] *e.g.* Hotel proprietors have a right of sale under certain prescribed conditions *per* the Innkeepers Act of 1878.
[40] See 13.75 above.
[41] *Invecta et illata.*

to landlords over the moveable items[42] of tenants for unpaid rent for up to one year, and to solicitors over the expenses awarded by the court in favour of his client in order to cover his own outlays in those court expenses. The Solicitors (Scotland) Act of 1980 allows the court to grant the solicitor a security over any property in the action.

---

[42] Again *invecta et illata*, but not clothes or money. *N.B.* that the feu superiors' hypothec will, if necessary, be given priority over the landlord's.

14. FAMILY LAW

14.1 Family law has two main elements, namely the law relating to husband and wife and the law relating to parent and child. Rapidly changing attitudes to the respective roles of family members in recent years have led to several major statutory initiatives designed to eliminate outdated common law thinking.

CONSTITUTION OF MARRIAGE

Introduction

14.2 For a marriage to be validly constituted under Scots law, two vital elements require to be satisfied. First of all there must be no legal impediment to the marriage, *i.e.* no legal reasons which render it impossible for the parties to marry. Secondly, the marriage must be constituted in the correct legal form.

14.3 The former law under which an engagement, as a "promise to marry," was regarded as a form of contract, and therefore gave rise to a "breach of promise" action if it was "broken off," was abolished under the Law Reform (Husband and Wife) (Scotland) Act 1984, and the only remaining vestiges of the old law are to be found in the surviving rule that presents given by the engaged couple to each other, in contemplation of the marriage, may be recoverable, and the general principle considered further in 14.35 below, that property bought by either or both of the couple prior to marriage, for use in the family home, becomes "matrimonial property" if the couple subsequently divorce.

Impediments to Marriage

14.4 As indicated in 14.2, it is an essential prerequisite of a legally binding marriage that there be no legal impediment to it taking place. If there is, then even though a ceremony of marriage correct in form may have been observed, there will be no valid marriage. Only a legal impediment, however, will stop a marriage being valid when the parties enter into it voluntarily; thus in *Lang* v. *Lang*[1] it was held to be no lawful impediment to a marriage that the wife had "conned" the husband into it by pretending that she was carrying his child.

14.5 The only legal impediments to a valid marriage are as follows.

Forbidden Degrees of Relationship

14.6 Two persons may not marry if they are too closely related to each other. Prior to 1978, the list of forbidden relationships was governed by an Act of 1567 which in turn was based on the Book of Leviticus, but a more rational modern approach was introduced with the passing of the Marriage (Scotland) Act 1977, as amended by the Marriage (Prohibited Degrees of Relationship) Act of 1986.

14.7 Schedule 1 to the Act distinguishes between "relationships by consanguinity" (*i.e.* blood relationships) and "relationships by affinity" (*i.e.* relationships by marriage). So far as consanguine relationships are concerned (whether of the full or half blood), persons may not marry if they are so related into the first, second or third degree (*i.e.* parent, child, brother, sister, uncle, aunt, grand-parent or great-grandparent).

14.8 Relationships of affinity extend only into the second degree (and so, for example, a man could lawfully marry his ex-wife's grandmother) and do not extend into the collateral line (*e.g.* brother or sister-in-law of a former spouse). The effect of the 1986 amendment is that a former spouse may marry a former father or mother-in-law provided that both parties are over 21, the younger party has never lived under the age of 18 in the household of the other party and been treated as his or her child, and both the former spouse and the former spouse's other parent are dead.

14.9 So far as concerns illegitimate relationships, the law since the passing of the Law Reform (Parent and Child) (Scotland) Act 1986 has been that they are the same as legitimate ones. So far as

---

[1] 1921 S.C. 44.

adoptive relationships are concerned, the only forbidden degrees are those of parent and child.

Subsisting Prior Marriage

14.10 Quite clearly, it will be a total legal impediment to a valid marriage under Scots law if one or other of the parties is still validly married. A party going through a ceremony of marriage knowing this in fact commits the crime of bigamy.

Party Under Age

14.11 If either of the parties is under the "marriageable age" of 16, at the time of the ceremony, then the marriage is invalid.

Mental Incapacity

14.12 If either of the parties is incapable of giving true consent,[2] or of understanding the nature of the ceremony, then any purported marriage ceremony will be invalid.

Parties of the Same Sex

14.13 A valid marriage cannot occur under Scots law between persons of the same sex.

Formalities of Marriage

14.14 Marriages under Scots law are classed as either regular (*i.e.* conducted by religious or civil ceremony) or irregular (*i.e.* recognised as a marriage even though not formally celebrated).

Regular Marriages

14.15 As the result of the Marriage (Scotland) Act 1977, which modernised and regularised the law on the subject, there are two forms of regular marriage, the "religious" and the "civil," although

---

[2] And this may be due either to insanity or intoxication. For an interesting recent application of the "sound mind" test, see *Scott* v. *Kelly*, 1992 S.L.T. 915.

each requires the preliminary formality of notice of intention to marry, publicity and absence of objection.

Notice of Intention to Marry

14.16 Each area of Scotland falls into a registration district with a Registrar of Births, Deaths and Marriages. Even when the marriage is to be conducted in church, each of the intending parties must submit a marriage notice in the prescribed form to the Registrar. This is in effect a notice of intention to marry and certain documentation[3] must accompany it. Alternatively, if either of the parties normally resides in another part of the United Kingdom, he or she may submit an approved certificate from his or her local Registrar.

Publicity

14.17 Once he receives the marriage notice, the Registrar must enter it into a marriage notice book, which may be inspected free of charge by anyone claiming to have a right to object to the marriage taking place. A list of the names of the parties and the proposed date of the marriage must also be displayed in a conspicuous place in the registration office until such time as that date has passed.

Objections

14.18 Anyone may make written objection to the Registrar to the marriage taking place; a medical certificate must accompany any objection based on alleged incapacity as described in 14.12 above. Any misdescription or inaccuracy in the marriage notice or approved certificate may be corrected with the approval of the Registrar-General of Births, Deaths and Marriages. Any other objection must be referred to the Registrar-General, and the marriage ceremony may then not go ahead until he is satisfied that there is no legal impediment to it.

---

[3] *e.g.* a birth certificate or divorce decree where relevant.

Marriage Schedule

14.19 Once the above formalities have been duly observed (and normally no earlier than 14 days after the issue of the marriage notice), the Registrar may issue a Marriage Schedule, which both certifies that the marriage is authorised to take place and acts as the official record of the marriage, after being signed by the two parties, two witnesses and the celebrant (*i.e.* the church minister or Registrar). The 14 day period may be shortened on written request by the parties to the Registrar, with the consent of the Registrar-General.

Religious Marriage

14.20 A religious marriage is essentially one conducted by an "approved celebrant," which means a minister of a church specified in the 1977 Act, or a person granted temporary written authorisation by the Registrar-General. The parties must produce the Marriage Schedule before the ceremony, and at least two persons other than the parties, each of whom profess to be at least 16 years of age, must be present during the ceremony, and sign the Marriage Schedule immediately thereafter along with the parties and the celebrant. Within the following three days it must be delivered or posted to the local Registrar, who enters the particulars from it into his Register of Marriages. The effect of the Law Reform (Miscellaneous Provisions) (Scotland) Act of 1980 is that thereafter the only challenge to the marriage on the ground of formal defect[4] can be on the ground that both parties were not present during the ceremony, or that the Marriage Schedule was not duly registered.

Civil Marriage

14.21 Only an authorised registrar (*i.e.* district and assistant registrars) may conduct a civil marriage ceremony, which will normally take place at the local registry office or some other place agreed to by the registrar on medical grounds when the ceremony cannot be delayed. As with religious ceremonies, both parties must be present, and there must be two witnesses at least 16 years of

---

[4] But not of course essential defect such as age.

age. The same rules apply with regard to the signing of the Marriage Schedule (which the registrar will have retained from his own records) and the subsequent registration of its contents.

Irregular Marriages

14.22 Prior to 1940,[5] a form of irregular marriage could be set up by the common law presumptions of declaration *de praesenti* (where the parties simply declared themselves to be married) and promise *subsequente copula* (in which a promise to marry was followed by sexual intercourse).

14.23 These only remain relevant in a diminishing number of cases involving disputed wills or presumptions of legitimacy (for which see 14.61 below) and since 1940 there has been only one valid form of irregular marriage, namely that based on "cohabitation with habit and repute."

14.24 This is in effect a presumption that a couple are lawfully married and is based on the fact that they have lived together for a considerable period (no minimum number of years is prescribed) and were generally believed to be man and wife. They must have intended to be married, and have been free to do so, although in neither case need this have been true at the start of the cohabitation. The use of the presumption is almost exclusively reserved for cases in which the parties have long since died, and the essential issue is the legitimacy of their offspring, although even this has been of less importance since 1986, as explained in 14.68 below.

THE LEGAL EFFECTS OF MARRIAGE

14.25 Nowhere is the change in society's attitudes towards the role of the family better illustrated than in the wholesale reform of common law brought about in the 1980s by a series of statutes including the Matrimonial Homes (Family Protection) (Scotland) Act 1981, the Law Reform (Husband and Wife) (Scotland) Act of

---

[5] And the Marriage (Scotland) Act 1939. For two recent examples of the successful application of the "cohabitation and repute" presumption see *Donnelly* v. *Donnelly's Exr.*, 1992 S.L.T. 13, and *Mullen* v. *Mullen*, 1991 S.L.T. 205.

1984 and the Family Law (Scotland) Act of 1985, the last of which had a considerable impact on the financial implications of marriage.

14.26 As a result, the legal rules relating to the duties and rights of partners in a marriage are a mixture of basic common law principles with statutory amendments grafted on. They may be summarised as follows.

1. Adherence.
2. Aliment.
3. Occupancy of the matrimonial home.
4. Ownership of household property.
5. Assurance policies.

Adherence

14.27 Each of the parties to a marriage is said to have a duty to "adhere" to the other, which in more modern language means that they have a duty to live with each other, unless one of the parties has reasonable grounds not to (*e.g.* the behaviour of the other party). The duty of adherence may be discharged by means of a court order which authorises "judicial separation," and which may be granted upon proof of the same grounds which since 1976 have justified divorce (for which see 14.53 below). Judicial separation must be distinguished from voluntary separation, which is a private agreement between the parties and not enforceable by the courts, except insofar as relates to arrears of agreed maintenance (aliment—see 14.29 below) payments.

14.28 A party who fails to adhere in the absence of a judicial separation order and without the reasonable grounds which might lead to one being granted, is said to be in desertion, which is itself a ground for a divorce petition by the deserted party (for which see 14.54 below).

Aliment

14.29 Aliment is the duty to maintain someone financially, and since the passing of the Family Law (Scotland) Act 1985, this duty has been owed by a husband to a wife, by a wife to a husband, by a parent to a child, and by a person to a child whom he or she has taken in and recognised as one of the family. A child for this purpose is a person under 18, or a person between 18 and 25 who is undergoing reasonable and appropriate further education and/or vocational training.

14.30 The amount of aliment will depend upon the economic status of the parties concerned, and an action for aliment may be brought by anyone seeking to establish that they should be alimented (*e.g.* a deserted wife) or seeking a more appropriate level of aliment. The needs and resources of all parties are considered as part of the overall circumstances of the case, and when a material change of circumstances takes place subsequently, the court may order a variation or recall of its original award, which will of course be legally enforceable.

14.31 Any informal alimentary agreement reached between the parties is always challengeable in the courts, normally the sheriff court.

Occupancy of the Matrimonial Home

14.32 Common law prior to 1981 operated very unfairly in cases in which one of the parties (usually the husband) was the owner or the registered tenant of the matrimonial home, since he could virtually evict the wife and family without legal restraint. The purpose of the Matrimonial Homes (Family Protection) (Scotland) Act 1981, as amended by the Law Reform (Miscellaneous Provisions) (Scotland) Act 1985 was to improve the protection given in law to the "non-entitled" spouse (*i.e.* the party with no direct occupancy right), to remain in the matrimonial home, or to enter into it if she[6] is not currently residing there. She is also entitled to have with her any "child of the family."

14.33 Where both parties are entitled spouses (*e.g.* in a joint ownership situation), the court may make an order regulating the occupancy rights of either or both spouses, taking into account the financial and other needs of all the parties concerned. This may

---

[6] And henceforward it will be assumed that the non-entitled spouse is the wife.

even extend to an exclusion order against even an entitled spouse (*e.g.* in the case of actual or threatened domestic violence), supported by interdict preventing the offender from even approaching the matrimonial home.[7] The court even has the power to transfer a tenancy into the sole name of the threatened spouse.

14.34 The provisions outlined above apply even to cohabiting couples; but in such a case occupancy rights will not normally be granted for more than six months at a time. A non-entitled spouse, whether married or not, may renounce her occupancy rights in the matrimonial home in a document sworn freely and voluntarily before a notary public.

Ownership of Household Property

14.35 The general rule with relation to the ownership of household property acquired during the course of the marriage is that it is owned in equal shares; the same applies to any money left over from the "housekeeping allowance" which is traditionally handled by the wife.

This general rule is now to be found in the Family Law (Scotland) Act 1985, which applies to "household goods" and includes, in addition to the obvious furnishings, ornaments, etc., any money or securities, any motor vehicle or caravan and any domestic animal.

14.36 Under the provisions of the Matrimonial Homes (Family Protection) (Scotland) Act 1981 referred to in 14.32 above, either spouse may make application to the court for an order permitting the use of furnishings in the home in association with occupancy rights.

Assurance Policies

14.37 Under the Married Women's Policies of Assurance (Scotland) Act of 1880—which remains in force—any policy taken out by a married man on his own life and declared to be for the benefit of his wife and/or children, is regarded as being held in

---

[7] Such a "matrimonial interdict" may also extend to prohibiting any other threatening conduct by the offender.

trust for her or them, and cannot later be revoked or alienated by him. It does not even form part of his estate upon his death, and his creditors have no claim over the policy if he becomes bankrupt.

14.38 The Married Women's Policies of Assurance (Scotland) (Amendment) Act of 1980 applied exactly the same principles to a life policy taken out by a married woman on her own life for the benefit of her husband and/or children.

14.39 The Family Law (Scotland) Act 1985, allows either type of policy to be varied or set aside if the parties are subsequently divorced.

TERMINATION OF MARRIAGE

Introduction

14.40 There are basically three ways in which a marriage may terminate, namely by nullity, death or divorce. The essential difference between nullity and the other two terminators of a marriage is that a null marriage never was valid in the first place, and the decree of nullity merely declares that fact. Death and divorce, on the other hand, bring to an end[8] what was, until then, a valid marriage.

Nullity

14.41 A declarator of nullity of marriage, as indicated above, is a statement to the whole world that a marriage once believed valid in fact never was. A distinction is made, however, between a marriage which was void *ab initio* (*i.e.* from the start) for one of the reasons specified in 14.4 to 14.13 above (*e.g.* because one of the parties was already married), and a marriage which is voidable, and remains valid unless and until the entitled party takes steps to nullify it.

14.42 The only valid ground upon which a marriage is voidable is the incurable sexual impotency of either party. The impotency may be physical or psychological.

---

[8] "Dissolve."

14.43 Whereas a voidable marriage may be kept valid by the entitled party, a void marriage never can be, however enthusiastic the parties may be. Also, whereas only the entitled party may challenge a voidable marriage, anyone with an interest to do so (*e.g.* an existing prior spouse of one of the parties) may challenge a void one.

14.44 A declarator of nullity is effective from the date of the purported marriage in the case of a void marriage, and the same is true of a voidable marriage, with the important exception that any children of the latter marriage remain legitimate.

Death

14.45 In general, it is of course obvious that the death of one of the parties will have the effect of dissolving the marriage. However, in some unusual cases it may not be certain whether or not the party has died (*i.e.* when he or she has simply disappeared or proved untraceable) and for that reason it is sometimes necessary to make use of the "presumption of death" declarator.

14.46 Under the Presumption of Death (Scotland) Act of 1977,[9] a declarator of death may be granted by the court (which *inter alia* will dissolve the marriage and leave the applicant free to remarry) when the person in question is not known to have been alive for a period of seven years, or when he may be presumed to have died (*e.g.* in a shipping accident). In the latter case, an approximate date of death can be entered into the declarator, whereas in the former case the court will simply declare that he died at the end of a period of seven years from the date upon which he was last known to be alive.

14.47 Any person having an interest may raise the action, and the declarator may be varied or recalled if the true facts emerge later, except that the marriage will not thereby be revived.

---

[9] Which also has application in succession law—see 15.3 below.

Divorce

14.48 Since 1983, actions for divorce (which are in effect the dissolution of marriage by court order) have been maintainable in both the Court of Session and the sheriff court. The only ground upon which an action may be brought in either court is that the marriage has "broken down irretrievably." In reality, this breakdown is evidenced by one or more of certain grounds which constitute the real reason why one or both of the parties is seeking a divorce, and they are as follows.

1. Defender's adultery.
2. Defender's behaviour.
3. Defender's desertion.
4. Two year separation with the defender's consent.
5. Five years separation.

14.49 These are the grounds specified in the Divorce (Scotland) Act 1976, and in the case of all but (4), the action may of course be defended, either on the alleged facts or on the ground of whether or not they justify divorce.

Adultery

14.50 One act of voluntary sexual intercourse between one of the parties to the marriage and a person of the opposite sex other than his or her spouse is sufficient to give that spouse grounds for divorce for adultery. However, the defender may be able to resist the divorce action if he is able to show either that the petitioning spouse "condoned" the adultery, or that he "connived" at it.

14.51 Condonation consists of the "injured" spouse, in full knowledge of the adultery, resuming sexual relations with the guilty spouse. There is, however, a statutory "reconciliation" period permitted under the 1976 Act, which in effect allows a trial reconciliation (with normal sexual relations) for up to three months. If the injured spouse continues cohabiting (in the sexual sense) with the guilty party after the end of that period, he or she is held to have condoned the adultery, and may not then use it as a ground for divorce.

14.52 Connivance[10] consists of a husband[11] creating opportunities for his wife to commit adultery or actively encouraging it. Failing to dissuade her from doing it, or simply "turning a blind eye" is not sufficient.

Defender's Behaviour

14.53 As indicated in 14.27 above, if the defender has been guilty of behaviour which justifies the innocent party failing to adhere to him or her, then the same behaviour may later be used as a ground for divorce. In effect the court is recognising that the petitioning party can no longer be reasonably expected to live with the defender, and all forms of mental[12] and physical cruelty will fall into this category, along with habitual drunkenness and mental abnormality. Sexually deviant demands would qualify, and the behaviour may consist of one single act, if sufficiently serious. The behaviour may be active or passive (*e.g.* refusing to communicate) and need not be directed at the pursuer.

Desertion

14.54 A failure to adhere[13] without reasonable cause is referred to as desertion, and entitles the deserted spouse to petition for divorce. However, simply moving out for a week or two will not suffice; to establish desertion as a ground for divorce, the pursuer must prove that following the desertion the parties did not cohabit for a continuous period of two years, and that during that period the pursuer has not refused a genuine and reasonable offer by the defender to adhere.

14.55 The 1976 Act introduced a maximum six month trial reconciliation period, during which the parties may resume cohabiting,[14] which will not break the continuity of the desertion period, but will not count as part of it. Cohabitation in excess of the six

---

[10] Known also as *lenocinium*.
[11] N.B. not a wife.
[12] *e.g.* as *Hastie* v. *Hastie*, 1985 S.L.T.146, unfounded allegations of incest.
[13] For which see 14.27 above.
[14] This is not the same as merely engaging in sexual intercourse.

months will nullify the original desertion. There is also a permitted three month period of trial reconciliation following the expiry of the two year period which will not negative desertion; after three months, however, it will.

Two Year Separation with the Defender's Consent

14.56 A so-called "quickie divorce" may be obtained when the parties have not cohabited for a continuous period of two years and the defender consents to the granting of the decree of divorce. The six month trial reconciliation period described in 14.55 above applies equally here. The consent must be positive, and in prescribed procedural form.

Five Years' Separation

14.57 If the parties have not cohabited for a continuous period of 5 years or more, then the pursuer may obtain a divorce whether the defender consents or not, assuming of course that the missing spouse has no reasonable grounds for not "adhering" (see 14.27 above). The 6 month trial reconciliation period described in 14.55 above once again applies. This is the only ground of divorce which gives the court a discretion as to whether or not to grant decree once the facts are proved.

Financial Provision on Divorce

14.58 Under the Family Law (Scotland) Act 1985, an action for divorce may be (and usually is) accompanied by a request for financial provision. This may take the form of a division of matrimonial assets, the making of a future alimentary[15] provision, and any number of incidental orders including the future use of the former matrimonial home. Custody of and access to any children of the marriage are also normally considered at this time, and these are explained in 14.78 and 14.80 below.

14.59 Such orders for financial provision will obviously take into account the relative economic positions of the parties, particularly

---

[15] See 14.29 above. *N.B.* that the duty to aliment does not necessarily terminate on divorce.

bearing in mind the need for one of the parties (normally the ex-wife) to look after young children and thus prejudice her earning capacity. On occasions, the parties draw up a full and formal divorce settlement agreement for the court to read into the decree as part of it.

LEGITIMACY

Introduction

14.60 As with many other areas of family law, the law relating to parent and child has undergone important statutory changes in recent years, in order to replace outmoded common law concepts with more modern lines of thinking. This is well illustrated in the matter of legitimacy, which has been substantially altered as a result of the Law Reform (Parent and Child) (Scotland) Act 1986.

Presumptions

14.61 A "legitimate" child is the offspring of parents who are lawfully married. In certain cases the law will assist the process of legitimation by making certain presumptions based on the relationship of the child's parents which fall little short of regarding the parents as having been married for the purposes of having legitimate offspring. Two of these presumptions arise out of common law, and two out of the 1986 Act.

1. *Pater Est Quem Nuptiae Demonstrant*

14.62 This amounts to little more than asserting the obvious, namely that a child born to a woman during a marriage is presumed to be the legitimate child of her husband, and this applies to any child which is born after the dissolution of the marriage, but at such a time as it must have been conceived during it. The presumption does not apply, however, if the child is born so soon after the marriage as to have obviously been conceived before it; in such a case, the second common law presumption takes over.

2. *Putative Father*

14.63 A man who marries a woman in the knowledge that she is pregnant will be presumed at common law to be admitting patern-

ity, assuming that the opportunity existed for pre-marital intercourse.

3. *Entry in Register*

14.64   By virtue of the 1976 Act, if a man and the child's mother
acknowledge in the Register of Births, Deaths and Marriages that
he is the father of her child, then he is presumed so to be.

4. *Declarator*

14.65   In terms of the 1986 Act, a decree of declarator following
an action for declarator of parentage[16] gives rise to a presumption
that the facts are as stated in the declarator, and this will override
anything to the contrary arising from the previous three presumptions.

Legitimation

14.66   Legitimation is the process whereby someone originally
illegitimate becomes legitimate, a process which at common law
could only occur when the child's natural parents subsequently
married, and were free to marry when the child was conceived.

14.67   This latter condition[17] was removed by the Legitimation
(Scotland) Act 1968, which allows the legitimation process to occur
regardless of any legal impediment which may have existed at the
time of conception. The legitimation cannot, however, be retro-
spective.

Legal Equality of Children

14.68   The importance of legitimacy, from a legal point of view,
was materially reduced by a provision of the Law Reform (Parent
and Child) (Scotland) Act 1986 to the effect that all children should
have legal equality regardless of whether or not their parents were
married. This means, for example, that they take equally in the

---

[16] More popularly referred to as a "paternity suit."
[17] Which, for example, bastardised forever the offspring of adultery.

wills or intestacies of their parents (for which see 15.34 *et seq.* below) unless any document executed by a parent is expressed to the contrary.

14.69 There are two important exceptions to this rule. First of all, while a natural mother will always enjoy "parental rights" (for which see 14.72 below) regardless of the legitimacy of her child, the father only enjoys such rights if he is married to the mother, or was so married at the time of conception or later.[18] Secondly, a child born out of wedlock takes the "domicile"[19] of its mother.

Declarator of Parentage

14.70 Reference has already been made to these in 14.65 above. They are in effect public statements as to the identity of a child's father, and are usually linked with claims for aliment (see below). Evidence has become increasingly scientific in recent years, and the 1986 Act cleared the way for the taking of blood samples for DNA testing from the child itself with the consent of the tutor, guardian or custodier of the child, whom failing by order of the court. The Law Reform (Miscellaneous Provisions) (Scotland) Act 1990 allows adverse inferences to be drawn from the refusal of either of the parents to give such a sample, or to give consent to a sample being taken from the child.

ALIMENT

14.71 Reference was made in 14.29 above to the duty of a husband to aliment his wife and a father to aliment his children. This applies whether they are legitimate or not, and as explained in 14.70 above, the mother may bring an action in the court for a declarator of parentage linked to a request for aliment. Alimentary provisions for children of a marriage will normally also be made during the course of divorce proceedings (see 14.58 above). As with all alimentary claims, the amount awardable will depend upon the relative economic positions of the parties.

---

[18] So that, for example, the "de facto" or "common law" husband of a woman never acquires parental rights over her children, even if they are also his.

[19] *i.e.* country of belonging.

PARENTAL RIGHTS

Introduction

14.72 After many years of common law confusion, the Law Reform (Parent and Child) (Scotland) Act of 1986 grouped "parental rights" into one, and defined them as "tutory,[20] curatory, custody or access, as the case may require, and any right or authority relating to the welfare or upbringing of a child conferred on a parent by any rule of law." The general rule also laid down under the Act is that while the child's mother always enjoys parental rights, the father only does so if he is married to the mother, or was so married at the time of conception or later.

14.73 The natural allocation of parental rights (which are joint if both father and mother qualify) may be varied by a court order following an action by "any person claiming interest."[21] Parental rights normally continue until the "child" is 18, but will vary according to the actual age of the child.[22]

14.74 The specific parental rights may now be examined more closely.

Guardianship

14.75 The "guardian" of a child is the person who will normally give consent for some process in respect of which the child itself cannot give consent (*e.g.* surgery). This has already been encountered in the context of making contracts (for which see 2.96 above) and normally the signature of either parent, as joint guardian, will suffice.

14.76 The guardian is referred to as a "tutor" if the child is a pupil (*i.e.* a boy under 14 or a girl under 12) and a "curator" if the child is aged 12/14 but under 18.

---

[20] For which see 2.96 above.
[21] *e.g.* a concerned grandparent; see *M. Petr*, 1989 S.L.T. 426, and *F. v. F.*, 1991 S.L.T. 357.
[22] *e.g.* custody and access rights extend only to 16; see 14.77 and 14.80 below.

Custody

14.77 Whereas in the normal situation the guardian(s) of a child will also have "custody" (*i.e.* the day-to-day residential control) of that child, this will not be the case if the guardians are separated or divorced, or custody has been granted to another party such as a grandparent. In such cases, day to day welfare matters such as schooling and health (custody issues) are in different hands from legal decisions (*e.g.* surgical operations or contracts) and conflicts can clearly ensue.

14.78 Custody issues on divorce will normally be resolved initially by the divorce court (see 14.58 above), and a similar procedure is normally followed in nullity or separation hearings. If not satisfied that either parent is fit to exercise custody rights, the court can give these to another relative, or to the local authority under the Social Work (Scotland) Act 1968.

14.79 Subsequently, or even before the dissolution of a marriage, a separate custody application may be brought before the court by any suitably interested party, in terms of the Children Act 1975. A local authority application will be brought under the Social Work (Scotland) Act 1968.

Access

14.80 A natural parent who does not enjoy custody rights is entitled to reasonable access to the child where it is in the child's interest to maintain contact with that natural parent. If the parties cannot agree informally, the court has power to grant access, either as part of an incidental order to a divorce decree,[23] or as the outcome of a specific access application.

ADOPTION

Introduction

14.81 Adoption is the legal process whereby the legal rights of one or more of the natural parents is taken over by a party who is

---

[23] For which see 14.58 above.

not a natural parent but who henceforth is regarded in law as having parental rights. The law on adoption is now largely to be found in the Adoption (Scotland) Act of 1978, and its primary objective is to maximise the welfare of the child, who will, following adoption, be regarded in law as being the legitimate child of the adopter(s).[24]

14.82 Adoption may only occur as the result of an order of the court.

Adoption Agencies

14.83 Adoption is normally the result of the efforts of an adoption agency actively seeking parents for children who need them. Every regional and island authority is statutorily bound to establish an adoption service as part of its social work function, and private adoption agencies must be registered (on a three year renewable approval) with the Secretary of State for Scotland before they may operate.

Adopters

14.84 Ordinarily, adopters will be married couples, and they must be 21 or over before they may apply. If the adoption order is granted, the effect of the order is to make the child the legitimate offspring of the marriage for all purposes except the consanguinity rules for marriage.[25]

14.85 A single person may adopt a child if the adopter is over 21 and unmarried, and the effect of the adoption order will be to make the adoptee the legitimate child of the adopter. The normal marriage rules considered in 14.84 above apply. Application may be by the mother or father of the child,[26] but the consent of the

---

[24] *e.g.* the child can claim in the adoptive parents' estate, and may claim aliment from him/her or them.
[25] Considered in 14.6 above. Thus, for example, an adopted boy could marry his adoptive sister. But marriage is still forbidden between adoptive parent and child.
[26] Where, of course, he or she is married to the natural parent as in the case of the stepfather.

outgoing natural parent must be obtained, and his or her absence satisfactorily explained.

Parental Agreement

14.86 The consent of the child's natural parents or guardian will normally be required before an adoption order will be granted; there is an exception in the case of the father of an illegitimate child, unless he has obtained parental rights by court order. This consent may either be at the time of the application for the adoption order,[27] or earlier in the life of the child, by means of an agreement freeing the child for adoption.[28] In such a case, the adoption agency acquiring the freeing agreement also acquires the parental rights over the child. Freeing orders may in some circumstances be revoked, but not once an adoption order has been made.

The Child

14.87 The potential adoptee must be aged between 19 weeks and 18 years, and must never have been married. His or her consent to adoption is required if over 12 for a girl or 14 for a boy, unless he or she is incapable of giving it. The child must have lived with at least one of the prospective adopters for at least 13 weeks, and the agency must have had an opportunity to see the child with the adopter(s).

14.88 A custody order may be granted in lieu of an adoption order where appropriate.[29]

---

[27] And will only be dispensed with if he or she cannot be found, is incapable of giving agreement, is refusing unreasonably, has abandoned or neglected the child, or has seriously or persistently ill-treated the child.

[28] A common procedure following the birth of an illegitimate child; the child must be at least six weeks old before this may occur. An adoption agency may apply for a freeing order if the parent(s) unreasonably refuse(s); for a recent example of this process, see *Lothian Regional Council* v. *A*, 1992 S.L.T. 858.

[29] The most common example being where the prospective adopters are the child's natural grandparents, seeking to adopt their daughter's child.

15. SUCCESSION

Introduction

15.1 The law of succession is that area of the law of Scotland which regulates the transmission of a person's property after his death. For A to succeed to the property of B, B must have died or be presumed dead, A must have survived him, all B's debts must have been paid in full, and A must not be excluded from succeeding by the "forfeiture" rules considered in 15.11 below. A must, finally, be entitled to succeed either in terms of B's will (testate succession) or in terms of the laws of intestacy (intestate succession).

15.2 The law of succession may therefore be considered under the following headings:

1. Presumptions of life and death.
2. Bars to succession.
3. Prior and legal rights.
4. Testate and intestate succession.
5. Executory procedure.

PRESUMPTIONS OF LIFE AND DEATH

15.3 At Common Law, a person is presumed to live for a "reasonable" time, and this may be taken to be for at least 80 years, unless cogent evidence[1] is adduced which persuades the court to conclude that he died at an earlier age. Since 1881, statutory rules have existed which permit this presumption to be replaced by a presumption of death, and the modern version is the Presumption of Death (Scotland) Act of 1977, which allows a court to grant a "declarator of death" if satisfied on a balance of probabilities that a missing person has died, or has at least not been known to be alive for a period of at least seven years.[2]

---

[1] *e.g.* of his lifelong ill health.
[2] There is a vast factual difference between the two.

15.4 Such an action may be raised by "any person having an interest,"[3] and if successful will result in a declarator to the effect that the person in question died on a certain date,[4] or at the end of a period of seven years running from the date upon which he was last known to be alive. The court may combine the declarator with any order relating to any interest in property which arises on that death.

15.5 Such a declarator may later be varied[5] or recalled[6] by a consequential court order, which may not, however, affect any property rights acquired under the original decree unless it is "fair and reasonable" in the circumstances to take this step under a supplementary order. Such an order will not be granted unless the variation was applied for within five years of the original declarator, and property rights acquired by innocent third parties in good faith and "for value" cannot be usurped.

15.6 Complex issues of fact can arise when two or more persons die in a "common calamity,"[7] and they were linked in the laws of succession, as for example in the case of a father and son. Assuming for the moment that the son stood to inherit in the estate of his father, then even if he survived him for a few seconds only, the effect of the normal operation of the law of succession would be that the son inherited for long enough to pass his father's estate through his and on to the grandchildren, if any, or whoever else stood to inherit from the son.

15.7 Unfortunately, in the "common calamity" situation, where there is no evidence of either party surviving the other, the common law did not presume that the younger of the two survived the older. This defect was remedied by the Succession (Scotland) Act of 1964, which provides that when two persons have died in circumstances which make it uncertain which, (if either) survived the other, then as a general rule the younger will be presumed to have survived the elder.

---

[3] *e.g.* his relatives or someone holding a policy on his life.
[4] *e.g.* the date of an air crash.
[5] *e.g.* as to the time or date of death.
[6] *e.g.* when the person turns up alive.
[7] *e.g.* a road accident.

15.8 There are two exceptions to this rule. The first is in the case of husband and wife, in which case the presumption will not be applied, and the normal effect will be that their estates will be distributed as if they had not been married.[8] The second arises when the elder of the two left a will in favour of the younger which contained a clause that in the event of the younger not surviving the elder then a named third party was to inherit *and* the younger person dies intestate. In such a special case, the elder is presumed to have survived the younger, so as to prevent the legacy passing in intestacy to relatives of the younger person.

BARS TO SUCCESSION

15.9 As indicated above, a person otherwise entitled to succeed to an estate may be barred from so doing if the estate is consumed by debt or the beneficiary is subject to the "forfeiture" rule.

Satisfaction of Debts

15.10 All estate debts must be met in full before any beneficiary may succeed, and since claims on the estate must be lodged within six months by all creditors except the undertaker and various government agencies, executors will normally wait for such a period before paying to the beneficiaries such money, etc. as remains following the satisfaction of all known estate debts.

Forfeiture

15.11 A long established rule of public policy bars from an inheritance anyone who unlawfully killed the person from whom he stood to inherit, for fairly obvious reasons. Under the Forfeiture Act of 1982, a court may vary the effect of this rule in all cases except those of murder, so as to allow such an inheritance to proceed despite the circumstances.[9]

---

[8] *i.e.* there will be no "prior right" of a surviving spouse; see 15.12 below.

[9] For examples of the rule in practice, see *Smith, Petr.*, 1979 S.L.T. (Sh.Ct.) 35, *Cross, Petr.*, 1987 S.L.T. 384, *Gilchrist, Petr.*, 1990 S.L.T. 494, and *Hunters' Exrs., Petrs.*, 1992 S.L.T. 1141.

PRIOR AND LEGAL RIGHTS

15.12 Prior rights, as the name suggests, are rights in succession which a surviving spouse enjoys in the estate of the deceased, ahead of all other claimants, in any case of total or partial intestacy.[10] Legal rights, on the other hand, are enjoyed by both the surviving spouse and the children of the marriage, and apply to both testate and intestate succession. They may be considered separately.

Prior Rights

15.13 Since prior rights apply only in an intestacy, they may be overridden by the terms of the deceased's will, but assuming that this does not occur, then prior rights come before any other claim on the estate, even ahead of legal rights. They may be claimed only by a surviving spouse (*i.e.* widow or widower), and take three separate forms, namely:

1. Dwelling house.
2. Furniture and plenishings.
3. Financial provision.

Dwelling House

15.14 The surviving spouse is entitled to claim the deceased's interest in any dwelling house in which the surviving spouse[11] was ordinarily resident up to a value of £110,000. If the deceased's share is valued at more than this, then the surviving spouse receives £110,000 in cash (assuming that it is available from the estate), and a cash payment is also all that the surviving spouse may claim when the house itself forms only part of property which is the subject of a tenancy, or when it forms part of the assets of a trade, profession or occupation, and the value of the estate as a whole would be diminished "substantially" by the separate disposal of the house.[12]

---

[10] *i.e.* where the deceased fails to dispose of his entire estate by will, see below.
[11] *N.B.* not necessarily the deceased.
[12] *e.g.* a craft museum.

15.15 When the surviving spouse was ordinarily resident in more than one house, then he or she may choose which one to exercise the prior rights over at any time during the six months following the death.

Furniture and Plenishings

15.16 The surviving spouse is entitled to the furnishings and plenishings of the dwelling house in which she or he was ordinarily resident[13] up to a value of £20,000. This rule applies even if the dwelling house itself is not part of the intestate estate, and is therefore not claimable by the surviving spouse as part of the prior rights. Once again, items used for business purposes are excluded.

Financial Provision

15.17 Once the prior rights in the dwelling house, and the furniture and plenishings, have all been satisfied in full (and not before), the surviving spouse is entitled to a further financial provision, which is £50,000 if the deceased left no "issue,"[14] and £30,000 if he did. If the intestacy is only partial and the surviving spouse is entitled to a legacy under that will (other than the dwelling house, furniture and plenishings), then the financial provision is reduced by the value of that legacy.

Legal Rights

15.18 Legal rights are not strictly speaking rights in succession at all, since they apply even before the rules of succession are applied, and come second only to the payment of the debts of the estate and the prior rights outlined above. They apply only in respect of "moveable" estate (*i.e.* everything other than land and/ or buildings).

---

[13] Which need not be the house chosen as described in 15.14 above, where there is more than one.
[14] Defined for succession purposes as children, grandchildren and more remote direct descendants.

Extent of Legal Rights

15.19 The legal rights themselves are referred to as:

15.20 1. *Jus relictae.* This is the common law right of the widow of a deceased to either one third of the moveable estate (if there are surviving issue) and one half if there are not.

15.21 2. *Jus relicti.* This is the equivalent right of the widower of a deceased to one half or one third of the moveable estate.

15.22 3. *Legitim.*[15] This is the right of the surviving issue to share in either one third or one half of the moveable estate, according to whether or not there is a surviving spouse to claim *jus relictae*, or *jus relicti*. Since 1964, even remote issue such as grandchildren or great-grandchildren have possessed the right to share in the estate in the place of those who have predeceased them; thus if A dies, and his son B has predeceased him, leaving C and D as the surviving grandchildren of A, then C and D share B's portion of the legitim.

15.23 In a larger family, this can lead to some fairly small divisions being made in the remoter categories *per stirpes* (*i.e.* in equal shares according to the branches of the family tree). When every claimant on the legitim fund is related to the deceased in the same degree (*e.g.* as sons) then the division is simple, and equal, *per capita* ("according to individuals"). To take a simple example, if A dies, leaving one son, B alive, but has been predeceased by a second son, C, whose children are D and E, then whereas B will take a one half *per capita* share of the legitim, the grandchildren D and E will *between them* take one half, that is they will receive a "stirpital" distribution of one quarter each.

15.24 As explained in 14.68 above, illegitimate issue enjoy the same succession rights as legitimate, and under the Succession

---

[15] Quaintly known in former days as "the bairns' part."

(Scotland) Act of 1964, adopted children enjoy the same status as natural children. Step-children, however, have no legitim rights.

Collation *Inter Liberos*

15.25 Under this principle, a claimant on the legitim fund who has received an advance on his share of the fund during the deceased's lifetime will have that amount deducted from the amount to which he is entitled. Technically, it will be "collated" (*i.e.* notionally put back into the fund) before the division is made. This applies to claims made by remoter issue (*e.g.* grandchildren) when advances were made to the issue whom they now represent (*e.g.* their deceased father). If the deceased in his lifetime makes it clear that the gift he is making is not collateable, or if it is clearly something else such as a loan, then the collation principle will not be applied.

Discharge of Legal Rights *Inter Vivos*

15.26 Both the potential surviving spouse and the issue may discharge their entitlement to legal rights by agreement with the deceased during his lifetime (*inter vivos*). Ideally, but possibly not out of legal necessity, such an agreement should be in "probative"[16] form. The effect of such discharge is to increase the share of the other claimants in the case of the legitim fund.

Satisfaction of Legal Rights by Testamentary Provision

15.27 Since legal rights apply in respect of both testate and intestate succession, a testator may, in his will, deprive either the surviving spouse or the issue of their legal rights. However, by a principle known as "approbate and reprobate,"[17] a claimant to legal rights may be required to "elect" between the legacy on the one hand and the legal rights on the other, if the will so prescribes. Alternatively, in wills made since 1964, if there is a provision in the will

---

[16] For which see 2.64 above.
[17] Which loosely translated means that a person cannot insist on the legality of a document for one purpose and reject it for another.

in that person's favour, this will impliedly be in satisfaction of legal rights unless the provision states to the contrary.

15.28 Any portion of legal rights lost by testamentary provision will not accresce to the remainder of the legal rights (*e.g.* it will not inflate the legitim fund), but will fall into the "dead's part."[18]

INTESTATE SUCCESSION

15.29 Intestacy[19] is the term used to describe a situation in which a testator has failed to leave all his estate under his will, or has failed to leave a will at all. In such a case, the estate is transmitted to beneficiaries in terms of what are called the rules of intestacy, which since 1964 have applied to both moveable and heritable estate.

15.30 The first group to stand to inherit (to the exclusion of other groups of beneficiaries) are the descendants (*i.e.* children, grandchildren, etc.), whom failing "collaterals" (*i.e.* brothers and sisters and their issue), whom failing the surviving spouse, whom failing ancestors and their issue. Where there is both a surviving parent and a brother or sister, the estate is divided in two between the two claimant groups.

15.31 In all cases *except* parents and spouses, "representation" is permitted, so that a person who would have succeeded had he survived the deceased is replaced by his issue; under this process, for example, a nephew or niece may inherit the share of the brother of the deceased. Once again, since 1968, illegitimate children have the same rights as legitimate ones for all succession purposes (see 14.68 above). Also *per stirpes* distributions may have to be made among groups of claimants in the same representation class (*e.g.* all the children of a deceased's brother); see 15.23 above.

15.32 Collaterals of the whole blood exclude collaterals of the half blood. If there is absolutely no claimant at all on the estate, it falls to the Crown as *ultimus haeres* (*i.e.* as "ultimate heir").

---

[18] *i.e.* the remaining 1/3 or 1/2 of the estate which is not affected by legal rights.
[19] Which may, as indicated above, be only partial.

15.33 The precise line of succession is therefore as follows:
1. Children and grandchildren, etc. (representation allowed).
2. Parents, brothers and sisters as explained above (no representation for parents).
3. Surviving spouse (no representation allowed).
4. Uncles and aunts (representation allowed).
5. Grandparents (no representation allowed).
6. Collaterals of grandparents (representation allowed).
7. Remoter ancestors (representation allowed).
8. The Crown.

TESTATE SUCCESSION

Introduction

15.34 Testate succession describes the situation in which the deceased's estate passes in terms of a will left by him; in such a case the deceased is normally referred to as "the testator." Whatever may have been his testamentary wish, of course, he cannot override the effect of the legal rights referred to in 15.18 above, so far as concerns his moveable estate, one third or one half of which will remain for him to leave under his will, depending upon whether or not he leaves a surviving spouse, or issue, or both.

15.35 No one may make a valid will unless he has the "capacity to test" in the sense that he is recognised by law as being capable of making a testamentary disposition of his estate. A "pupil"[20] has no such capacity, nor has an insane person, except during a lucid interval. A will may also be challenged when the alleged testator was so drunk as to not understand what he was doing, as may a will obtained by misrepresentation,[21] force and fear,[22] facility and circumvention[23] and undue influence.[24]

---

[20] *i.e.* a boy or girl under 12; see s.(2) of the Age of Legal Capacity (Scotland) Act 1991.
[21] For which see 3.26 above.
[22] For which see 3.70 above.
[23] For which see 3.71 above.
[24] For which see 3.72 above.

Form of Will

15.36 Any will which disposes of property worth more than £8.33[25] must be attested, holograph or adopted as holograph.[26] Despite the prevalence of commercially induced pre-printed will forms, no particular form of words is required in a will, provided that the testator makes his intentions clear, leaves no room for uncertainty, and makes it clear that these are his final wishes in the matter. A later edition to the main will may be made and is referred to as a "codicil."

15.37 A will may be revoked at any time by the testator, whether by intentional formal cancellation, physical destruction, or implication from the fact that he has made a later, inconsistent, will. Intentional revocation or destruction must be such as to illustrate *animus revocandi*[27]; accidental destruction, for example, will not invalidate a testamentary document, which will still be enforceable if its contents can be satisfactorily proved (by means of an "action for proving the tenor of the will" brought in the Court of Session).

15.38 A will may also be revoked by the operation of law under the principle known as the "*conditio si testator sine liberis decesserit*," which arises when a will makes no provision for children not yet born, and children are born to the testator subsequent to the date of the will. The presumption is that the testator would have wished to make provision for such issue, but it may be rebutted by evidence to the contrary. Only the subsequently-born child may invoke the condition so as to "reduce" the will; the effect of this is not, however, to revive any earlier will, with the result that the deceased will die intestate.

15.39 Wills may be made "mutually" by two or more persons at once, but the legal complications to which they can give rise make them inadvisable in all but the simplest cases (*e.g.* husband and wife with one child).

---

[25] The modern equivalent of £100 Scots.
[26] For which see 2.65, 2.67 and 2.68 above respectively.
[27] *i.e.* the desire to revoke.

Interpretation of Wills

15.40 The main objective of any court seeking to interpret the terms of a will is to give effect to the wishes of a testator insofar as this may be deduced. This will normally be done by giving the words used by the testator their normal meaning, and only in special cases will extrinsic interpretation be used, for example to translate a foreign language, to show special facts known to the testator (*e.g.* family nicknames) or to resolve ambiguities and uncertainties.

15.41 If doubts still remain, the courts will tend towards an interpretation which avoids partial or total intestacy; if even that fails, then so does the particular legacy which depended upon that portion of the will being interpreted.

Classification of Legacies

15.42 Legacies may be general (*e.g.* a sum of money), special (*e.g.* a specific item such as a house or a car) or demonstrative (*i.e.* in which the testator indicates where the legacy is to come from, as in the case "first choice from my vintage car collection").

15.43 A special legacy will "adeem" (a process known as "ademption") if it ceases to be part of the testator's estate by the date of his death, in which case the "special legatee" has no further claim on the estate.

15.44 Once general and special legacies have been honoured,[28] the balance of the estate is referred to as the "residue," and unless the testator has made provision for a "residual bequest," that part of his estate will fall into intestacy, to be distributed in the manner outlined in 15.33 above.

15.45 Two or more legacies in the same will, or in a series of wills, to the same legatee may be either "cumulative" (*i.e.* all due) or "substitutional" (in which case only the latest in date is effective). They are in fact presumed to be cumulative unless they are in the same document and for the same amount.

---

[28] And, of course, after all debts and prior and legal rights have been met.

Abatement of Legacies

15.46 Legacies will be "abated," or cut down, when the testator's estate proves insufficient to meet all the bequests which he attempted to make. He may indicate the order of any potential abatement in the will, but if not then residual bequests abate first,[29] general legacies abate next,[30] and special legatees receive priority.

Identification of Legatees

15.47 If an intended legatee cannot be identified, then the bequest fails; this will not, however, prevent a trust being set up under the will which allows the trustees themselves to choose the beneficiaries from a class nominated by the testator (*e.g.* "any two of my nephews").

15.48 When a legacy is bequeathed to a group of persons, whether named individually or by virtue of membership of a class, there is a presumption that the division is to be *per capita* (*i.e.* equal shares to each legatee).

15.49 "Accretion" will occur if some of the intended legatees die before the testator, and their share will be available for distribution to the other legatees (and normally of course the residuary legatees). This will not occur, of course, if the legacy is "several" as opposed to "joint,"[31] but there is a presumption that any bequest to two or more legatees is intended to be joint, unless the testator uses "words of severance" such as "in equal shares," so as to indicate that each legatee is to take his own share, which will pass into residue if the legatee dies before the testator. Even this rule does not apply if the testator clearly indicates that the words of severance are not to exclude accretion, or they are applied to a class of legatees (*e.g.* "to my nephews in equal shares"). In such cases, accretion will still occur.

---

[29] And residual legatees receive nothing unless and until other legatees are paid in full.
[30] Proportionately, so that each legatee receives the same percentage of what was bequeathed to him.
[31] For which distinction, see 13.104 above.

15.50 To prevent a particular bequest falling into residue, the testator may provide for a "destination-over" (*i.e.* "to A, whom failing to B"), to ensure that the legacy passes specially or generally.

Vesting of Legacies

15.51 A legacy "vests" in a legatee when it becomes his own property, at which point he may dispose of it as he wishes, either in his own lifetime (*inter vivos*) or by will (*in mortis causa*). His right to immediate possession may, however, be delayed by the intervention of a trust with conditions relating to the eventual possession by the legatee.[32]

15.52 A legacy which is unconditional will vest in the legatee immediately upon the death of the testator, and for this purpose a fee subject to a life rent is regarded as unconditional. When, on the other hand, a legacy is subject to a "suspensive condition" (*i.e.* one which postpones vesting until the condition has been fulfilled[33]), then vesting will not occur at all unless and until that condition is fulfilled.

15.53 If the condition is "resolutive" (*i.e.* it does not postpone vesting, but makes it liable to be defeated if a prescribed event occurs), then the legacy is said to "vest subject to defeasance."

Conditio Si Institutus Sine Liberis Decesserit

15.54 In certain special cases, in which a person intended to be a legatee dies before the testator, but leaving issue, the issue will be allowed to "represent" the deceased legatee and inherit. This is based upon the presumption that had the testator known what was to happen, he would have expressly provided for the issue to take the place of the parent.

---

[32] A classic example of which is a testamentary life rent and fee, in which the possessory rights of the fiar are subsidiary to the rights of the life renter during his or her life rent; see 13.120 above.

[33] *e.g.* "to A when he attains age 18."

15.55   The conditio applies only to the requests to the testator's own direct descendants,[34] or to nephews and nieces whom he has treated as his own children. It will also be defeated by clear language in the will which indicates that it is not to apply, or by a separate bequest in the will to the issue of the predeceasing legatee.

Void Conditions

15.56   A condition attached to a legacy will be regarded in law as void (*i.e.* of no legal effect), if it is uncertain, impossible, illegal, immoral or contrary to public policy.[35] The legacy will then take effect without the condition.

Repugnant Conditions

15.57   A condition attached to a legacy is said to be "repugnant" when it is inconsistent with it; once again the legacy will take effect without the condition.

Accumulation of Income

15.58   The Accumulations Act of 1800,[36] as amended in 1961 and 1966, prevents the accumulation of income for more than 21 years after the testator's death; after that it is paid to the beneficiary who would have received it had accumulation not been specified under the will.

15.59   Thus, in *Elder's Trs.* v. *Treasurer of the Free Church of Scotland*,[37] trustees were directed to hold the residue of an estate until the death of the testator's widow, and then and only then to disperse the money for church purposes. The widow survived for more than 21 years, and it was held that since the suspensive condition (*i.e.* that the widow die) had not been fulfilled so as to release the money for church purposes, the surplus income fell into intestacy.

---

[34] *i.e.* children, grandchildren and remoter issue.
[35] *e.g.* preventing a person from marrying, or having children.
[36] The "Thellusson Act."
[37] (1892) 20 R.2.

EXECUTORS

15.60 The "executor"[38] of an estate is the person who "ingathers" it, pays off the debts and distributes the estate according to either the terms of the will or the laws of intestacy, subject of course to legal and prior rights when appropriate.

Appointment of Executor

15.61 An executor appointed under the testator's will is known as an executor-nominate; in a case of testate succession in which the executor has not been appointed, or declines to act, then any testamentary trustee or residual legatee may be deemed to be the executor. If all else fails, and in all cases of intestate succession, an executor-dative is appointed by the sheriff court following a petition for his or her appointment.

15.62 The order of priority for such appointment is the surviving spouse (if he or she has prior rights which exhaust the estate), the "next of kin," other persons in the order in which they may succeed in an intestacy, creditors, legatees,[39] the procurator-fiscal or a judicial factor.

Confirmation of Executors

15.63 Both executors-nominate and executors-dative must apply for confirmation of their office from the sheriff court, and this is then their statutory authority to "intromit" with the estate in the manner outlined in 15.60 above. Executors-dative must "find caution"[40] before confirmation will be granted. Small estates[41] may be confirmed on by executors who then leave the completion of the inventory of estate[42] to the sheriff-clerk.

---

[38] *N.B.* that the female equivalent is known as the "executrix."
[39] In a partial intestacy.
[40] *i.e.* lodge a fidelity bond in practice supplied by insurance companies in return for a premium.
[41] *i.e.* less than £17,000 in total at the time of writing.
[42] Normally completed and presented to the court as part of the confirmation application.

15.64   The effect of confirmation is to vest the estate in the executor, who then becomes the deceased for the purpose of paying off estate debts and ingathering money due to the estate, prior to disbursing the final estate in terms of either the will or the laws of intestacy. Certain debts are preferential when the estate is insufficient to meet them all, and high in the list are confirmation and funeral expenses. Ordinary creditors are then paid *pari passu* (*i.e.* in equal shares) taking only a percentage payment when this is all that the estate can pay.

INDEX